The Research Process in Political Science

THE
RESEARCH PROCESS
in
Political Science

Edited by
W. Phillips Shively
University of Minnesota

F.E. PEACOCK PUBLISHERS, INC.
ITASCA, ILLINOIS 60143

CONTRIBUTORS

Terence W. Ball
    University of Minnesota
Jeffrey L. Brudney
    University of Georgia
Sandra Van Burkleo
    Wayne State University
Barbara G. Farah
    University of Michigan
Stanley Feldman
    Brown University
George E. Marcus
    Williams College
James E. Piereson
    University of Pennsylvania
W. Phillips Shively
    University of Minnesota
John Sprague
    Washington University
John L. Sullivan
    University of Minnesota
James A. Stimson
    University of Houston

Contents

*Written for this volume

*Written for this volume

Introduction: What's Involved in Doing Research?

I assume that most of you who are reading this book are students, that you have *read* many works of research, but that you have not done a great deal of it yourself. You might well be asking yourself the question with which I've titled this chapter, "Just what is involved in carrying out a piece of research?"

I hope that this book will help to answer that question, since reading narratives about how a piece of research was done is probably the best way—other than carrying out your own project—to learn what actually goes on when people do research. We have gathered seven scholars' accounts of how they did some piece of research. In all the essays except Terence Ball's we have printed the research report, plus a narrative recounting how the research was done (Ball blends the two together in one essay.) I would urge you in reading these articles to pay particular attention to the narratives, rather than the research reports. Each report appears before the narrative that goes with it, so that you may skim over it to see what the author is talking about in his or her narrative, but the important parts of this book for you are the narratives. You have read plenty of research reports before; what you have not read often enough is an account of how the research was done.

There is no cut-and-dried way to do good work. Represented here are works that involved digging through official records; works that required the use of a mass survey; works that simply involved an exercise of the mind. Similarly, in doing any of these particular tasks, there is no set "correct" procedure. The scientific method is often presented to students as if it involved a clear and inflexible set of steps: (1) take a theory; (2) derive hypotheses from it; (3) develop measures to fit the terms of the hypotheses; (4) go out and measure those things in the field, in order to test the hypotheses and thereby strengthen or weaken our belief in the theory.

While it is true that this is the intellectual structure of what we do, it is *not* true that this structure must be recapitulated in full in each individual research project. Often a researcher will develop only one or another facet of this structure in a project. John Sullivan and his coauthors, for instance, sought in their work primarily just to measure political tolerance better than had been done before.

Or, in a particular project a researcher may do things in a different order from what the pure scientific method would prescribe. As you will see, Sandra Van Burkleo found that she had to adjust her theories and hypotheses—in fact, to some extent, her very focus—as she got more thoroughly into her materials and knew more about her subject. This ran counter to pure scientific method, and in doing so she ran some risk of presenting a finding that appeared to be general, but was in fact a function of the idiosyncracies of the case she was looking at. But it would have been silly for her to have refused on principle to adjust her research design as she learned more about her subject.

There are many ways, then, to do good research, and this is in fact one of the messages I hope you will take from this book. However, I don't wish to suggest that therefore all is chaos, that anything goes. Some research is done well, and some is not. What makes the difference between the two?

It is easier to see what is required in good research if we remember that research is no different from any other inquiry that we might make from day to day. "Research" is not some special and isolated thing. Detectives, children learning to walk, chefs designing a new pastry, students selecting courses to take are all doing something that is not different in its logic from scholarly research.

"Research" consists of asking a question about the world and presenting a convincing answer to that question. "Scholarly research" is simply research in which the question which is asked is one that addresses bodies of theory with which scholars are concerned.

What marks good research? What things should you be looking for as you read the essays in this book?

First of all, good research must address an interesting question. If the question you address is not of interest to those reading your report, it does not matter how "well" you have done your work; it will be greeted with a yawn. What makes a question interesting is, of course, highly subjective. Someone once said that we could tell good work by the "interocular subjectivity test" (Does the work hit you between the eyes?), but that simply restates the question. What will make work hit scholars between the eyes?

In general, any research question is interesting to the extent that it promises to accomplish the goals of that research. For a detective, a question is interesting to the extent that it offers a chance to break open a case. For a business executive, it is interesting to the extent that it offers a chance to increase profits. "Scholarly research," we have said, is any research that addresses bodies of theory for their own sake. In scholarly research, then, a question is interesting to the extent that it promises to have a bearing upon theories. The more chance there seems to be that the answer to a question will affect our theories, the more interesting that question will be.

As one example of an interesting question, a political scientist once noted that West Germany is a major exception to one of the best-established theories about parties and elections: that proportional electoral systems produce multiparty systems while first-past-the-post electoral systems produce two-party systems.[1] He formulated a highly interesting research question, "Why has postwar West Germany, with its proportional electoral system, had essentially a two-party system?" Notice that given the existing theories, it would not have been nearly so interesting for him to have asked, "Why does Great Britain, with its first-past-the-post electoral system, have essentially a two-party system?" Since West Germany went against the grain of the theory, examining it closely offered some hope of adjusting the theory. Great Britain's case, like most cases, fit with the theory; looking at it would not have seemed likely to lead to much change in the status of the theory.

Good ways to formulate an interesting question are to look for logical inconsistencies in a theory, or to look for new cases, or improved measures, which will shed a different light on the theory. All the authors in this book formulated their questions in one or another of these ways.

John L. Sullivan and his coauthors noted a weakness in previous studies of tolerance, in that all of them had measured tolerance only toward left-wing groups. Thus, people who were intolerant of right-wing groups might erroneously be classed as "tolerant"; Sullivan thought this might have helped lead to the then-current theory that university education increased one's tolerance of others.

James A. Stimson noted that the research on which prevailing views of the complexity of American voters' belief systems were based had been conducted in the 1950s and early 1960s. If the electorate were changing radically, as some had suggested, looking at a later election might be illuminating. Thus his study of the 1972 election.

Terence Ball found implausible all the prevailing explanations for why John Stuart Mill became a pioneer feminist in the nineteenth century, so he set out to reinvestigate the question.

For *Barbara G. Farah*, West Germany's unusual electoral system offered a unique chance to test how important a representative's personal tie to constituents is in influencing the representative's behavior.

Jeffrey L. Brudney found that two theories of organizational power, which were apparently inconsistent, could be tested by the research he designed.

Sandra Van Burkleo thought that earlier explanations for Kentucky's attempt in the early nineteenth century to remake its constitutional relationship with Virginia and the other states—a case of constitutional development which has figured importantly in constitutional history—were too limited by one or another discipline and its outlook. Economic histories looked only at the Panic of 1819 and its outcome, legal historians looked only at legal doctrines, and so on. By working across all these concerns, she could construct a more complete picture of what had happened, and *why*.

John Sprague was struck by an odd paradox in American elections—the fact that the Democratic party has consistently dominated the House of Representatives since the Second World War, a period in which control of the presidency has see-sawed back and forth between the Republicans and Democrats. The same voters participated in both kinds of election; how is it that they can yield such different results? He propounded a formal model to account for the paradox.

This is really the most difficult part of a piece of research: coming up with a question that is worth your own and your readers' time. The rest, though it certainly requires a good deal of concentration and creativity on your part, follows more or less straightforwardly.

What is required, once you have posed a question for yourself and your readers? You now must provide an answer (or perhaps a couple of competing answers), together with evidence that will convince your readers that those answers are reasonable.

How you provide evidence that will convince your readers is beyond the scope of these comments. All the techniques of measurement, of statistical analysis, of logical reasoning that you are being taught will come into play here—plus a large admixture of simple common sense. It is worth noting one thing, however, about "convincing your audience." We are all accustomed to convincing people through conversation, and consequently we tend to model our writing after our verbal experiences with argumentation. You should be conscious of one major difference between writing and conversation, though. In a conversation we make a point, listen to the response of the person to whom we are talking, rebut that response, and so on and on. We can allow our audience to raise doubts, respond skeptically, and so on, and then we respond to what they have raised. If we can handle their doubts satisfactorily, we can convince them of our case.

When we are writing, however, we don't have the audience physically with us to respond to what we have written. *In order to convince them of our case, it is necessary to anticipate their doubts and respond to them in advance.* A very common flaw in student research is to present a case straightforwardly enough, but not to have anticipated problems or doubts a reader might reasonably raise. When your audience reads your piece, doubts, alternative explanations, and other questions occur to them. Unless you have included your rebuttals in advance, they will not hear your rebuttals and they will be unconvinced by your argument.

It is hard to develop an argument which you are convinced is true and to anticipate reasons why someone might disagree with it simultaneously. A useful technique in this regard is to have a friend read a first draft of your piece and raise any objections that come to mind. This will help you to avoid missing important counterarguments that you need to deal with in advance.

Enough of this. I don't want so much to tell you here how to do research, as to get you on to reading the examples in this book and the authors' accounts of how they went about doing the research piece you'll have read. Stay alert in reading these to see how the authors picked a question for examination, how they developed alternative answers to the question, how they picked the answer or answers that they thought were right, how they developed evidence to convince their readers that they were correct, and how they tried to handle readers' objections in advance.

I have tried to present examples here of the full variety of research methods that students in political science are likely to use. Ball and Van Burkleo provide examples of historical research, with Ball providing an example also of literary analysis in political philosophy; Sullivan and his coauthors conducted an original mass survey, while Stimson carried out a secondary analysis of survey data; Farah and Brudney did field research; Sprague's piece provides an example of formal modeling. I hope that these will give you a good sense of how research is done.

A few other books you might like to read along lines similar to this one are:

Richard Fenno, *Home Style: House Members in Their Districts* (Boston: Little, Brown, 1978). This is an important study of how members of Congress cultivate their constituents and of what effect this has on their work in Congress. It is elegant research, as we can expect from Professor Fenno. And most importantly for our purposes here, it includes a substantial appendix in which he tells how he conducted the field research for the book. This is a piece written in just the spirit I have looked for in this book.

M. Patricia Golden, ed., *The Research Experience* (Itasca, Ill.: F. E. Peacock Publishers, 1978). This book provides for sociology what I am attempting to provide here for political science. There are a number of excellent essays in it that would be as applicable for political science as for sociology.

James D. Watson, *The Double Helix* (New York: Atheneum, 1968). This book recounts the discovery of the molecular structure of DNA, a dramatic breakthrough which led to the development of modern genetics. It is a dramatic story, told well by one of the co-discoverers. It reads like a novel.

Charles Lave and James March, *An Introduction to Models in the Social Sciences* (New York: Harper & Row, 1975). This is an introduction to formal modeling, which may or may not be what you are interested in. But the first three chapters are about research in general and are pure delight. There are many examples of interesting research questions and of what it is that makes them interesting. The presentation is informal and playful.

NOTES

1. Gerhard Loewenberg, "The Remaking of the German Party System," 1 *Polity* (#1, Fall, 1968), pp. 86–113.

CHAPTER ONE

The Sources of Tolerance: A Multivariate Analysis

1. The Sources of Tolerance: A Multivariate Analysis

Sullivan and his coauthors take on here what had been rather well-accepted doctrine—that the well-educated are more tolerant of opposing viewpoints and are more likely to extend the protection of democratic norms to them than are the less-educated. As you will see, Sullivan et al. thought that tolerance had not been measured properly in the studies on which this doctrine was based, and they did not think that relationships between education and other factors and tolerance had been properly assessed. The problem of measurement is handled straightforwardly in their article, but I should introduce you briefly to the problem of "specifying a model" in case you are not familiar with it.

When we try to explain why a given thing varies—in this case, tolerance—it may be that a few different independent variables in combination all affect that thing. For instance, one's education, acceptance of democratic norms, and political ideology might all affect how tolerant one was of the Communist party. Now, if the things that affect tolerance of the Communist party are themselves related to each other, and if we look at only one of them in isolation as a possible cause of tolerance of Communists, we may get a quite false picture of the relationship between that thing and tolerance for Communists. If highly educated people tend to be liberals and liberals tend to be tolerant for Communism, then if we look only at education and its relationship to tolerance of Communism, we will exaggerate the effect of education on tolerance. In fact, we may perceive a relationship where none really exists. In this example, for instance, it might be that there is nothing about education per se that leads to tolerance; one might just be picking up the historical accident that educated people tend to be liberals; conservative educated people might be no more tolerant of Communists than any other conservatives are.

Looking at some, but not all, of the relevant explanatory variables in an attempt to account for something yields what is called an *improperly specified model*. That is, to explain something properly, we must look at the simultaneous effects of all relevant explanatory variables, not look at some in isolation from others.

The multivariate model that Sullivan and his coauthors devise is designed to do this. It is not necessary that you understand the statistical technique of LISREL in order to follow the argument of their article, but it is important that you understand why it was necessary for them to use some sort of technique that would allow them to look at the simultaneous direct and indirect effects of all explanatory variables. A number of statistical terms are referred to in the article, but I think you can follow the argument adequately even if these are unfamiliar to you. Most represent side-checks on the evidence presented and are not vital to an understanding of the piece.

Sullivan's narrative of how this research came about is pleasing in many ways, but I am personally most pleased at the way in which it exemplifies the basic unity between teaching and research. This research approach was suggested to Sullivan by his undergraduate students, and he developed it in its early stages in undergraduate class projects.

_____ RESEARCH ARTICLE

1A.   The Sources of Political Tolerance: A Multivariate Analysis

JOHN L. SULLIVAN, GEORGE E. MARCUS, STANLEY FELDMAN AND JAMES E. PIERESON

The study of political tolerance has been a major component of public opinion research in the 25 years since Stouffer's seminal contribution (1955). Over this time, a number of findings on the determinants of tolerance have become accepted. Yet there are two reasons to suspect the general conclusions of these studies. First, as we have attempted to show earlier (Sullivan, Piereson and Marcus, 1979), previous studies of political tolerance were flawed in their measurement of the dependent variable. The use of items developed by Stouffer, all with left-wing targets (communists, socialists, and atheists), creates problems that will affect the distribution of political tolerance and will bias estimates of relationships between tolerance and other variables. The content bias resulting from using only left-wing targets means that respondents who are intolerant of *other* groups may erroneously be classified as generally tolerant. Such measures confound the willingness to extend rights to objectionable groups (tolerance) with indifference or perhaps even support of the groups specified. Correlations involving these measures of tolerance are thus difficult to interpret since they invariably tap attitudes toward the group in question as well as the construct of tolerance.

The second problem with previous studies of political tolerance has been their reliance on simple correlations to establish the relationships between tolerance and a number of independent variables. Bivariate correlations, however, can be misleading when other important factors influence both variables in question. This sort of specification error can affect the magnitude and even the direction of parameter estimates. Yet, so far as we have been able to find, no study presents or evaluates a well-specified model of political tolerance. As a result, many currently accepted findings on the determinants of political tolerance may be based on severely biased estimates of the relationships between key independent variables and tolerance.

We wish to acknowledge the support of the National Science Foundation, grant SOC 77-17623, in conducting this study. Professor Michal Shamir provided invaluable assistance.

This article was reprinted from *The American Political Science Review* with permission from the American Political Science Association.

We report here an analysis of the determinants of political tolerance that attempts to correct these problems. We use a content-controlled measure of tolerance to remedy the content-bias of previous measures. This measure is used in a multivariate analysis to evaluate a more fully specified model of political tolerance. In addition, we rely on maximum likelihood confirmatory factor analysis (LISREL) to fit the model to our data. The advantage of this approach to model fitting is that it incorporates a measurement model into the data analysis. We are thus able to examine the reliability and appropriateness of our indicators as one part of the overall evaluation of the model. This will further raise confidence in our results since parameter estimates will be free of the effects of measurement error and the major constructs will be more clearly defined.

POLITICAL TOLERANCE AND DEMOCRATIC THEORY

Much of the theoretical significance of political tolerance derives from its role in varieties of democratic theory. Its importance depends on two sets of empirical questions. The first of these questions involves the distribution of levels of tolerance in society and the relationship of tolerance to political activism. Given the hierarchy of political roles available to citizens today, from those uninvolved in politics to those in formal positions of authority, the citizen's opportunity (and thus responsibility) to sustain the "rules of the game," including ensuring political access to potentially objectionable groups, may vary across these roles in a systematic way. Empirical findings suggesting that those with greatest responsibility have greater commitment to the norms and maintenance of political tolerance would support the continuing hierarchy of influence among political roles as necessary to sustain the tolerant character of the regime. Alternatively, finding the aggregate level of political tolerance to be fairly uniform across different political roles would support a more equitable redistribution of political influence. Thus how tolerant various classes of people are in various political roles has been one of the abiding areas of dispute in the contention between "elitist or revisionist" theories of democracy and "participatory" theories of democracy (see Walker, 1966; Pateman, 1970; Thompson, 1970).

A second important way in which the empirical study of political tolerance can affect views on democratic theory lies in the question of the relationship of political tolerance to other factors. As societies change, for example by becoming more educated, more industrialized and more urban, these changes may alter the extent and nature of tolerance in the political culture. We need, therefore, to explore the determinants of political tolerance and how changes in these determinants are likely to affect the level and distribution of political tolerance. For example, while finding low levels of political tolerance,

Stouffer (1955) also found powerful links between tolerance and education which he expected would lead to increased tolerance in the future. The extent to which political tolerance is linked to determinants likely to go through progressive changes that will in turn ameliorate political intolerance is thus an important empirical question. The answer will add fuel to the controversies as to which type of democratic theory is best suited to our values and circumstances (see Pennock, 1979; Thompson, 1970). Some varieties of democratic theory, for example, have strong developmental expectations. According to such theorists as J. S. Mill, the political culture and the political judgment of the electorate can be expected to improve as formal education and practical political experience become more widespread throughout the public. A model of the development of political tolerance can help to assess the empirical status of such theories.

DEVELOPMENT OF THE MODEL

We will consider variables taken from two sources. First, we will review the major independent variables that previous studies have shown to have significant relationships with political tolerance. Such variables fall into three broad categories: social (or demographic) characteristics such as education, occupation, age and religion; psychological (or personality) characteristics such as self-esteem, authoritarianism and dogmatism; and political characteristics such as political ideology, political involvement and commitment to democratic norms. Second, we will consider those factors that are theoretically important even if research has not yet demonstrated significant relationships.

THE DEPENDENT VARIABLE: POLITICAL TOLERANCE

As we noted in our previous work (Sullivan, Piereson and Marcus, 1979) a measurement procedure is needed which allows respondents themselves to specify the groups they most strongly oppose. In an attempt to obtain such a measure, we developed and tested the following measurement approach on a national survey of 1509 respondents conducted for us by the National Opinion Research Center in the spring of 1978. First, we provided each interview respondent with a list of potentially unpopular groups that ranged from communists and socialists on the left, to fascists, John Birch Society members, and Ku Klux Klan members on the right. We also included a number of groups, such as atheists, pro-abortionists, and anti-abortionists, which we expected in some ways to represent positions that are independent of the left/right dimension. Respondents were then asked to identify the group they liked the least, and we made it very clear that they could also select a group not on the list. Respondents were then presented with a series of statements in an agree/disagree format which elicited their views about a range of activities in which members of that group might have participated. The following statements were among those included in the series:

1. Members of the _____ should be banned from being president of the United States.
2. Members of the _____ should be allowed to teach in the public schools.
3. The _____ should be outlawed.
4. Members of the _____ should be allowed to make a speech in this city.
5. The _____ should have their phones tapped by our government.
6. The _____ should be allowed to hold public rallies in our city.

The statements were read as they appear above with the blanks filled with the group selected by each respondent.

Our intention was to avoid contaminating the tolerance/intolerance dimension with the respondents' political beliefs. If we had merely asked all respondents whether communists should be allowed to hold public office, their responses would have depended not only on their levels of tolerance, but also on their feelings toward communists. The advantage of our procedure is that it creates a situation in which the evaluation of each respondent toward the group in question is held constant. Clearly, our measures are not "content-free" since there is a context and a specific group toward which each respondent must react. We thus call it a "content-controlled" measure, to emphasize that we have attempted to "control for" the content by allowing respondents to select functionally equivalent groups.

In the following analysis, we rely upon a six-item political tolerance scale, based on the six political tolerance items reviewed above. Since each item has five-point agree/disagree response categories, scores on the six-item scale range from 6 to 30. The mean score for the six-item scale is 16.1, well below the midpoint of 18.

Social Determinants of Tolerance

Since Stouffer's in-depth empirical study of tolerance, a number of basic demographic variables have been thought to influence political tolerance. Foremost among these is education. Education is thought to increase familiarity with diverse ideas and people. Moreover, the citizen must *learn* that a free market of ideas is vital to American democracy and that nonconformists are not necessarily bad. This is basically a cognitive explanation; one learns the principle that free exchange of ideas is necessary and that to be different is not necessarily to be bad and dangerous. Thus education plays a dual role in increasing levels of information and increasing the willingness to accept hitherto threatening information.

While this argument makes no attempt to tie education into the more general aspects of the social structure, high social status is also likely to be linked to increased experience (hence acceptance of diversity of opinion) and increased security from threat (hence greater willingness to allow others to hold potentially threatening ideas and to display potentially threatening behavior). This reasoning would lead us to expect social status to be related to tolerance in somewhat the same way as education is (see Korman, 1975).

In our study, we examine the impact of both education and social status, the latter measured by income and occupational position. Social status is measured by the Hodge-Siegel Prestige Score, which is assigned to the reported occupation of the respondent (or in the case of the unemployed, of the respondent's spouse; for details see Siegel, 1971).

Previous researchers have found a relationship between age and political tolerance. Because younger respondents are likely to be more educated, and because the younger cohorts of respondents have experienced a political climate that should be more liberalizing and enlightening than that of their elders (a period effect), age should be inversely related to tolerance. The increasing commitment to civil rights for blacks, women and the poor, particularly on the part of the young in the 1960s, may have given the younger respondents a greater commitment to political tolerance, or so the argument runs. Thus, while the link between age and tolerance may be strongly affected by the influence of education (Stouffer, 1955; Nunn et al., 1978; Cutler and Kaufman, 1975), it appears from other studies that even after the influence of education is removed, age may still have a conservative effect on political tolerance.

Past studies (Stouffer, 1955; Nunn, et al., 1978) have also uncovered what appears to be a relationship between religion and tolerance of ideological nonconformity. Following Stouffer, Nunn and his associates found that in 1973, Jews and non-religious people were the most tolerant, followed by Catholics and Protestants, with little difference between the latter two religious groups. The percentage differences discovered were substantial, as approximately 46 percent of Protestants, 59 percent of Catholics, 88 percent of Jews, and 87 percent of non-religious people were categorized as "more tolerant" on Nunn's scale.

Other researchers have discovered the relationships between tolerance and additional social variables such as sex, size of city, and region. Our research, reported elsewhere (Sullivan et al., 1982) shows that all of these social background variables relate with target-group selection in such a way that the content-bias of the traditional measurement procedures may have produced misleading conclusions about the correlates and determinants of political tolerance. For example, the following respondents are most likely to select rightwing targets: those with more education, younger respondents, Jewish or non-religious respondents, urban residents, residents of the East, and so on. On the other hand, the following respondents are mostly likely to select left-wing targets, precisely those groups included in previous studies of tolerance: the uneducated, those of the older generation, Catholics or Protestants, rural residents, residents of the South and Midwest, and so on. Thus previous studies may have "stacked the deck" by asking about groups which are, in some sense, harder for certain respondents to tolerate.

Psychological Determinants of Tolerance

In addition to the studies which have focused on the demographic determinants of political tolerance, other studies have examined mainly the psychological and personality sources of political tolerance (Knutson, 1972; Zellman and Sears, 1971; Zalkind, Gaugler and Schwartz, 1975). The most consistent finding links self-esteem (or a closely related concept) to political tolerance. Most analysts have examined self-esteem within a trait conceptualization of personality, although Sniderman (1975) viewed low self-esteem as a hindrance to the social learning of political norms, including tolerance. Sniderman argued that low self-esteem leads to intolerance because it interferes with social learning. Although the norms of society may be tolerant ones, a significant portion of the public will neither learn nor adhere to these norms because this requires a facility for abstract thought that many do not possess. In particular, people with low self-esteem will "reject the norms of democratic politics not because they are motivated to do so but largely because their negative self-attitudes have impeded the learning of these values" (p. 178). While he concentrates on the social learning argument, Sniderman also argues that low self-esteem may interfere with motivation to learn norms and ideals such as tolerance.

Sniderman used three different measures of self-esteem that correlate highly with one another and produce similar results. In the interests of parsimony, we selected his eight-item personality unworthiness scale as the measure of self-esteem we would use in our multivariate analysis. The scale has a reliability (coefficient alpha) of .69.

Probably the most dominant tradition in political psychology is research into the authoritarian personality (see Sanford, 1973). In essence, the authoritarian personality construct is based on a trait approach—an approach which assumes personality to be a collection of traits within the individual. Authoritarianism consists of a number of important characteristics including authoritarian submission, defined as a basic need to obey those in authority and to command subordinates; aggression toward outgroups, which means redirecting underlying hostility of authorities toward weaker scapegoats;

stereotyped thinking—that is, intolerance of ambiguity and a strong tendency to think in terms of black and white categories—and other similar characteristics. Seen in these terms, the relationship of authoritarianism to political intolerance is probably close, although tolerance is an attitude rather than a personality trait and the two must be separated analytically.

A serious problem, from our point of view, are the criticisms that the traditional measure of authoritarianism, the F-scale, is appropriate to measure authoritarianism on the political right but not on the left. Theoretically, there is no reason why left-wing belief systems cannot be rigid or authoritarian. One major alternative to the F-scale is Rokeach's work on dogmatism (1960) which attempts to measure the degree of people's open-mindedness and flexibility without regard to ideological content. We include seven dogmatism items which create a scale with a coefficient alpha of .77.

Another strategy is to employ an indirect measure that taps a central aspect of the authoritarian syndrome. To accomplish this, we have included three items from Rosenberg's faith in people scale (1956) and two items from Martin's and Westie's threat orientation scale (1959). Since an important characteristic of the authoritarian personality is distrust of other people, their motives and their impulses, we deem the five items an appropriate, if simple, measure of the affective component of authoritarianism. These items create a scale with a coefficient alpha of .69.

Another major approach is that of Knutson (1972) who relies on the conceptualization of personality developed by Maslow. In this scheme, human personality is dependent on the satisfaction of various needs, ranging from the most basic (physiological and safety needs) to the more complex (affiliation, self-esteem, and self-actualization needs). These needs form a definite hierarchy with the more basic needs requiring satisfaction before the needs on the next level of the hierarchy can be met. Knutson has characterized these as lying along a continuum with "concern with self" at one end and "concern with self in relation to one's environment" at the other. The self-centered person is unlikely to experience empathy; since most of that person's energies are directed toward meeting personal, basic needs, abstract ideas such as tolerance are unlikely to receive much attention from such a person. Thus, at one end, individuals are expected to be self-centered and most of their behavior should be directed at immediate, concrete goal fulfillment. At the other end, individuals are expected to consider and examine broader perspectives and to be concerned with how they relate to others and to the social environment more generally. Using Knutson's formulation, we would anticipate a monotonic relationship with higher levels on the need hierarchy linked to greater tolerance.

In order to assess people's positions on Maslow's need hierarchy, we asked people in our national study to select their most important value from a list provided them. We selected one value that represented each level on the need hierarchy (see Inglehart, 1977; Marsh, 1977). The values are listed in Table 1.1 along with the need level they purport to measure and the percentage of our national sample selecting each as most important. The relationship is generally monotonic. There is a strong increase in political tolerance as one moves from the safety-security need level to the affiliation need level.

To anticipate our findings somewhat, we did not find that these four psychological variables were able to discriminate among the various approaches to personality and political tolerance. Our analysis showed all to be linked to political tolerance, and furthermore, that the most powerful analysis was to incorporate the four indicators as alternative measures (multiple indicators) of a single concept: personality. Since the four indicators are so highly intercorrelated and the measurement approach we use corrects correlations for attenuation due to unreliability, multicollinearity problems require us to use them as multiple indicators. Conceptually then, we combine the four personality variables in a single factor, perhaps best defined as "psychological security." The four indicators have much in common because each focuses, in importantly different ways, on the ability of the individual to confront reality and social experience, and to deal with a world that is complex, ambiguous and threatening. The variance shared by these indicators suggests that people vary in the extent to which they are psychologically prepared to engage a socially and politically complex environment.[1]

Political Determinants of Tolerance

The most serious omission in previous studies of political tolerance has been the failure to examine *political* tolerance as an inherently *political* concept with its source in *political* processes. We will attempt to correct this deficiency by examining the importance of three sets of political variables, including political ideology, political threat, and support for the general norms of democracy.

The differences between liberals and conservatives are sometimes thought to account for various degrees of political toleration. At times, the terms "tolerance" and "liberalism" are used interchangeably so that the acceptance of norms of toleration is said to be a liberal position and the rejection of tolerance, or a more guarded acceptance, is said to be a conservative or "illiberal" position (see Lipset and Raab, 1970, pp. 432–33). Those who make this connection, however, are usually careful to distinguish between economic and non-economic issues, where the former refers to questions of the distribution of wealth and the latter to those of cultural conformity and nonconformity. In this sense, tolerance is understood to be part of the social or non-economic dimension of domestic liberalism. Tolerance is thus associated with issues such as the legalization of drugs, acceptance of cultural nonconformity and opposition to traditional women's roles.

TABLE 1.1
Respondents' Choice of Most Important Need

Maslow Need Hierarchy	Value	Percent of Sample	Mean Tolerance Score*
1. Physiological Needs	Comfortable Life	24	14.9
2. Safety and Security Needs	Security	31	15.0
3. Affiliation and Love Needs	Affection	19	16.7
4. Esteem Needs	Esteem	20	17.7
5. Self-Actualization Needs	Originality	6	18.0
N = 1509			

Source: Computed from 1978 Political Tolerance Survey conducted by the National Opinion Research Center, University of Chicago.

*On the six-item scale which ranges from 6–30.

From another perspective, social scientists such as McClosky (1960) and Eysenck (1954) have suggested that ideological identification is linked to personality characteristics that might lead us to anticipate a link with tolerance. Specifically, McClosky argues that support of certain conservative beliefs signals a personality unlikely to engage in political discourse, to adapt to social change, to extend universal norms to strangers, and to engage in stereotyping and discriminations. Thus this non-economic dimension of ideology may relate to tolerance in part because of certain underlying personality characteristics. While previous studies of political tolerance may have overestimated the impact of ideology due to an inherent left-wing bias, we advance the tentative hypothesis that those on the left will be more tolerant of extremist groups on the right than those on the right will be tolerant of corresponding groups on the left.

Two measures of ideology, in the left/right sense, have been adopted. The first is an index of ideological self-placement, a seven-point liberal/conservative scale on which respondents were asked to locate themselves. The second measure is based on the ideology of respondents' two least-liked groups. As we demonstrated earlier (Sullivan, Piereson, and Marcus, 1979), respondents at the liberal end of the spectrum were most likely to select targets from the right, and vice versa. It is therefore possible to contrive a measure of ideology based on the target groups selected. Thus, those who chose two right-wing groups were classified as the most liberal, while those who chose two left-wing groups were classified, on a three-point scale, as the most conservative. Those who picked one group from each end of the spectrum were placed in the middle of the scale.

Previous studies have also shown that the level of intolerance in individuals is directly related to their perceptions of dissident groups as posing a threat (see Stouffer, 1955, Ch. 8). Thus intolerance arises from people's perceptions that dissident groups threaten values important to them or constitute a danger to the constitutional order. Yet it is also true that many people who perceive dissident groups as threatening are nevertheless prepared to tolerate them and to defend their procedural claims. It is appropriate, therefore, to test this general proposition within a multivariate framework with our data.

We attempted to measure the threat posed by each respondent's least-liked group by presenting a series of semantic differential adjectives about the group in question. We began with eight adjective pairs, which were factor-analyzed. The five adjective pairs with the highest loadings on the first factor extracted were selected for use as indicators of perceived threat: honest/dishonest; trustworthy/untrustworthy; safe/dangerous; nonviolent/violent; and good/bad.

While previous studies (Prothro and Grigg, 1960; McClosky, 1964) have concluded there is little relationship in the mass public between support for some general democratic principles and the specific applications of these principles, this conclusion—based on a comparison of marginal distributions—needs more examination. The observed consensus in favor of the abstract statements and the lack of any such consensus on the specific items were taken to mean that there was no relationship between the two. A more appropriate way to approach the problem is to measure the relationship between the degree to which individuals support the abstract principles and the degree to which they apply them in practice.

To examine this question, we repeated in our survey two of the questions used by Prothro and Grigg and four used by McClosky. These items, along with the distribution of responses in our survey, are summarized in Table 1.2. The first four items express democratic principles in highly abstract form, while the last two are more specific and hence more controversial. The distribution of responses to these items is very close to those reported in the earlier studies, despite Prothro's and Grigg's use of local samples, and the passage of nearly 20 years. It is still true that the overwhelming proportion of the American public supports the principles of minority rights, majority rule, equality under the law, and free speech when these principles are posed in an abstract form, as they are in the first four items of the table.

Although the marginal distributions of responses to questions ascertaining support for abstract principles and to questions ascertaining support for specific situations of political tolerance may vary substantially, it does *not* follow that there is no relationship between the two categories of questions. Among recent writers, only Lawrence (1976) has been sensitive to this problem as he tried to measure the relationship between respondents' positions on the general norms regarding tolerance and their willingness to apply them in practice. Using different items, Lawrence found considerable consistency between support for general norms and their application to specific circumstances, concluding: "Large majorities of the population in fact apply

TABLE 1.2
Support for General Principles of Civil Liberties (Percent)

General Statement[a]	Agree	Uncertain	Disagree	Agree with Prothro-Grigg or McClosky[b]	Correlation[c] with Six-Item Tolerance Scale (Specific Acts)
1. People in the minority should be free to try to win majority support for their opinions.	89	9	2	94–98	.25
2. Public officials should be chosen by majority vote.	95	3	2	94–98	.27
3. No matter what a person's political beliefs are, he is entitled to the same legal rights and protections as anyone else.	93	4	3	94	.22
4. I believe in free speech for all no matter what their views might be.	85	7	9	89	.29
5. When the country is in great danger we may have to force people to testify against themselves even if it violates their rights.	35	16	48	36	−.14
6. Any person who hides behind the laws when he is questioned about his activities doesn't deserve much consideration.	52	16	32	76	−.23

N = 1509

Source: Computed from 1978 Political Tolerance Survey, conducted by National Opinion Research Center, University of Chicago.

[a]The first two questions listed are taken from the Prothro-Grigg (1960) questionnaire, while the last four are taken from McClosky's (1964). Our questions were presented in the form of five-point agree-disagree scales. The agree column reports the percentage that agree or strongly agree while the disagree column reports the percentage that disagree or strongly disagree. In the original studies, these questions were presented dichotomously so that respondents either had to agree or disagree.

[b]Reported in Prothro and Grigg (1960) and McClosky (1964).

[c]Correlations are Pearson's r.

their tolerant general norms consistently on even the hardest . . . issues"
(p. 93).

Although the proposition is often taken for granted that abstract beliefs
influence responses to practical situations, it is not surprising to find that there
is not a one-to-one relationship between the two. Competing values usually
operate in practical circumstances, so that people are forced to find some
compromise between or among them. Hence, we hypothesize that the
stronger their commitment to the general norms of democracy, the more
willing people should be to act on those norms. Table 1.2 presents the simple
correlations between the various questions measuring support for the general
norms and our six-item tolerance scale, which is based on responses to
specific situations and political groups. These correlations, while not particularly high, are all in the expected direction. In interpreting these correlations,
readers should bear in mind that there is little variation in the responses to
these four items (note the distributions in the table), a circumstance that will
usually reduce the size of the correlations.

In addition to the variables of left/right ideology, perceptions of threat and
support for general norms concerning tolerance, additional political variables
such as political interest, participation, and information were also examined.
There is sufficient theoretical reason to expect a strong relationship between
an individual's political involvement, for example, and political tolerance.
Participatory democracy theorists (such as Pateman, 1970) have argued that
the process of political participation is an educative one, and that tolerance is
one of the natural outcomes of such a process. Empirical studies have found
large differences in tolerance between the participatory elite and the non-
participatory masses (cf. Stouffer, 1955, p. 57). We find that most of these
differences are probably the result of the content-bias of the Stouffer-based
questions, because in our national sample we find that political participation
relates strongly to target group selection, but not to tolerance (the higher
participants dislike right-wing groups more). The parameter estimates in our
model are unaffected by excluding these additional political variables.

MULTIVARIATE ANALYSIS OF POLITICAL TOLERANCE

In this section, we specify a more complete model of political tolerance
including variables from each of the three sets. In general, we assume that
social variables are causally prior to psychological variables, which in turn
precede political variables. Certainly these are dynamic relationships. As our
analysis uses a cross-sectional survey, it must necessarily be a static one. We
assume that this general causal ordering represents the major processes
underlying the relationships among these variables.

Figure 1.1 presents the hypothesized relationships among endogenous and
exogenous variables in our model of political tolerance. We assume the most

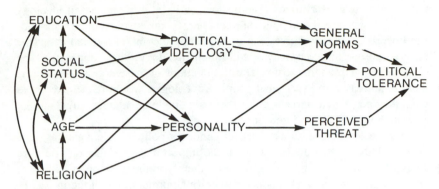

Source: Compiled by the authors

FIGURE 1.1
Fully Specified Model of Political Tolerance

important immediate causes of tolerance to be twofold: adherence to the general norms of civil liberties, and the perceived threat posed by the group toward which the tolerance (or intolerance) is directed. The reasons for our expectations are outlined above, and there is no compelling reason to expect that the impact of these two variables would be mediated by any of the other endogenous variables.

An individual's perception of another group as threatening is undoubtedly affected by psychological processes rather than resulting solely from realistic assessments of the danger of a particular disliked group. Some respondents may be psychologically predisposed to perceive threats whether they exist or not; and, thus, some people may be predisposed to be intolerant while others may not. The psychological characteristics discussed earlier, such as dogmatism and low self-esteem, might therefore explain perceptions of threat and, indirectly, tolerance and intolerance. If this argument were completely true, then levels of tolerance and intolerance in the society would be independent of actual political developments. We take the view here that perceptions of threat do involve evaluations of the political strength of, and the danger posed by, dissident groups, although since such perceptions are subjective, they will be affected by psychological variables such as personality.

Turning to political ideology, we have already noted the liberal sources of tolerance. There is considerable reason to expect liberals to be more tolerant than conservatives. We fully expect some of this impact to operate through support for general norms of democracy, since the norms of democracy are themselves liberal norms. Thus liberals should be more likely to adopt these norms than are conservatives. There should also be some impact of ideology which operates directly on political tolerance, because while not all rank-and-file liberals and conservatives can be expected to comprehend and adopt the general norms most consistent with their ideology, they might well be expected to adopt the more concrete implications of these norms.[2] However, there is no reason to expect that people's ideologies would relate directly to what they perceive as threats, since there are ample threatening targets in the eyes of both liberals and conservatives.

The role of personality as to its influence on political tolerance has been discussed above. It is unclear whether the impact of personality on tolerance should be expected to be direct, or to be merely indirect, through its link to perceptions of threat and support for toleration norms. Some of the impact of psychological factors is no doubt indirect, as we noted in its role in the development of the perceptions of threat from other groups and ideas. In addition, those respondents who are more dogmatic, low on Maslow's need hierarchy, low in self-esteem and low in trust in people, can be expected to be more conservative than their opposite counterparts, and to be less likely to learn accurately the norms of the political system, leading us to expect a relationship between inner security and the support for general norms of democracy (Sniderman, 1975).

It is less clear what to expect regarding the direct impact of personality on political tolerance. Certainly, Sniderman's analysis (1975) suggests a direct impact, but it is plausible to explain this as working through the impact of personality on the learning of general norms. Perhaps those with low self-esteem are less tolerant merely because their lack of esteem interferes with learning general norms of democracy so that they cannot therefore apply them in specific situations. On the other hand, in addition to affecting the learning of general norms of democracy, low self-esteem may enhance the tendency to project personal inadequacies onto hated scapegoats, as suggested by the traditional literature on personality and politics. This could operate above and beyond this indirect effect, and in a sense, a comparison of the direct and indirect effects of personality on tolerance may provide a crude test of the social learning hypothesis as against the more traditional personality-trait hypothesis. The indirect effect of personality on toleration through support for general norms of democracy may represent the effect of personality through social learning, while the direct effect may represent its effect through traditional personality traits such as authoritarianism

The four sociological variables in our model (all exogenous) include education, social status, age, and religion. Education is expected to have a major direct impact on three variables: political ideology, personality, and understanding general norms. Education has been shown to be related to tolerance in many studies, reviewed above, but these studies have not attempted to discern whether its impact is mediated by other variables. Furthermore, our evidence suggests that education relates more strongly with the selection of target groups than with tolerance per se (Sullivan et al., 1982).

There is good reason to expect education to have an impact on at least three endogenous variables other than political tolerance. It ought to have two opposite impacts on ideology. Previous studies have shown that education leads to greater economic conservatism, and greater social liberalism (Erikson and Luttbeg, 1973; Ladd, 1978). Thus the composition of our political ideology variable—social rather than economic—determines the direction of the relationship between education and ideology. Education also ought to affect personality—particularly those aspects of it that we have discussed here—self-actualization, dogmatism, and self-esteem. Persons with higher levels of education ought to be more competent in their environment, generally better able to manipulate and understand the forces which affect them, and thus better able to close the gap between the ideal self and the perceived self, i.e., to have higher self-esteem. They should also learn about diverse points of view and ways of experiencing life, thus becoming less dogmatic, even if they had a tendency toward closed-mindedness before achieving a high level of education. Finally, education ought to enable people to learn better the general norms of democracy. Since these norms are abstract, and require the ability to understand concepts, the highly educated should be more adept at learning and understanding them. Indeed, this was one of the major findings of both Prothro and Grigg (1960) and of McClosky (1964). The major unanswered question about the impact of education is similar to the question regarding the impact of personality: does it have any direct effect on political tolerance, above and beyond its impact on personality and support for general norms?

Social status should have an impact similar to that of education, while age should affect two of the political variables directly—older respondents should be more conservative (both on social and economic issues), and they should be more dogmatic and have lower self-esteem (see Erikson and Luttbeg, 1973). Religion is defined as secular detachment. We have found that specific religious preference is related to target group selection, rather than political tolerance.[3] Secular detachment should have basically the same impact as age.

The model in Figure 1.1 presents the variables that we expect to have direct and significant impacts on one another. It is not a fully recursive model because several possible recursive relationships are not expected to be significant and have therefore been deleted. In estimating the parameters of the model, we estimate a fully recursive model, although generally we will report only those coefficients which are statistically significant. In this way, our a priori expectations can be compared with the modeling results; it will become clear which of the hypothesized direct paths, in Figure 1.1, are erroneous and should not have been specified, and it will likewise be clear which unspecified paths do in fact appear to exist between variables.

PARAMETER ESTIMATION

We rely on maximum-likelihood confirmatory factor analysis (LISREL) to fit the model to our data. The problem of measurement error is addressed by allowing the researcher to specify first a set of theoretical relationships among unmeasured, theoretical constructs; and second, to specify a set of measurement relationships between these theoretical constructs and their empirical indicators. Using only information about the relationships among indicators, the researcher is able to obtain estimates of the relationships among the theoretical constructs (called *structural parameters*) and estimates of the relationships between each theoretical construct and its empirical indicators (called *epistemic correlations*).[4] The details of these statistical procedures are presented in Jöreskog (1969, 1970, 1973); a brief summary may be found in

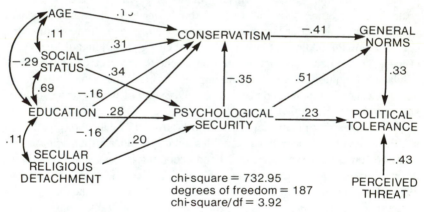

chi-square = 732.95
degrees of freedom = 187
chi-square/df = 3.92

Source: Computed from 1978 Political Tolerance Survey, National Opinion Research Center, University of Chicago.

Note: Disturbance terms have been omitted for sake of clarity.

$x^2 = 732.95$
degrees of freedom = 187
$x^2/df = 3.92$

FIGURE 1.2
Model of the Sources of Political Tolerance

the appendix. Most of the theoretical constructs are measured by several empirical indicators. The epistemic correlations help both to determine which indicators are the most reliable measures of each construct, and to assess the "true nature" of the construct.[5] Table 1.3 presents the epistemic correlations for those constructs with multiple indicators and for the six-item tolerance scale.[6] Single-indicator exogenous variables are not presented in this table.

The epistemic correlations are consistent with the definitions given to the constructs. Interestingly, the general norms construct seems primarily defined by the political process rules (majority vote and free speech) rather than by legal rules. The single value-actualization item relates only weakly to personality, and the common semantic differential format of the perceived threat indicators introduces some minor correlated error ($-.13$ between honest/dishonest and safe/dangerous).

Regarding the personality construct, the dogmatism scale is the "best" indicator. It practically defines the construct, although the self-esteem scale also has a large epistemic correlation. The other two variables—the value measure of self-actualization and the faith in people scale—are of lesser importance than dogmatism and self-esteem in defining the personality construct. Thus, although we label the construct psychological security, it is closely related to the traditional dogmatism-authoritarianism syndrome presented in the personality and politics literature, and in personality research generally. A lack of self-esteem is often hypothesized to underlie this syndrome, and the epistemic correlations suggest that this is the case here. The dogmatism scale also has the highest bivariate correlation with political tolerance.

The relationship between the theoretical constructs is called structural parameters (*partial* path coefficients, corrected for measurement error). The structural parameters represent the strength of the relationships between each of the theoretical constructs included in the model, controlling for the other constructs. Figure 1.2 presents the political tolerance model with the exogenous and endogenous variables included. As we previously noted, political involvement is not included inasmuch as no direct or indirect relationships with political tolerance were found.

The perception of others as posing a threat has the strongest direct impact on political tolerance; the coefficient of $-.43$ shows that the more respondents perceived a threat from the target group the less their political tolerance. The general norms construct also has a strong impact ($.33$), confirming the hypothesis that the general norms of democracy do force some constraint onto specific applications of tolerance. There is a slight tendency for conservatives to exhibit less tolerance, all other things being equal, but the coefficient is small ($-.10$) and is statistically insignificant. We assume that the only reason conservatives are less tolerant than liberals is that they are less supportive of

TABLE 1.3
Epistemic Correlations among Indicators in Political Tolerance Model

Theoretical Construct	Indicator	Epistemic Correlation
Social Status	Occupation	.53
	Income	.87
Psychological Security	Value-Actualization	.43
	Self-Esteem	.67
	Dogmatism	.81
	Trust in Others	.50
Conservatism	Self-Placement	.44
	Least-Liked Group	.58
General Norms	Minority Rights	.44
	Majority Vote	.53
	Equal Legal Rights	.32
	Free Speech	.58
	Fifth Amendment	.32
	Legal Protection	.24
Perceived Threat	Honest/Dishonest*	.67
	Trustworthy/Untrustworthy	.63
	Safe/Dangerous*	.89
	Non-Violent/Violent	.62
	Good/Bad	.66
Political Tolerance	Six-Item Tolerance Scale	.89

Source: Computed from 1978 Political Tolerance Survey, conducted by National Opinion Research Center, University of Chicago. Complete listing of the actual items, and the questionnaires, are available from the authors.

*Correlated error terms between these two items, $r = -.13$.

the general norms of democracy, since ideology and support for general norms are strongly related ($-.41$).

Psychological security has the hypothesized effects on political ideology and general norms. Respondents who are less dogmatic and have greater self-esteem tend to be both more liberal and more likely to support the general norms of democracy above and beyond that expected by their liberalism. Personality's direct effect on the general norms construct is in fact quite powerful, suggesting that support for the norms of democracy is not purely cognitive, nor is it purely a function of political ideology—the affect component of personality has a powerful influence on this support. Unexpectedly, psychological security and perceptions of threat are unrelated to one another. Our expectation, that perceptions of threat would be greater when the level of inner security is low, is clearly proved wrong.

The first question mark—whether psychological security has a direct influence on political tolerance—is answered in the affirmative (.23) in addition to its rather powerful indirect effect through the general norms construct. Persons with flexible, secure and trusting personalities are much more likely to be tolerant beyond that expected because of differences between them and people with opposite personalities as a consequence of the indirect effects through general norms of tolerance. The evidence is thus consistent with Sniderman's results (1975).

In Figure 1.2 four exogenous variables are included in the model—secular detachment, education, social status, and age. All but the third are single-indicator variables for which we assume perfect measurement. There is one significant correlation among error terms, here between income and age. Since age is assumed to be perfectly measured, the correlated error is between the error terms for the indicator (income) and the construct (age).

None of these exogenous variables has *any* direct effect on the constructs for general norms, political tolerance, or perceived threat. However, psychological security is strongly influenced by education (.28) and social status (.34); and political ideology is affected by social status (.31) while the impact of education is minimal ($-.16$). These results are discussed elsewhere (Sullivan et al., 1982), especially the finding that an individual's social status is positively related to the degree of conservatism, but is negatively and only indirectly related to psychological factors. Space considerations preclude the extended discussion necessary to unravel these relationships.

The model fits the data quite well, with a chi-square to degrees of freedom ratio of 3.92, generally considered acceptable.[7] The R^2 for the endogenous variables are: psychological security, .42; conservatism, .22; general norms, .60; and for political tolerance, .57. So the model does go a long way toward explaining support for the general norms of democracy and specific applications of these norms to least-liked political groups.[8]

CONCLUSIONS

We have examined the impact of social, psychological and political variables on levels of political tolerance toward people's least-liked political groups, as reported by a national sample of respondents. From the analysis reported herein, we conclude the following:

1. Social variables generally have very little impact on individuals' support for the general norms of democracy or for political tolerance. Such variables have no direct impact, and have only minor indirect effects, mediated through such variables as political ideology and personality. Variables such as sex, region, race, and size of city, which previous research has suggested are strongly related to political tolerance, do not correlate with political tolerance once the content-controlled measurement strategy is adopted. Secular detachment, education, and age have a very small indirect impact on political tolerance, while, surprisingly, social status has a somewhat larger indirect

impact, as it is one of the major factors influencing personality and political ideology.

2. Personality variables have both a powerful indirect impact on tolerance, through support for general norms of democracy and a fairly strong direct impact on political tolerance. Our results are quite consistent with those reported by Zellman and Sears (1971) and Sniderman (1975). We were unable to separate various aspects of personality, to examine the relative impact of self-esteem and self-actualization, for example, in order to test the relative merit of the Sniderman (1975) and Knutson (1972) theses. The presence of both indirect and direct effects *suggests* that the impact of personality is exhibited both by improving the learning of society's political norms, as suggested by Sniderman, and directly through the affective aspects of personality, as suggested by Knutson. We cannot press this line of inquiry too far, but it certainly suggests that both social learning and more traditional psychoanalytic and humanistic formulations should be taken seriously in any examination of political tolerance.

3. Two political variables—general norms and perceived threat—have a strong direct impact on political tolerance, though other political variables such as political interest, information and participation had no discernible impact. Our work is thus consistent with Lawrence's finding (1976) but somewhat inconsistent with the conclusions of Prothro and Grigg (1960) and McClosky (1964). Surprisingly, perceived threat is an exogenous variable in the model and thus is not merely or even partially a projection of psychological insecurity onto disliked political groups. The common view that inner needs dictate perception of threat is clearly not appropriate here.

On the other hand, general norms are strongly influenced both by political ideology and personality. Support for the general norms of democracy are thus partially the result of a political-ideological calculation of the importance of tolerance compared with other political values, but also partially the result of the degree to which individuals are open, flexible, and secure personally. Surprisingly, education does not have a direct effect on general norms, and even its indirect effects through ideology and personality are weak. It is plausible to suggest, therefore, that support for general norms is more the result of personality predispositions than of cognitive processes such as might result from civic education.

We by no means regard this analysis as definitive and the debate as closed. We do, however, suggest that we have taken the analysis a step further by adopting a content-controlled measurement strategy and by working with a more fully specified multivariate model, particularly one which takes an explicit measurement model into account in conducting the analysis.

The varieties of democratic theory are many and it would be inappropriate to say that these findings uniformly and consistently support any of these theories. However, some brief suggestive points may be made. The failure of political involvement—broadly investigated to include information, interest and participation—to have any direct or indirect effect on political tolerance, and the weakness of the ability of education to strengthen political tolerance suggests that participatory and populist versions of democratic theory have placed too much emphasis upon the presumed salutory impact of these variables, at least with regard to the American setting. On the other hand, the failure of measures of social status to play a powerful role in differentiating the politically tolerant from the intolerant suggests that conservative variants of democratic theory have placed too great a weight on the ability of the "better classes" to sustain the political norms of tolerance.

APPENDIX

Since we had several measures of many of the important constructs in our model, we wanted to take advantage of this excess information to estimate the parameters of the model free from the effects of measurement error. Multiple-indicator models are appropriate in such a situation but the complexity of the model means that more sophisticated methods are needed (Sullivan and Feldman, 1979). To accomplish this, LISREL requires the specification of three sets of equations. The first is the set of equations giving the (hypothe-sized) relationships among the *true* or latent variables. To define those latent variables, two other sets of equations are necessary. One set specifies the *indicators* of the endogenous (dependent) variables as functions of these variables' true scores plus a rando error component for each indicator, while the other set of equations does the same for the indicators of the exogenous (independent) variables. Thus, on the basis of these three sets of equations, all the relationships in the main and auxiliary (measurement) theories may be clearly specified as one of three types: free parameters (to be estimated), fixed parameters, and constrained parameters (unknown but set equal to some other parameter to be estimated).

In this form it is not possible to estimate directly the free or constrained parameters since there are too many unknowns in the equations. It is possible, however, to derive the variance-covariance matrix for the indicators on the basis of the hypothesized factor structure. Details may be found in Jöreskog (1973). This derived variance-covariance matrix should then equal the observed variance-covariance matrix of the indicators assuming correct specification of the model. The problem then becomes one of estimating the values of the free and constrained parameters so as to maximize the fit between the derived and observed variance-covariance matrices. If the model is identified, maximum-likelihood estimation procedures are used because for large samples these estimates are consistent (unbiased), efficient (having as small a variance as any other estimator), and approximately normally distributed. The estimators are also scale-in-variant, meaning that if the units of measurement have no real significance, as is the case here, the correlation matrix may be analyzed instead of the variance-covariance matrix. And finally, maximum-likelihood estimation generates a convenient statistical test for evaluating the adequacy of the model, the likelihood-ratio test which, for large samples (the case here) is distributed as chi-square and allows a test of the null hypothesis that the model specified by the fixed and constrained parameters is a perfect fit to the observed data. This simultaneously tests the fit of the structural relationships *and* the measurement component of the model. A large chi-square indicates that the hypothesized model does *not* fit.

NOTES

1. The excessive intercorrelations of these personality measures prevents any direct comparisons among the various psychological explanations. Such a result is not totally unexpected; unfortunately it may be predicted from several theoretical perspectives. Knutson (1972) demonstrates that the need hierarchy formulation can account for the development of a number of personality characteristics, including the ones used here. The data are also consistent with Rokeach's argument (1960) that low self-esteem will lead people to develop dogmatic belief systems and to exhibit little faith in other people. These results are consistent with the broad outlines of the theory of the authoritarian personality.

2. Although in the United States we fully expect even most conservatives to adopt the norm of tolerance, at least in the abstract, we do believe that conservatives will be more likely than liberals to trade off tolerance against other political values, such as stability and security. It is, of course, a matter of degree.

3. We divided our sample into the same four religious groups: Protestants, Catholic, Jewish, and non-religious respondents. Using our content controlled measure we found almost no difference among Protestants, Catholics and Jews in their levels of political tolerance, although we did find some large differences in percentages selecting left-wing groups as least-liked targets. This again suggests the importance of the content bias of the original Stouffer questions, as Jews are more tolerant of left-wing groups but not of right-wing groups. We find that people who adhere to no particular religious faith are more tolerant than the more religious respondents, and in fact the differences are large. The only difference in tolerance scores among the various Protestant denominations is that Baptists are less tolerant than the others. To maximize the relationship with tolerance, we coded Baptists 1, non-religious people 3, and all others 2. When this is done, the correlation with our tolerance index is .26. Thus, although religion appears to be an important variable in understanding political tolerance, it is primarily a secular detachment from religion that is important, not whether one is Jewish, Catholic, or Protestant.

4. Since almost all of the variables in this analysis are attitude or personality scales which have arbitrary units of analysis—and since the major concern is a comparison of

the relative impact of different variables—we have relied on standardized rather than unstandardized coefficients.

5. Readers versed in factor analysis can interpret the epistemic correlations as factor loadings and the abstract constructs as factors. The pattern of loadings helps to label and interpret the factors.

6. The epistemic correlation between the tolerance scale and the underlying construct is obtained by taking the square root of the scale's estimated reliability. Coefficient alpha for the tolerance scale is .79, so the epistemic correlation is fixed at .89. The other epistemic correlations are estimated using the excess information, provided by the over-identified model, using the LISREL program. In the case of the personality construct it will not generally be true that the epistemic correlations equal the square root of the estimated reliabilities. This is the case because the epistemic correlations reflect both the reliability of the appropriate scale and its relationship to the more general personality construct.

7. While the chi-square statistic provided by the LISREL program does yield a probability level for evaluating the goodness-of-fit of the model, this is not very useful in practice since the chi-square is a direct function of the sample size. Thus, for the number of cases we have here, any non-trivial model will fail to pass this test of statistical significance. A more useful test of fit in this case is to compute the ratio of chi-square to degrees of freedom. As a rule of thumb, ratios of less than five (for this number of cases) are indicative of a well-specified model (see Wheaton et al., 1977).

8. In our national sample, we included a subset of four items from Stouffer's 15-item tolerance index. When a scale of these four items is used in the model, several important differences occur. Briefly, the Stouffer index produces a significant negative path between conservatism and tolerance, confirming our suspicion of bias in the Stouffer items. We elsewhere describe this and other differences more fully (Sullivan et al., 1981).

REFERENCES

Cutler, Stephen J., and Robert L. Kaufman (1975). "Cohort Changes in Political Attitudes: Tolerance of Ideological Nonconformity." *Public Opinion Quarterly* 39: 69–81.

Erikson, Robert S., and Norman R. Luttbeg (1973). *American Public Opinion: Its Origins, Content and Impact*. New York: John Wiley.

Eysenck, Hans Murgen (1954). *The Psychology of Politics*. New York: Praeger.

Inglehart, Ronald (1977). *The Silent Revolution: Changing Values and Political Styles*. Princeton, N.J.: Princeton University Press.

Jöreskog, K. G. (1969). "A General Approach to Confirmatory Maximum Likelihood Factor Analysis." *Psychometrika* 34: 183–202.

———— (1970). "A General Method for Analysis of Covariance Structures." *Biometrika* 57: 239–51.

———— (1973). "A General Method for Estimating a Linear Structural Equation System." In A. S. Goldberger and O. D. Duncan (eds.), *Structural Equation Models in the Social Sciences*. New York: Seminar Press.

————, and Dag Sörbom (1975). "Statistical Models and Methods for Analysis of Longitudinal Data." Research Report 75-1. Uppsala University, Statistics Department.

Korman, A. K. (1971). "Black Experience, Socialization, and Civil Liberties." *Journal of Social Issues* 31: 137–51.

Knutson, Jeanne (1972). *The Human Basis of the Polity*. Chicago: Aldine-Atherton.

Lawrence, David (1976). "Procedural Norms and Tolerance: A Reassessment." *American Political Science Review* 70: 80–100.

Lipset, Seymour Martin, and Earl Raab (1970). *The Politics of Unreason*. New York: Basic Books.

Marcus, George E., James Piereson and John L. Sullivan (1980). "Rural-Urban Differences in Tolerance: Confounding Problems of Conceptualization and Measurement." *Rural Sociology* 45: 731–37.

Marsh, Alan (1977). *Protest and Political Consciousness*. Beverly Hills, Calif.: Sage Publications.

Martin, John G., and Frank E. Westie (1959). "The Tolerant Personality." *American Sociological Review* 24: 521–28.

McClosky, Herbert (1964). "Consensus and Ideology in American Politics." *American Political Science Review* 58: 361–82.

McClosky, H., P. J. Hoffman and R. O'Hara (1960). "Issue Conflict and Consensus Among Party Leaders and Followers." *American Political Science Review* 54: 406–29.

Nunn, Clyde Z., Harry J. Crockett and J. Allen Williams (1978). *Tolerance for Nonconformity*. San Francisco: Jossey-Bass.

Pateman, Carole (1970). *Participation and Democratic Theory*. London: Cambridge University Press.

Pennock, J. Roland (1979). *Democratic Political Theory*. Princeton, N.J.: Princeton University Press.

Prothro, James W., and Charles W. Grigg (1960). "Fundamental Principles of Democracy: Bases of Agreement and Disagreement." *Journal of Politics* 22: 276–94.

Rokeach, M. (1960). *The Open and Closed Mind*. New York: Basic Books.

Rosenberg, Morris (1956). "Misanthropy and Political Ideology." *American Sociological Review* 21: 690–95.

Siegel, Peter H. (1971). "Prestige in the American Occupational Structure." Ph.D. Dissertation, Dept. of Sociology, University of Chicago.

Sanford, Nevitt (1973). "Authoritarian Personality in Contemporary Perspective." In J. Knutson (ed.), *Handbook of Political Psychology*. San Francisco: Jossey-Bass.

Sniderman, Paul (1975). *Personality and Democratic Politics*. Berkeley: University of California Press.

Stouffer, Samuel (1955). *Communism, Conformity, and Civil Liberties*. New York: Doubleday.

Sullivan, John L., and Stanley Feldman (1979). *Multiple Indicators*. Sage University Papers on Quantitative Applications in the Social Sciences, 07-015. Beverly Hills, Calif.: Sage Publications.

Sullivan. J. L., G. E. Marcus, J. Piereson and S. Feldman (1979). "The Development of Political Tolerance: The Impact of Social Class, Personality and Cognition." *International Journal of Political Education* 2: 115–39.

Sullivan, J. L., J. Piereson and G. E. Marcus (1979). "An Alternative Conceptualization of Political Tolerance: Illusory Increases, 1950s–1970s." *American Political Science Review* 73: 781–94.

———— (1982). *Political Tolerance and American Democracy*. Chicago: University of Chicago Press.

Thompson, Dennis (1970). *The Democratic Citizen*. London: Cambridge University Press.

Walker, Jack L. (1966). "A Critique of the Elitist Theory of Democracy." *American Political Science Review* 60: 289–95.

Werts, C. E., R. L. Linn, and K. G. Jöreskog (1971). "Estimating the Parameters of Path Models Involving Unmeasured Variables." In H. M. Blalock (ed.), *Causal Models in the Social Sciences*. Chicago: Aldine.

Wheaton, Blair, Bengt Muthen, Duane F. Alwin, and Gene F. Summers (1977). "Assessing Reliability and Stability in Panel Models." In David R. Heise (ed.), *Sociological Methodology*. San Francisco: Jossey-Bass.

Zalkind, Sheldon, Edward Gaugler and Ronald Schwartz (1975). "Civil Liberties, Attitudes and Personality Measures: Some Exploratory Research." *Journal of Social Issues* 31: 77–91.

Zellman, G., and David Sears (1971). "Childhood Origins of Tolerance for Dissent." *Journal of Social Issues* 27: 109–35.

1B.   On Students and Serendipity in Social Research

JOHN L. SULLIVAN

Describing the anatomy of a research project that began in the fall of 1974 and ended in the spring of 1982 is a task that is at least partially doomed from the start. Problems of simplification, incompleteness, and vagaries introduced by faulty memory and the necessity of reconstruction will plague any such analysis. I make the attempt, however, at least in part because of one of the main points I will emphasize: that there is a reciprocal relationship not only between teaching and research, but between teachers and their students. My hope is that efforts such as this will encourage students to engage in the research process not merely because they accrue narrow benefits—an increase in research-related skills, a better grade in a class or seminar—but because they should realize their role in educating their professors and in shaping and acquiring new "knowledge."

I really write this chapter, then, for myself. I wish to excite and encourage students so that they will help my colleagues and me in our own efforts to come to grips with significant questions about human behavior, about politics, and about any aspects of the social sciences that we find interesting. But I am ahead of myself, not to mention the reader. This chapter has three parts, not necessarily equal in length or importance. The first is a brief chronology of the political tolerance project described in the accompanying report, reprinted from the pages of the *American Political Science Review*. The second discusses the reciprocal relationships mentioned immediately above, between teaching and research, and between students and teachers. And finally the third discusses the importance of serendipity in the research process.

THE POLITICAL TOLERANCE PROJECT

During the fall of 1974, I taught an undergraduate course at Indiana University entitled "Elements of Political Analysis." It was, basically, a semester-long course in research methods, including statistical analysis. I had taught it twice previously, and both times I had assigned the students a research project that included designing and carrying out a survey of the local community. They were to write the questions, select the sample, do the interviewing and the data processing, and finally write a paper based on the results. Both times, the work load had been excessive both for the students and for me. As a result, the third time through the course, I decided that the students should survey their student colleagues rather than the larger community of Bloomington, Indiana. This, I reasoned, would make the load easier for all concerned.

Most students who are reading this chapter will no doubt only vaguely recall the nature of the times in 1974. The country was just emerging from a period of intense political conflict, highlighted by civil rights demonstrations and counterdemonstrations, protests against the course of action in the Vietnam War, and less violent but equally intense conflicts on behalf of women's rights. The year 1974 was toward the end of that era, when things had begun to calm down. Many of the older students in the class had been active in protests and were themselves part of the "New Left" counterculture. The younger students were markedly more conservative and even occasionally hostile toward them. As a result, the older students wished to construct the questionnaire around issues of tolerance, thereby exploring the attitudes of their fellow students toward "hippies" and other labels often attached derogatorily to themselves. They examined the meager literature on political tolerance, including works by Stouffer (1955), Prothro and Grigg (1960), and McClosky (1964). During classroom discussions of how our current efforts could be guided by previous research, we began to express a diffuse sense of unease and restlessness, almost an anxiety, that something was amiss.

That "something" was not immediately clear. First it took the form of objections and dissatisfactions with the wording of questions used in previous research and ways they could be adapted to the current situation. But eventually it became clear that the fundamental problem revolved around the targets to be examined in our research. As I recall, several of the more left-wing students were generally opposed to the idea of empirical research in the first place, and while expressing their general objections, they noted that we couldn't really measure political tolerance by asking our student respondents about hippies or left-wingers, since we would be asking some hippies and left-wingers if they would tolerate themselves! The absurdity of this was, of course, evident to them, and eventually to me as well. After several additional sessions discussing this matter, we decided to tailor the target group used in each question to each individual respondent's personal prejudices. A rudimentary form of the content-controlled strategy described in the accompanying article emerged, although none of us realized its significance as yet. My own view was merely that this was an interesting approach to the problem, but my main concern was its pedagogic value, and I did not give it much further thought because I had a rather full research agenda at the moment.

The students completed the survey, wrote their papers, and the semester ended. I recall nothing remarkable about their papers, other than that more than usual were quite good. About five months later, however, I resigned from Indiana University, and Professor James Piereson, a colleague filling a temporary position at Indiana, accepted a position elsewhere. We decided to write a joint article to commemorate our time together at Indiana University. We realized that hardly any work had been done on political tolerance since the 1950s and early 1960s and decided to have a look at the data from the students' survey.

To check the validity of the data, our first action was to examine that old reliable, the relationship between social class background and political tolerance. Since the respondents were all college students, we used measures of parents' education and income as indicators of social class background. The results were staggering. We discovered a strong but *inverse* correlation between class background and political tolerance! Everyone who had looked at this question until then had found that middle- and upper middle-class people were more tolerant than those of lower status.

This could have indicated a fairly serious data problem, but after reconstructing all data collection and processing procedures, we convinced ourselves that "data errors" was not a plausible explanation for these unexpected findings. We slowly became convinced that these results were the result of one of two factors: either the measurement strategy, which differed so greatly from the usual measurement strategies employed, vitiated the usual relationship between tolerance and education and somehow inverted it; or, alternatively, the uniqueness of college students could explain away our findings as lacking external validity, or generalizability.

It seemed reasonable to assume that lower- and working-class college students were somehow unusual and atypical members of their social class. They might well have been exceptional in a number of ways other than their levels of political tolerance, and thus, if a poll were conducted in the community using the content-controlled strategy, perhaps the class-tolerance relationship would assert itself in the "proper" direction once again.

As is the case in most research projects, we did not have the luxury of testing these alternative explanations, and so we arbitrarily attributed the results of the student survey to the measurement strategy. We wrote up the results and submitted them to a scholarly journal. Our manuscript was rejected for two fundamental reasons, one of which we judged to be legitimate, the other illegitimate. The first reason was political scientists' innate suspicion of students as subjects in research projects. No doubt a psychology journal would have been more sympathetic. The second reason for the rejection was one reviewer's insistence that we had not measured tolerance properly and that the original studies, criticized as content-biased, had actually done a better job of valid measurement. The more we considered this matter, the more certain we became that we were in fact on the right track and that the traditional literature was misguided.

In the rejected paper, we had described in rather matter-of-fact terms the alternative measurement strategy we had employed. We did not emphasize it, nor did we yet fully realize what we had stumbled upon and how we would later elaborate upon it. At about this time, we began to discuss these ideas with Professor George Marcus of Williams College. He and I were conducting some different research together, and he began to see that these seemingly different projects were related and that they were arriving at similar theoretical conclusions about democratic theories and the differences (or lack thereof) between elites and masses in the political system. As our discussions expanded, we determined that we did indeed need to pursue the matter to eliminate the "external validity" objection. That is, we needed to try the new measurement technique in a community sample, not just on a sample of students.

By this time, almost a year had passed since the original data were collected. We raised some research monies, and in 1975 Professor Marcus supervised a poll in New England which provided us with a small pretest of nonstudents. The relationship between tolerance and social class was virtually nil in this sample. We then conducted the Twin Cities Survey during 1976, and some of the results from that data set are presented in Sullivan, Piereson and Marcus (1979). In this survey, we found a very small positive relationship between class and tolerance, and we conducted a multivariate analysis reported in Sullivan, Marcus, Piereson, and Feldman (1979), showing that background variables had little if any direct impact on political tolerance. On the basis of these results, we obtained a National Science Foundation grant to conduct the 1978 national survey that is described in the attached article. Our book, published in 1982 by the University of Chicago Press, marks an end of sorts to this particular project.

ON RECIPROCITY IN TEACHING AND RESEARCH

Students at major research universities in the U.S. have occasionally been known to allege that their professors place research above teaching, and that in many departments, professors seldom engage in serious undergraduate instruction, leaving such menial tasks to graduate students and junior faculty members. One also, again only occasionally, hears the charge that the best researchers obtain the greatest prestige and other rewards, while the best teachers sometimes lose their jobs, although more frequently they merely lose their colleagues' esteem. Most tenured professors—and especially tenured administrators who seldom teach or do significant research—counter that teaching and research, by their very nature, are interrelated activities that enjoy a reciprocal relationship. According to this view, one cannot really be a good teacher without also being a competent scholar. Thus the undergraduate view is seen as a misconception based on a rather self-interested desire to have teachers who entertain, effectively competing with the mass media. The academic view is often that these "desirable" teachers mislead more than they inform students, particularly about the nature of social scientific knowledge and how it is acquired.

Caricatures aside, I tend to fault the professorial profession not for its emphasis on the reciprocity of teaching and research, but for not taking that view far enough. Most active scholars recognize the pedagogic benefits of conducting research and of remaining abreast of published and unpublished research in their fields of specialization. It is true that the skills necessary to condense and interpret this research for undergraduate consumption are, to put it mildly, unevenly distributed among the professoriate. I suspect that this latter skill is randomly distributed across the different types of research scholars ranging from the most active and prolific researchers to those whose research efforts are minimal or nonexistent. But skill or no skill, professors who conduct little research themselves and who generally do not remain current in their field do a disservice to their undergraduates. This much is generally recognized, at least by a large number of my colleagues. Another point, generally recognized as well, is that by offering graduate seminars, faculty members are forced to organize and synthesize recent work in their field and thereby are compelled to generate ideas for further research. This is true to a much lesser extent at the undergraduate level, but most recognize the interplay that takes place: teaching fuels research, and research in its turn generates a more sophisticated content in courses at both the graduate and undergraduate levels of instruction.

Less recognized is the symbiotic relationship between instructors and their students. Occasionally, I hear comments from professors that reflect a view that the relationship is basically parasitic. These comments are often mirrored by graduate students, only the roles of host and parasite are reversed. It seems clear, however, that students play a poorly understood role in teaching their professors both how to teach (and few of us learned anything about teaching before we became teachers) and how to conduct their research. They could teach us a great deal more if we gave them the opportunity. In the political tolerance project, it seems clear that the students in my class in 1974 were unwilling to accept what had by then become, for the political science profession, entrenched and un-self-conscious methods of studying attitudinal tolerance, nor were they willing to accept at face value the substantive conclusions generated by such methods. In a sense, they intuitively understood the point we make, about measuring tolerance, in the accompanying article reprinted from the *Review*, a point that appears not to have occurred to many political scientists between the 1950s and the 1970s. The undergraduates brought to bear an uncluttered notion of common sense, which is often destroyed (or at least partially damaged) *of necessity* by the kind of training and socialization that takes place in the finest graduate schools of the land. Graduate training must be thorough; it must instill a sense of how to conduct research and of what kinds of questions to ask; and it must thereby incur some costs in the form of a type of "blinder" which sometimes hides the obvious from such well-socialized professionals. Partially socialized amateurs are a helpful check on such excesses.

A rather painful illustration of this argument involves the political tolerance project. As a well-trained but thick-headed political scientist, I did not really become terribly interested in the ideas generated during our discussions in that undergraduate class so long as they revolved narrowly around how to measure tolerance among an ideologically bimodal population of undergraduates. Once we discovered the serious damage done to previous empirical conclusions merely by adopting a slightly more idiographic measurement procedure, my interest was immediately piqued. My own working-class background had always left me with an uneasy and defensive reaction when I read the widely accepted findings showing that education and social class were the major "causes" of such valued commodities as political tolerance, issue voting, and ideological sophistication. During my own graduate training in the late 1960s, such findings were virtually unchallenged, at least among empirical, behavioral political scientists.

My resonance on this point was heightened as I noted what I believed to be intolerant discussions and statements uttered by my highly educated colleagues over lunch and at cocktail parties. Had I heard such remarks uttered about racial minorities or unpopular left-wing groups, I would have concluded that they indicated an underlying attitude of intolerance. For these reasons, I was predisposed to accept the basic validity of our findings and was thus highly motivated to follow up on their implications. Nevertheless, it is clear that the initial catalyst for this project was the fresh and untrained eye of the undergraduates, not an abstract theoretical discussion among colleagues.

Another example of the usefulness of presenting research to a naive audience brings the political tolerance project full circle. After conducting the national survey mentioned above, I presented elements of the tolerance project to another undergraduate class. Whereas the earlier class had helped to generate new ideas for significant research, this class assisted in highlighting several of the major weaknesses of that same research. I mention only one here. When our first article on tolerance was reviewed by several referees for the *Review*, it contained much stronger statements about the levels of tolerance in the 1970s relative to the 1950s, essentially stating more forcefully that levels of tolerance were probably about the same in both decades. Those statements were watered down before publication. The official reviewers failed to take issue with our conclusions on this matter, but several undergraduates immediately invoked their intuitive sense of experimental design: before drawing such conclusions, we needed to demonstrate that levels of tolerance for least-liked groups in the 1950s were not appreciably different from levels of tolerance for Communists, socialists, or atheists, and of course we could not do that. In fairness to my colleagues in the profession, several of them did eventually point this out, but the ease with which several undergraduates went straight to the point without the benefit of formal training was impressive. As a rule, my undergraduates are less impressed by this research than our colleagues are.

In summary, I wish to emphasize the role of undergraduates in educating and drawing out the best research efforts from faculty members. Undergraduates are, of course, less socialized into the profession and therefore they are less likely to recognize the importance of our best research efforts. This makes it difficult for us to awe them, and this lack of awe may prompt them to provide us with honest, direct, and helpful reactions to our work. It is true that their lack of methodological training and sophistication will make it easier, on the one hand, for us to bury them with what they believe to be irrelevant detail, but on the other hand it forces us to be clear about what we have done and why, all obfuscation aside. Unlike many of our graduate students, their immediate career goals are not likely to be affected by our judgments of their abilities or by our own defensive reactions to criticisms or objections to our best efforts. And, finally, as a source of new ideas and conceptualizations, undergraduates have an advantage over all of us. They are unfamiliar with our truisms, our "common knowledge," and our unchallengeable empirical findings, so no matter how often and under how many different circumstances these findings have been replicated, such students retain their open posture toward our work. As such, I urge my colleagues to take advantage of this rich but generally untapped resource.

ON SERENDIPITY IN RESEARCH

Many important research discoveries take place almost accidentally, as a result of luck or an almost random set of circumstances. Merton (1957) has labeled this the "serendipity pattern," and Barber and Fox (1958) have investigated this pattern by studying two medical researchers. Both researchers discovered, accidentally, that the injection of an enzyme called papain into a rabbit's ear produced unexpected floppiness in the ear. Both of them made initial modest attempts to discover why this happened, and both failed. Eventually, one researcher discovered the cause, while the other researcher merely filed it away in his brain as one of those interesting but inexplicable phenomena that clutter the gray matter of serious scholars. Barber and Fox attempted to locate the major sources of what they called "serendipity gained" and "serendipity lost."

Both medical researchers had made their discovery while conducting research projects unrelated to the effects of papain on rabbits' ears. Both made an immediate attempt to discover the explanation for this phenomenon. Both followed regular procedures which were dictated by their previous training as research scholars. Both failed to discover anything unusual—they could find no inflammation, no tissue damage of any kind.

One researcher failed to follow up on this curious discovery because he did not see it as terribly important; it did not relate to his own basic research interests; he had a full research agenda which continued intact for a fairly long period of time; and he had made several other, similar serendipitous discoveries about the same time, so this particular effect did not stand out. In short, the basic reason that this researcher did not pursue his discovery after his initial attempts at explanation failed, involves his own preconceptions as a trained and sophisticated research scholar. The first element was his strong preference for basic over applied research, and the discovery involving papain had no obvious relationship to his theoretical research interests. The second element—whose details I cannot yet reveal since it would prematurely disclose the key to explaining this discovery—involves a certain preconception shared by both researchers, which in a sense blinded them to the obvious. More will be said about this shortly. The final element was that this researcher's other work was going very well, and thus he had no need to pursue it further.

The second researcher experienced some of the same difficulties, but several fortuitous events conspired to provide him with the opportunity to explain this significant discovery. Just as in the case of the first researcher, the second failed to discover anything significant about the rabbit's ear tissue. There was no apparent damage, and the floppiness eventually disappeared. He made an effort to discover the cause, but nothing seemed to work. As in the case of the first researcher, he returned to his normal research schedule and filed this floppy-eared effect away for future reference. Unlike the first researcher, however, he returned to it several years later, for largely accidental reasons. He was more impressed with the regularity of the phenomenon than the first researcher was, and in the meantime had demonstrated it to several colleagues, who found it amusing but were equally unable to explain it. Furthermore, his own research agenda was not progressing as he had hoped it would, and so his interest was again engaged.

He was teaching a class of second-year medical students, and as was his custom, he decided to share with them certain aspects of his own research efforts. Since his regular work was not progressing smoothly, he decided to show them the effects of papain on rabbits' ears, intending to amuse them. This time, he did something he should have done long ago—something the first researcher and his colleagues should also have recognized as critical in this case. Now, in front of the students, he decided to stick closely to the experimental method. He injected the papain, the ears flopped, and then he cut a cross section to show the students that the tissue was undamaged. Then he cut a cross section of ear from a rabbit that had not been injected with papain. It became immediately apparent that there were significant differences between the cartilage of the two sections. This ultimately led to an explanation of the phenomenon.

The key to the problem was totally overlooked by everyone involved for two reasons. The first reason was that both researchers had forgotten about the major desideratum of the experimental method: the need for a control group. This is the same difficulty that we experienced in the political tolerance project, and which, as I noted above, several undergraduates did not forget. The second reason was the preconception among medical researchers that cartilage is relatively inert material and thus it was an unlikely source of the floppy-eared effect. Our assumptions and unstated conceptions about the subject matter that we study are often instilled during our graduate training, and this of course has serious costs associated with it, as noted above in the political tolerance project.

My project with Professors Piereson and Marcus has had some significant effects on the way our colleagues view political tolerance and how they study it. No doubt our efforts will shortly be supplanted, but for the time being, they appear to be well received in most quarters. If our work has fundamental validity, then it will have some lasting effect on our knowledge about political attitudes. It must be obvious from the research narratives outlined above that there are many serendipitous aspects to this project and its findings.

First, I have no doubt that the project would never have been carried out if the students in my undergraduate class had not acted as catalysts. If I had taught a different class that semester, or if different students had taken the class, or if I had steered the survey toward some preordained topic, the research generated by this project would never have occurred. Second, as in the case of "serendipity gained" noted above, my research agenda was filled and thus any curiosity I may have felt about the newly developed measurement strategy in the students' survey was suppressed at first. Later, even though I did not lack a research agenda, being involved in collaborative work both with Professor Marcus and with several graduate students, Professor Piereson and I wanted a unique project on which we could work together.

This was mere circumstance, and turning to the students' tolerance survey was also merely a stroke of luck. Third, had the first manuscript, written using only the student data, been accepted, we would undoubtedly have let things drop at that point. It is difficult to say with any certainty what impact that manuscript would have had, since it was based on data collected on and by students, and since it was submitted to a journal whose visibility and readership were considerably less than that of the *Review*'s. The fact that we submitted it to a lesser journal reflected our own judgment of its merits. Luckily, the referees for that journal did not find our work convincing, and we persisted, in spite of the blinders we were wearing about the significance of our alternative measurement strategy. And, finally, several of the more important findings that we report in the attached chapter, and elsewhere, were discovered accidentally. Our main concern was with the education-tolerance connection and how it seemed to be altered with our measurement instrument, but several equally important findings emerged, almost offhandedly. One example of this is the major point of the Sullivan, Pierson and Marcus (1979) article, that Americans' levels of tolerance are not very high. We initially had no interest in showing this, and in fact we had hoped things would be otherwise.

CLOSING COMMENTS

In this paper, I have provided a narrative about a research project, which includes the kinds of details seldom discussed in academic publications. There are exceptions, of course, but the accidental pathways and informal discussions that powerfully influence the research process and hence much of human knowledge seldom find their way into our textbooks on research methods. As Bachrach (1967) notes, "People don't usually do research the way people who write books about research say that people do research." Perhaps the serendipity pattern is even more common than the formal research pattern outlined in texts on experimental and ex post facto designs.

Several of my earlier comments may have conveyed an exaggerated sense of cynicism about professional training and its role in providing the academic disciplines with creative researchers. Make no mistake about this matter—and it is a matter of the utmost importance—good, in-depth training in research methods, statistics, and the substance of a discipline are, in truth, almost necessary (but certainly not sufficient) conditions for the conduct of significant scholarly research in the modern world. I merely wish to emphasize here the negative side to such professional socialization, and to reemphasize the need for well-trained scholars to remain open to suggestions that well-accepted and "proven" conclusions might be wrong, or at least misleading. We must be ready to perceive anomalies in our systems of knowledge when they occur, and we must remain curious about any unusual observations of any kind that come to our attention. The cost of failure is an adherence to a kind of "normal science" that may mislead more than it enlightens us. We have no way of knowing how many important potential breakthroughs in our knowledge have been overlooked because of rigid professional training and its concomitant perceptual orthodoxy.

REFERENCES

Bachrach, Arthur J. 1967. *Psychological Research*. New York: Random House.

Barber, Bernard, and Fox, Renee 1958. "The Case of the Floppy-Eared Rabbits: An Instance of Serendipity Gained and Serendipity Lost." *American Journal of Sociology* 54: 128–36.

McClosky, Herbert 1964. "Consensus and Ideology in American Politics," *American Political Science Review* 58: 361–82.

Merton, Robert K. 1957. *Social Theory and Social Structure*. Glencoe, Ill.: Free Press.

Prothro, James W., and Grigg, Charles M. 1960. "Fundamental Principles of Democracy: Bases of Agreement and Disagreement." *Journal of Politics* 22: 276–94.

Stouffer, Samuel 1955. *Communism, Conformity, and Civil Liberties*. New York: Doubleday.

Sullivan, John L.; Marcus, George E.; Piereson, James E.; and Feldman, Stanley 1979. "The Development of Political Tolerance: The Impact of Social Class, Personality, and Cognition." *International Journal of Political Education* 2: 115–39.

Sullivan, John L.; Piereson, James; and Marcus, George E. 1979. "An Alternative Conceptualization of Political Tolerance: Illusory Increases, 1950's–1970's," *American Political Science Review* 73: 233–49.

Sullivan, John L.; Piereson, James; and Marcus, George E. 1982. *Political Tolerance and American Democracy*. Chicago: University of Chicago Press.

CHAPTER TWO

Belief Systems: Constraint, Complexity and the 1972 Election

2. Belief Systems: Constraint, Complexity, and the 1972 Election

Stimson sought to measure how "organized" Americans' beliefs about different issues are. Do Americans tend to have complex systems of political belief in which numerous issues are all related to each other (a belief in the evils of high taxes going together with opposition to social progress, anti-Communist foreign policy, and so on), or are our minds unsystematic vessels of free-floating beliefs (an anti-tax person is as likely to favor social progress as to oppose it)? Do our beliefs fit into only a single simple ideology, or do we simultaneously operate with a blend of several different dimensions along which our beliefs relate to each other?

I may need to explain two statistical techniques briefly before you can read this paper: the "correlation coefficient" and "factor analysis." I will not explain these in detail, just the broad outlines. If you are already familiar with these, feel free to skip the rest of this introduction to Stimson's article.

THE CORRELATION COEFFICIENT

The correlation coefficient is a statistic designed to measure how tightly two variables are tied to each other. (Stimson uses it in this study to measure how tightly attitudes on different issues are connected.) Take the case in which we want to see how tightly people's incomes are tied to their education. We may array people's educational income on what is called a "scattergram" as in Figure 2.1. Each person is entered on this graph as a dot showing a combination of a certain number of years of education and dollars of income. For instance, the person represented by dot A has had thirteen years of education and earns an annual income of $19,000.

As you can see, there is a fairly tight relationship between the two variables. It could be tighter, but in general high incomes accompany high education and low incomes accompany low education. The *correlation coefficient* is used to measure how tightly two variables such as these are bound together. It is set up so that when all dots fall on a single line, as in Figure 2.2, the correlation coefficient will equal 1.0, its highest possible value. If all dots fall on a straight line, there is one and only one value of one variable, for any given value of the other. That is, the two variables are as tightly tied together as they could possibly be.

If the dots are randomly scattered as in Figure 2.3, this means that all incomes are just as likely to accompany, say, five years of education as fifteen or twenty. The variables are not connected at all. Under this circumstance the correlation coefficient takes on a value of zero. The more a scattergram approaches the pattern illustrated in Figure 2.2, the higher the correlation coefficient becomes. Thus the correlation coefficient is a measure, ranging from zero to one, that indicates how tightly interconnected two variables are.[1] It is a single number which summarizes a whole scattergram.

We can see how useful such a statistic can be when we see Stimson compare how tightly interconnected forty-five different pairs of variables are, in Table 2.5. Imagine how we would goggle if he presented us with 45 scattergrams to compare visually! Looking at forty-five single numbers is difficult enough.

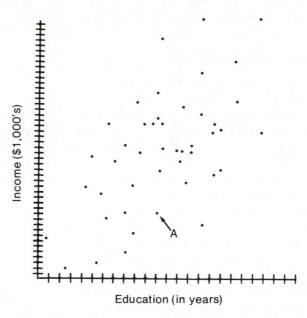

FIGURE 2.1
The Relationship Between Education and Income: A Hypothetical Example

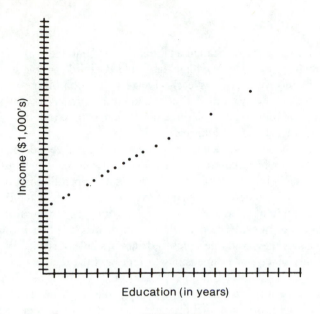

FIGURE 2.2
An Example in Which the Correlation Coefficient is 1.0

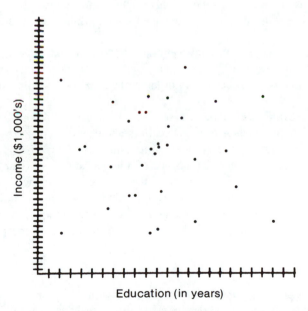

FIGURE 2.3
An Example in Which the Correlation Coefficient is 0.0

FACTOR ANALYSIS

For the two variables, education and income, we required two dimensions to portray their relationship. We might have added a third variable such as age (What income do we expect for each given combination of age and education?). In this case we would need to use three dimensions to represent the relationship, with dots floating in three-dimensional space to portray varying combinations of age, education, and income.

If we had a hundred variables, we could represent their combined relationships in a one-hundred-dimensional space, if you can imagine such a thing. However, with so many variables it might happen that two were not independent of each other. For instance, assume we had been stupid and had included in a study of tolerance two variables, "tolerance of minorities" and "tolerance of majorities." These would be mirror images of each other, and without any loss they could be combined into a single variable. We would now need only ninety-nine dimensions to represent the relationships among them.

Now let us assume that we're willing to operate a bit on the rough and ready, and accept less than a total dependence of two variables on each other as a basis for combining them. For instance, we might assume that several variables—support for nationalized industries, a progressive income tax, and labor unions, perhaps several more—all are variants of "left-right orientation" and could be collapsed. Even though this might involve a few errors, it would reduce markedly the number of dimensions with which we would have to work.

Factor analysis is a statistical technique by which one can take a large number of variables and by very "rough and ready" operations assess the number of dimensions necessary to organize them in their relationships with each other.

Stimson uses this technique to assess the number of different ideological dimensions along which Americans' beliefs about issues appear to be simultaneously organized. What is the minimum number of dimensions which is required to display the interrelationships of a larger number of issue beliefs?

I have passed over here a number of technical details of factor analysis, several of which are referred to in Stimson's article. If you are unfamiliar with them, don't worry about it. The broad outlines of the technique, as explained here, are all that you need to follow the line of argument in the paper.

NOTE

1. It only happens once in Stimson's article, but where a relationship is *negative*, that is, where high values of one variable are associated with low values of the other, the correlation coefficient will vary between zero and -1.0. The closer it is to -1.0, the more tightly the two variables are interconnected.

_____ RESEARCH ARTICLE

2A. Belief Systems: Constraint, Complexity, and the 1972 Election

JAMES A. STIMSON

There is little agreement about the degree to which the American electorate structures its beliefs about salient aspects of the political scene. Disagreement arises in large part from the use of differing concepts of belief structuring. Some researchers look for evidence of consistency, simplicity, and power in belief systems and do not find it in large measure. Others look for complexity and multidimensionality and do find it. Both believe they are measuring belief sophistication.

Both schools expect to find greatest evidence of sophistication among the educated and well informed and least among the uneducated and uninformed. The 1972 electorate is stratified by education and political information, and operational indicators of both "constraint" and "complexity" notions of belief structure are examined.

When the authors of *The American Voter* (Campbell, Converse, Miller and Stokes, 1960, p. 250) first concluded that "the concepts important to ideological analysis are useful only for that small segment of the population that is equipped to approach political decisions at a rarefied level," they set off a debate about the structure of belief systems in the American electorate that is as lively today as when *The American Voter* was first published. It is a fruitful debate because both sides are increasingly asking the sort of questions amenable to empirical answers. It is unresolved because both sides are finding evidence in support of their position. It is vital because the answer has direct implications for democratic theory.

_____

*Funds for this study were provided by the Research Foundation of the State University of New York. The Center for Political Studies 1972 Election Study data were provided by the Inter-University Consortium for Political Research. I have been aided in this work by the assistance of Elizabeth Plumb and Alan Negin, and have been the beneficiary of the ideas and critical scrutiny of Edward Carmines, John Sinclair, Richard Zeller, and John L. Sullivan. Data included in an earlier version of this paper were generously provided by George Marcus, David Tabb, and John Sullivan.

This article was reprinted from the *American Journal of Political Science,* Vol. xix, No. 3, Aug. 1975, pp. 393-417. Austin, TX: University of Texas Press.

This article brings new evidence to bear on the belief systems question. The 1972 elections extend the debate in time. Our mode of analysis extends its direction.

THE DEBATE ABOUT BELIEF SYSTEMS

A brief examination of the belief systems debate is in order to set the stage for the analysis to come. If *The American Voter* started the rumblings of controversy, Philip Converse (1964) articulated what will here be called the "empiricist" position so precisely that it remains ten years later the most influential statement. Converse spelled out what a political belief system worthy of the name "ideology" would look like; it would have abstract *objects of centrality*, wide *scope*, and would be *constrained*. The constraint concept refers to internal consistency, and the way Converse uses the concept implies consistency along a single powerful underlying dimension.

The Converse school will be called "empiricists" from their scientific world view (the usage is borrowed from Diesing, 1971). They tend toward building theory out of small-scale testable hypotheses. They might also be called "elitist" (because they find the mass public wanting in comparison with political elites), but that term has broad normative implications that are probably inaccurate. They are also "unidemensionalists," but that tag fails to capture much of the scope of their position.

The opposing school will be denoted as "rationalists," because their common denominator is the assertion that the electorate has the cognitive apparatus necessary for rational choice. A more normative characterization is "populist," because they find great virtue in the common man. With some significant exceptions (Marcus, Tabb, and Sullivan, 1974), their implicit ontology is formalist.[1] They build theory deductively; starting with formal models, they make inferences about what the electorate would look like if their models "fit," delimit the scope of confirming evidence, and test. A significant new trend in rationalist approaches is the postulation of multi-dimensional belief systems (Weisberg and Rusk, 1970; Marcus et al., 1974).

Why, if both sides appeal to empirical evidence in support of their theories, does the debate continue? Part of the answer is that they are interpreting the same "facts" differently. The rationalists are searching for *some* evidence of rational choice in the electorate and finding it. The empiricists look for belief structuring and find it only in a minority of the electorate. The two findings are not inconsistent (as indeed they ought not to be, since both sides frequently exploit the same data!). It is, in part, the classic, "The glass is half full." "No, it is half empty," interpretation problem.

A second barrier to agreement is differing emphasis. The empiricists look for belief structuring and are only secondarily concerned with rationality. The rationalists look for evidence of rational choice and are only secondarily concerned with its proximate causes. Thus, the two sides never address exactly the same phenomenon.

A last, and more speculative, explanation for the less than total convergence of the two sides is that the rationalists believe they have time on their side. The major election studies may provide slim support for the rationalist position; but they might as well support an assertion that the electorate is changing, becoming more rational (and more ideological) every four years. Why strike an unfavorable bargain with the empiricists, the rationalists might say, if the voters are moving toward our position? If this is the case, the 1972 election study is not just new data, another case, but an important indicator of the future.

Ideological Choice in 1972

If ever a good case of ideological choice in American presidential elections could be found, it would be 1972. From the first Democratic primary of March through the postmortems of November, contrasting candidate ideologies were a constant focus of media and (presumably) popular attention. The New Hampshire contest was described as "left" versus "center"; Florida, "left" versus "center" versus "right"; California and New York, "left" versus "center," and so on. Only extraordinary inattention to politics could have left a voter unaware that George McGovern represented the "left" segment of the Democratic Party and was indeed widely regarded as a "radical" in his own party.

It may well be that the candidate whose ideology was less well known was Richard Nixon, the incumbent president. Nonetheless, the less visible Republican primaries included ideological challenges from both "left" (McCloskey) and "right" (Ashbrook). If the lines were as sharply drawn, they were probably not as salient to the electorate, since few apparently regarded the Republican challengers as serious threats to the Nixon candidacy.

Issue positions were unusually sharply defined in 1972. In most cases, the McGovern position was a clear challenge to the status quo. The Democratic candidate called for radical alterations in taxes and welfare, for peace in Vietnam with something less than Nixon's "honor," and for massive government spending to reduce joblessness. He was publicly associated with groups who pushed for the legalization of marijuana and the radical restructuring of the role of women in American society. His most prominent status quo position, on busing school children, was unfortunately for him an immensely unpopular status quo, ably exploited by Nixon from the right.

McGovern, a "prairie populist" to those in the press who liked him, simply a "radical" to those who didn't, was widely regarded a captive of the small and intensely ideological constituency he molded to achieve the Democratic nomination. That tiny constituency, compensating for lack of numbers by extraordinary organizational skill and hard work, was just barely enough to impress in some states and to win in others, aided by the low turnout and rampant chaos of presidential primaries. It was not enough to seriously contest the presidency.

McGovern could not win in November without compromising his issue positions, but could not compromise without relinquishing his only strategic advantage, his zealous army of volunteer campaign workers—most apparently more concerned with McGovern being right than president. In the end, he did attempt some small and tentative compromises, but appeared to have gained only alienation of some of his workers and a new reputation for indecisiveness for his effort.

It is often argued that voters fail to discriminate on ideological grounds because "tweedledum-tweedledee" candidates and parties in the American system offer no perceptible choice. It is arguable whether this contention is accurate even for the contests normally cited as illustrations, the Eisenhower-Stevenson elections of the placid fifties. Few but the most extreme ideologues could deny that the 1972 contest presented ideological cues of unprecedented clarity and consistency.[2] As a high water mark in the clarity of ideological choice, the Nixon-McGovern contest allows the examination of belief-structuring hypotheses under conditions which do not allow the attribution of ambiguous responses to ambiguous stimuli.

The Data

To examine questions of belief structuring, we will employ the Center for Political Studies' 1972 American National Election Study. The 1972 sample of 2705 respondents was divided into sets who responded to partially overlapping interview schedules. Primary emphasis here will be on the subsample of 1119 respondents who responded to pre- and postelection versions of the "Form 1" interview. The Form 1 respondents were asked to position themselves on ten issue dimension scales and a similar liberal-conservative scale. In each case, questions defined the poles of the scale and asked respondents to place themselves at one of seven points along it (see Appendix). . . .

IDEOLOGY IN THE 1972 ELECTORATE

For a first approximation of the impact of ideological thinking on the 1972 electorate, we examine the simple relationship between position on the seven-point liberal-conservative scale and 1972 vote. Table 2.1 reveals a

TABLE 2.1
1972 Two-Party Vote by Ideology (Liberal-Conservative)

	Ideology							
	Most Liberal						Most Conservative	
Vote	1	2	3	4	5	6	7	Total
McGovern	92%	88%	61%	29%	14%	10%	8%*	34%
Nixon	8*	12	39	71	86	90	92	66
Total	100%	100%	100%	100%	100%	100%	100%	100%
N	13	66	72	218	139	87	12	607

*Only one case in cell

strong and consistent relationship between position on the scale and reported vote. Moving across the scale from "most liberal" to "most conservative," the Nixon proportion of the two-party vote rises in steps from a low of 8% to a high of 92%. Arbitrarily coding the vote (0, 1 for McGovern and Nixon, respectively), the data of Table 2.1 produce a healthy product moment correlation of .51, substantially higher than would be expected from earlier voting studies.

Before the impact of unidimensional ideology on the 1972 electorate is confirmed, some selection biases of Table 2.1 should be noted. Its 607 respondents are only 54% of the 1119-member (Form 1) sample. Its more evident (and perhaps admirable) bias is that it, of course, includes only those who reported casting a presidential vote in 1972. A more serious bias is that nearly one-third of the sample did not place themselves on the liberal-conservative scale. Thus, a more limited conclusion is in order: *Of those voters for whom the liberal-conservative dimension seems meaningful*, there is a strong and consistent relationship between scale position and 1972 vote.

Enduring party loyalty may account for part of the relationship between ideology and vote of Table 2.1. Party loyalists might be presumed to be closely anchored to their party's position and cast votes which give the appearance of ideology, but are, in fact, caused by partisanship. Table 2.2 decomposes the responses of Table 2.1 into party loyalists (strong or weak identifiers of each party who voted for their party's candidate) and others (independents and defectors from party) to examine this hypothesis.

An examination of Table 2.2 leads to further caution about the relationship between ideology and vote. The relationship is actually much stronger among the party faithful (r = .59) than among the more dynamic element of the electorate (r = .43), leading to some doubt about the degree to which ideology may be used to account for electoral *change*. Not only is the relationship between ideology and vote weaker for the independents and defectors, but it is different. Table 2.2-A shows the expected break between liberals and conservatives, McGovern garnering most liberal votes and Nixon

TABLE 2.2
Nixon-McGovern Vote by Ideology (Liberal-Conservative) for
Party Loyalists and Others

2-A: *Party Loyalists: Weak and Strong Identifiers Who Voted for Their Party's Candidate*

| | | | | Ideology | | | | |
| | Most Liberal | | | | | | Most Conservative | |
Vote	1	2	3	4	5	6	7	Total
McGovern	88%	98%	85%	42%	16%	14%	0%	44%
Nixon	13*	2*	15	58	84	86	100	56
Total	101%	100%	100%	100%	100%	100%	100%	100%
N	8	41	34	104	64	56	6	313

2-B: *Others: Defectors and Independents*

| | | | | Ideology | | | | |
| | Most Liberal | | | | | | Most Conservative | |
Vote	1	2	3	4	5	6	7	Total
McGovern	100%	72%	39%	17%	12%	3%*	17%*	23%
Nixon	0	28	61	83	88	97	83	77
Total	100%	100%	100%	100%	100%	100%	100%	100%
N	5	25	38	114	75	31	6	294

*Only one case in cell

winning most conservative votes and more than his share of the neutrals. In Table 2.2-B we expect McGovern to do badly, since defection in 1972 is overwhelmingly defection to Nixon; but what is unexpected is that McGovern does not do well even among the minority who class themselves "liberals." Of the 68 liberal respondents in the nonloyalist sample, only 38 (56%) report a McGovern vote. If the 1972 contest had been decided by ideology, without the restraining effects of party loyalty, these data suggest that the McGovern landslide defeat would have been unmitigated disaster. McGovern would have won majority support only from the two most leftist positions, which together account for slightly more than 10% of the electorate.

What of the nearly one-third of the 1972 sample who could not place themselves on the liberal-conservative scale? There is widespread agreement that the liberal-conservative dimension is not common to all voters (Converse, 1964; Marcus et al., 1974; Wilker and Milbrath, 1970). Large numbers of voters fail to refer to it when asked to explain their partisan preferences (Campbell et al., 1960), to define it in a way that captures much of its breadth (Converse, 1964), or even to associate it with the two parties (Converse, 1964).

Converse (1964) has found the use of the concept of a liberal-conservative ordering dimension to be associated with level of formal education (as well as levels of political activity and information). Presumably, the skills required to associate an abstract ordering dimension with the concrete issues of day-to-day politics are nurtured in formal education. Others have argued that not lack of perceptual skills, but the use of *alternative* dimensions differentiates those of higher and lower educational backgrounds (Marcus et al., 1974; Wilker and Milbrath, 1970).

Because differences in the use of the liberal-conservative ordering continuum by voter cognitive ability are expected, a simple index of cognitive ability is developed which, in the ensuing analysis, will be used to stratify the 1972 electorate. The index is a linear combination of two variables presumed to be related to cognitive skills, *education*, and *political information*.[3] The former is expected to be related to ability to manipulate abstract concepts. The latter, based on the number of correct answers to six objective questions about basic features of American politics (e.g., How many years in a senator's term?), measures command of factual information. Cognitive ability rests in perceiving "facts" and integrating them into a larger framework. The index taps both facets of this process.[4]

Table 2.3 displays the simple correlations between ideology and vote, stratified (approximately at the quartiles) by the cognitive ability index. It shows that the obtained correlation between ideology and vote is based upon very uneven levels of correlation for the four ability strata and a dramatic selection bias that effectively weights the behavior of respondents from the higher ability levels out of proportion to their numbers in the sample.

TABLE 2.3
Liberal-Conservative Ideology and the 1972 Vote,
Stratified by Level of Cognitive Ability

Cognitive Ability	Product-Moment Correlation between Ideology and Vote	Explained Variance (r^2)	N
Group 1 (Lowest) (n = 295)*	.31	.10	69
Group 2 (n = 292)	.43	.19	144
Group 3 (n = 267)	.55	.30	178
Group 4 (Highest) (n = 264)	.61	.37	215
Sample	.51	.26	606

*Unevenness in group size is due to the discontinuous distribution of the ability index. The between-group cut points on the index approximate the quartiles.

TABLE 2.4
Reported Voting Turnout and Response to Liberal-Conservative
Scale, by Cognitive Ability Strata

Cognitive Ability Group	N	Percent of Sample	Percent Reporting Vote	Percent of All Voters	Percent Responding to Liberal-Conservative Scale	Percent of All Scale Respondents
1 (Lowest)	295	26%	44%	17%	43%	16%
2	292	26	72	27	65	24
3	267	24	80	27	83	28
4 (Highest)	264	24	87	29	93	31
Total	1118	100%		100%		99%

Thus, we introduce a further note of caution. When we examine the ideology of the mass public, we are quite likely to overstate its impact because the evidence of impact is most slight for that part of the electorate that systematically selects itself out of such analyses by not voting and not responding to measures of ideology. Table 2.4 illustrates the point.

THE STRUCTURE OF BELIEFS

Having seen that position on a liberal-conservative scale was a potent predictor of voting for many respondents in 1972, the question is raised here of what respondents *meant* when they classified themselves on the scale. More specifically, we raise the question: What are the attitudinal correlates of the liberal-conservative dimension? It is a question often asked and often answered. The answers are, unfortunately, various.

Form 1 of the 1972 election study includes ten respondent attitude scales in the same seven-point format as the liberal-conservative scale. Nine of these are employed here to locate the issue correlates of the liberal-conservative scale.[5] The correlations between these scales and the liberal-conservative scale begin to tell the meaning of the presumed liberal-conservative dimension for the 1972 respondents. The nine issues were a mixture of economic (on government action to control inflation, to guarantee jobs, to provide health insurance), foreign (on ending the war in Vietnam), racial (on protection of minority rights and "busing"), civil liberties (on the rights of accused criminal suspects), and social (on legalization of marijuana and the role of women in American society). They are a good selection of issues, new and old, hypothesized to be relevant to wide-ranging conceptions of political life.

Table 2.5 presents correlations of the nine issues with the liberal-conservative scale, first for the whole sample and then for each ability stratum. As the slightest glance at the table will tell, the liberal-conservative dimension has more meaning for the higher ability respondents than for their lower ability counterparts. More issues are related to the liberal-conservative dimension (and those more strongly) for those high in cognitive ability. Because many issue positions are related to these respondents' location on the liberal-conservative scale, their conception of the meaning of the dimension may be said to be broad and abstract—at least relative to lower ability respondents.

It is much more difficult to say what the liberal-conservative dimension means for the two low ability groups, or even if it exists as anything more than an item in a survey interview. Low correlations could result from lack of constraint between the abstract (liberal-conservative scale) and the concrete (the issue scales), from a concrete interpretation of the liberal-conservative scale (as something other than the nine issues), from concrete, but nonconsensual definitions of the scale, or from some combination of the three. We can say that the liberal-conservative dimension does not seem to be used as a structuring principle by many lower ability respondents, nor does it seem powerful for those who do employ it. For the electorate as a whole, the evidence suggests that these widely used concepts have no shared connotations. What is "liberal" to one citizen may not be "conservative" to another, but it is quite likely irrelevant to his conception of "liberalism."

It is at this point that we begin to encounter the objections of the various "rationalist" positions. All these objections speak to the problems arising from the use of the notion of a liberal-conservative continuum to assess the mass public's conception of the political world. The objections are taken up here in order of severity.

The mass public may use the liberal-conservative continuum, it is argued, but be unable to *articulate* responses to survey questions on it. The argument here is that *use, recognition of use,* and *articulation of position* may be a good deal less than perfectly correlated. Large numbers of people might have reasonably accurate "gut" impressions of the ordering of candidates and parties in American elections, but be unable to say so. The articulation of subtle concepts is clearly related to cognitive ability, but the implication of this first rationalist argument is that *use of the liberal-conservative dimension to structure the political world is not related to cognitive ability.*

The notion of a liberal-conservative ordering dimension has wide currency among the American political elite. It is widely held to be "central" to the belief systems of political activists. That it is central to the beliefs of political scientists may explain, according to a second rationalist objection, why we look for it in the mass public. Might it not be the case that members of the mass public have belief systems equally constrained along some abstract dimension other than the liberal-conservative dimension? The implication of

TABLE 2.5

Correlations of Issue Dimensions with the Liberal-Conservative Scale, by Ability Group

		Ability Group			
	Whole Sample	1 (Lowest)	2	3	4 (Highest)
.47					Busing .47
.46					Minority .46
.45				Jobs .45	Health Ins. .45
.43					Vietnam .43
.42				Minority .42 / Busing .42	
.41				Vietnam .41	Jobs .41
.40					Marijuana .40
.39				Marijuana .39	
.38	Minority .38 / Busing .38				
.37				Rights of Acc. .37	Rights of Acc. .37
.35	Vietnam .35				
.34				Health Ins. .34	
.31	Jobs .31 / Rights of Acc. .31				
.30			Minority .30		
.29	Marijuana .29 / Health Ins. .29	Minority .29	Busing .29		

	695–786	110–128	165–191	201–221	224–245
26					
25	Women	Vietnam .25	Vietnam .25		Women .25
24			Jobs .24		
23			Rights of Acc. .23		
22	.22	Women .22		Women .22	
21		Rights of Acc. .21			
20		Busing .20	Women .20		
19					
18					
17				Inflation .17	
16		Marijuana .15			
15		Health Ins. .15			
14					
13					
12			Marijuana .12		
11					
10					
9					
8		Jobs .08			
7	Inflation .06		Health Ins. .07		Inflation .07
6					
5					
4					
3					
2			Inflation .02		
1					
00	Inflation	Inflation −.06			
N	695–786	110–128	165–191	201–221	224–245

this argument is that *at various cognitive ability levels we should expect to see perhaps different ordering dimensions, but dimensions that are equally abstract and powerful in all groups.*

The final objection holds that voters do not structure their beliefs along any single dimension but use several; and more important, it holds that multiple-dimension belief systems show more "cognitive complexity" than the uni-dimensional (Marcus et al., 1974). By implication, multidimensional and complex are more appropriate to rational choice than unidimensional and simple. This objection, preferring complexity, rejects constraint as a desirable property of belief systems. The multidimensional argument implies that *those of higher cognitive ability use more dimensions to structure their political perceptions.*

All three rationalist arguments lead to testable propositions. The first holds that people at all ability levels employ the liberal-conservative continuum, although they may not articulate it. The second holds that people at all ability levels use a single abstract dimension, but it may not be the liberal-conservative dimension. The third holds that the number of dimensions used increases with cognitive ability.

As a means of simplifying some rather substantial correlation matrices to bring summary data to bear upon each of the three propositions, we have performed a principal components factor analysis. Factor analysis is not an ideal method for examining belief systems. The number of dimensions "found" is quite clearly in part a function of the number and centrality of issues chosen for analysis. Factor analysis may also overstate the number of real dimensions. And interpretation of rotated factors is always hazardous.

None of these deficiencies of factor analysis is particularly severe for our purpose. The "number of factors" problem is more problematic for inferences about the whole electorate than for comparisons between respondents. The number and substance of items do affect the number and substance of resulting factors, but here all respondents are subject to the same items.[6] Interpretation, too, is sometimes problematic, particularly for residual factors, but on the whole requires few leaps of faith. Factor analysis does speak to central questions—"How many dimensions?" and "What are they?"—without forcing either particular dimensions or levels of articulation on respondents.

The factor analysis is based on the intercorrelations of the nine issue scales of Table 2.5 and the liberal-conservative scale. The liberal-conservative scale was included to ease factor interpretation after ascertaining that its inclusion did not materially affect the factor structure.[7]

The first question to be approached is: How many dimensions? In more operational terms: How many of the factors explain how much variance? Figure 2.4 diagrams, for each ability group, the amount of variance explained by each factor with an eigenvalue greater than 1.0. It speaks clearly to the

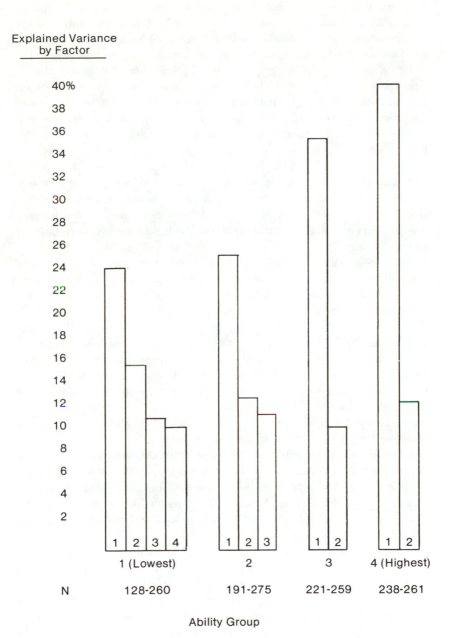

FIGURE 2.4
Dimensionality of Belief by Ability Group, 1972

argument that number of dimensions used increases with cognitive ability. Exactly the opposite is the case. Moving from those of low cognitive ability upward on the scale, the number of dimensions used declines (from 4 to 3 to 2 for the highest two groups), and the variance explained by each increases. The evidence of Figure 2.4 suggests that for those of lowest cognitive ability, structure—if it exists at all—is multidimensional. The upper strata of the sample show evidence of a tendency toward attitude constraint and *perhaps* unidimensional constraint. Both upper strata groups show impressive differences between the proportions of variance explained by the first and second factors, suggesting that the latter are unimportant residual dimensions.

We have yet to deal with the *meaning* of structuring dimensions. Is the structure of the lower ability groups the structure of higher ability groups writ small? Or do different dimensions structure the beliefs of different ability strata? In Table 2.6, we examine the content of the factors derived for each group. Question marks indicate skepticism about the inherent interpretability of some factors.

It is a good deal more problematic to tell what factors mean than to tell how many of them there are and how much variance each explains. It is particularly difficult for the lower ability respondents, because it is not clear that the presumed dimensions are real.

Despite these difficulties, some clear patterns are to be observed from Table 2.6. One is a clear separation of issue types at the lowest cognitive ability level. For the most part, the issues that load together on any given factor are high in superficial similarity. Racial issues load with other racial issues, economic issues with other economic issues, and social issues with other social issues (except the role-of-women item, which loads on a minor factor all by itself). Perhaps most conspicuously, the liberal-conservative scale loads highly on none of the factors.[8] Beginning in the second group, and increasing in the third and fourth, the first factor cuts across issue types. In both of the higher strata, seven of the ten items load highly on the first factor, including all of the issue types except the new issues of 1972, the role of women and the legalization of marijuana. In sum, the *scope* of particular dimensions is narrow for lower ability respondents and broad for those from the upper strata of cognitive ability.

Scope of belief systems is broader for higher ability respondents because the objects of centrality—the fundamentals—are far more abstract. Dimensions for the upper level respondents that correlate with attitudes toward race, economics, and the Vietnam War are evidently approaching the kind of abstract structuring principles implied by the concept of Ideology. Those in the lowest ability groups just as clearly lack such abstract structuring principles. If dimensions cannot be derived that cut across policy types, then ordering may be no more abstract than the policies themselves.

TABLE 2.6
The Derived Factor Structure, by Ability Group

Factor	Eigenvalue	Interpretation	Defining Variables
Group 1 (Lowest)			
1	2.39	Race	Minority, Busing
2*	1.47	Social Issues	Vietnam, Rights of Accused, Marijuana
3*	1.03	Economic Issues	Inflation, Jobs, Health Insurance
4	1.01	Women	Women
Group 2			
1	2.42	Social: Crime, Race, Vietnam	Rights of Accused, Minority, Vietnam, Liberal-Conservative
2	1.25	Economic Issues	Health Insurances, Jobs
3	1.13	?	Marijuana, Women, (Inflation—)
Group 3			
1	3.45	Left-Right	Liberal-Conservative, Jobs, Health Insurance, Minority, Vietnam, Rights of Accused, Busing
2	1.01	New Social Issues	Women, Marijuana
Group 4 (Highest)			
1	3.90	Left-Right	Jobs, Busing, Minority, Health Insurance, Liberal-Conservative, Vietnam, Inflation
2	1.21	Social Issues	Marijuana, Women, Rights of Accused

*Factors 2 and 3 are reversed when the liberal-conservative scale is not included in the analysis.

How *constrained* are respondent beliefs? Before answering that question, we note the implicit bias of the constraint concept. It is a parsimony concept, clearly implying that few structuring dimensions are better than many. By extension, one structuring dimension (e.g., left-right) is better than multiple dimensions. This constraint notion is specifically rejected by scholars who look to multiple structuring dimensions as evidence of belief complexity, presumably more appropriate to rational choice.[9]

What evidence would demonstrate belief constraint? Converse (1964) and more recent studies (Bennett, 1973; Nie, 1974) employ correlations of specific attitude scales. The 1972 election study has similar evidence, but the unwieldiness of analysis of four 10-by-10 correlation matrices leads to factor analysis as a summary device.

A number of similar indicators from the factor analysis are operational measures of belief constraint. All point to the same conclusion. The higher ability groups have fewer factors (according to the arbitrary 1.0 eigenvalue cut off). The first factor explains more variance for the higher ability respondents, and more variables load on it. (See Table 2.7.) The average variance explained by each factor increases with cognitive ability; and,

TABLE 2.7
*The Factor Structure as Evidence of Belief Constraint, by
Cognitive Ability Group*

Cognitive Ability Group	Number of Factors	Number of Variables with Highest Load on First Factor	Variance Explained by First Factor	Mean Variance Explained	Item Content Sensitivity
1 (Lowest)	4	2	23.9%	14.7%	High
2	3	4	24.2%	16.0%	Moderate
3	2	8	34.5%	22.3%	Low
4 (Highest)	2	7	39.0%	25.6%	Low

finally, the obtained factor structure is insensitive to marginal changes (addition or deletion of items) for the higher ability groups, but extremely sensitive for the lowest group. In sum: *those of higher cognitive ability have more constrained belief systems.*

What then were the dimensions of belief current in the 1972 electorate? It is a question which appears not to be answerable *for the electorate.* We can say that roughly the upper half in cognitive ability seem to have structured their beliefs, at least on traditional political issues, around the left-right continuum. For the lower half, belief dimensions are more complicated, more issue-specific, less stable and less powerful.

We have shown that the number of belief dimensions used by the 1972 respondents to structure responses to issue dimensions declines as level of formal education and political information increase. If any element of the electorate can be expected to choose rationally among political alternatives, most would concur that the expectation of rationality would be highest among the educated and informed. Since those most likely to be rational use the fewest dimensions, the evidence then suggests that few dimensions, rather than many, are linked with rational choice.

If the number and content of belief dimensions extracted by factor analysis are more than testimony to the power of computers to undertake the creative manipulation of nonsense, they should predict attitudes and behavior. To say that a belief dimension is meaningful is to say, in a most important sense, that it is related to real political choices. Two such choices are candidate evaluation and vote.

Candidate evaluations, as Stokes (1966) has noted, are the most variable elements in American presidential elections; but it is not clear to what degree they are composed of more than fluff—reactions to projected images of sincerity, piousness, and the like—rather than more genuinely political content. A candidate's character is undoubtedly important, but it fails to

TABLE 2.8
*Affect toward Candidates: Multiple Correlations of Belief Dimensions
with Candidate Feeling Thermometers, by Ability Group*

Ability Group	McGovern Feeling Thermometer			Nixon Feeling Thermometer		
	Multiple Correlation (R)	Variance Explained	N	Multiple Correlation (R)	Variance Explained	N
1 (Lowest) Four Dimensions	.448	20.1%	262	.290	8.4%	272
2 Three Dimensions	.456	20.8%	287	.402	16.2%	288
3 Two Dimensions	.515	26.5%	266	.514	26.4%	267
4 (Highest) Two Dimensions	.605	36.6%	263	.655	42.9%	264

convey important information about what he will do if elected. Knowing only character is not to know the shrines of a candidate's political faith, the groups he will appease and those he will ignore, or the programs he will sponsor.

Table 2.8 examines the degree to which candidate evaluation may be predicted by the dimensions of political belief previously isolated for the four ability groups. Dependent variables are McGovern and Nixon "feeling thermometers," measures of affect toward the two candidates. Independent variables are factor scores representing the dimensions of belief derived for each ability group. These dimensions are derived from items that make no reference to either party or candidate, but only issue dimensions, and hence may be thought of as relatively pure indicators of enduring beliefs, little affected by the fluff of campaign and candidates. Candidate evaluations heavily influenced by fundamental beliefs about politics would seem to be prima facie evidence of rational choice. The lack of such influence indicates either nonrational evaluation or some form of policy-irrelevant rationality.

The message of Table 2.8 is clear: Even though more dimensions of belief are allowed to contribute to the predicted evaluations of lower ability groups, higher ability groups are substantially more predictable. In the highest ability group, a mere two dimensions of belief account for about 37% and 43% of the variance in evaluation of McGovern and Nixon respectively. In the lowest group, four dimensions account for 20% and 8% respectively. Those who use fewer dimensions appear more to evaluate candidates on the basis of rational considerations. This is true both relatively (variance explained per dimension) and absolutely (total variance explained).

Another message of Table 2.8 is that McGovern evaluations are more uniformly predictable among ability groups than Nixon evaluations. It seems reasonable to postulate that the frequent public reference to McGovern as "radical" made him uncommonly easy to evaluate by ideological criteria. Nixon's less ideological appeal seems to have captured many voters of lower cognitive ability in spite of—not because of—their beliefs.

Table 2.9 takes us to the final question about belief structure: What impact does it have on the vote? To answer that question, we introduce party identification both as a baseline and as a control. As a baseline it allows comparisons between the impacts of structures of belief on the one hand and simple party loyalty on the other. Since it may interact with belief structure, we also examine party identification jointly with belief dimensions.

Those of higher cognitive ability, which is to say those who use few dimensions to structure their political beliefs, cast votes which are far more predictable from their beliefs than do those of lower ability. The range of multiple correlation coefficients is from about .38 for the lowest ability group to .68 for the highest. These levels of predictability are remarkably similar to the predictability of voting gained by examination of party identification for each group. For both belief dimensions and party identification, predictability increases with cognitive ability, the only significant deviation occurring among those of highest ability, where belief predictability increases and party predictability declines.

The combination of belief dimensions and party identification to predict vote shows that both factors have substantial independent predictive power. The impact of party is not so neatly related to cognitive ability as is the case with belief dimensions, and indeed there is no reason to expect that it should be. Differences between the first two and second two groups are, however, substantial.

We may infer from Table 2.9 that few voter defections from party identification occur among those of high cognitive ability (and constrained beliefs), *and* that those defections which do occur are more predictable from fundamental voter beliefs. The lower ability groups, on the other hand, are less tied to party *and* less predictable when they depart from party loyalty. Those of high cognitive ability structure their beliefs simply and behave in a manner consistent with theories of rational choice. Those of low ability do not show evidence of simple and powerful belief structuring, and their more complex derived belief structures are far less predictive of their behavior at the polls.

A CONCLUDING IRONY

A picture has been sketched here of a conflict between unidimensional and multidimensional approaches to belief structuring, between simple structures

TABLE 2.9
Belief Dimensions and 1972 Vote: Multiple Correlations of Belief Dimensions with Reported Vote, by Ability Group

Ability Group	N	Multiple Correlation: Belief Dimensions and Vote	Simple Correlation: Party Identification and Vote	Multiple Correlation: Party, Belief Dimensions, and Vote
1 (Lowest) Four Dimensions	131	.378	.384	.509
2 Three Dimensions	211	.466	.420	.559
3 Two Dimensions	213	.588	.622	.743
4 (Highest) Two Dimensions	230	.675	.599	.741

and complex structures. We have found simple structures more associated with high levels of cognitive ability, more powerful in predicting attitudes, and more predictive of two important political choices, candidate evaluation and vote. All of this would seem to suggest simply enough that the Converse approach to measuring belief structure has been fundamentally correct all along.

But the conflict about the proper way to conceptualize belief systems was part of a larger debate about the level of belief structuring present in the American electorate. Differing conceptualizations led to differing conclusions; unidimensionalists found little structure, multidimensionalists found it widespread. A strange thing has happened on our way to a conclusion. The same data that shore up the validity of the unidimensional approach lead to a conclusion about the level of belief structuring that is strikingly different from Converse's. They show that at least half of the eligible electorate (and more of the actual electorate) displays evidence of belief structuring that is consistent with the standards originally laid down by Converse; that is, the upper two ability groups show evidence of using the left-right dimension in a manner which is sufficiently abstract to encompass a wide scope of more specific political attitudes, and which is demonstrably important in predicting their responses to the choices offered by the political system.

How can Converse be both right and wrong? The 1972 data do not speak directly to the point, but a recent article by Norman Nie and Kristi Andersen (1974) demonstrates what many have long suggested: that a very substantial change has occurred in American politics since 1960 and that the presidential elections which were the subject of Converse's analysis were vastly less ideological in the minds of voters than all those which have occurred since then. The 1972 data would seem to confirm the Nie et al. hypothesis. It remains to be seen whether this change is a prelude to future quiescence or a lasting rearrangement of the shape of American politics.

APPENDIX

1972 Election Study Issue Dimension Scales

The same format is followed for each scale; a descriptive lead-in is followed by the question: "Where would you place yourself on this scale, or haven't you thought much about this?" Only the lead-ins are listed here.

G1. Suppose people who believe that the government should see to it that every person has a job and a good standard of living are at one end of this scale—at point number 1. And suppose that the people who believe that the government should let each person get ahead on his own are at the other end—at point number 7.

G2. As you know, in our tax system people who earn a lot of money already have to pay higher rates of income tax than those who earn less. Some people think that those with high incomes should pay even more of their income into taxes than they do now. Others think that the rates shouldn't be different at all—that everyone should pay the same portion of their income, no matter how much they make.

G3. Some people think that the use of marijuana should be made legal. Others think that the penalities for using marijuana should be set higher than they are now.

G4. There is much discussion about the best way to deal with racial problems. Some people think achieving racial integration of schools is so important that it justifies busing children to schools out of their own neighborhoods. Others think letting children go to their neighborhood schools is so important that they oppose busing.

G5. There is much concern about the rapid rise in medical and hospital costs. Some feel there should be a government insurance plan which would cover all medical and hospital expenses. Others feel that medical expenses should be paid by individuals, and through private insurance like Blue Cross.

G9. Recently there has been a lot of talk about women's rights. Some people feel that women should have an equal role with men in running business, industry, and government. Others feel that women's place is in the home.

J3. With regard to Vietnam, some people think we should do everything necessary to win a complete military victory, no matter what results. Some people think we should withdraw completely from Vietnam right now, no matter what results. And, of course, other people have opinions somewhere between these two extreme positions.

J4. There is a great deal of talk these days about rising prices and the cost of living in general. Some feel that the government must do everything possible to combat the problem of inflation immediately or it will get worse. Others say the problem of inflation is temporary and that no government action is necessary.

J5. Some people are primarily concerned with doing everything possible to protect the legal rights of those accused of committing crimes. Others feel that it is more important to stop criminal activity even at the risk of reducing the rights of the accused.

J6. Some people feel that the government in Washington should make every possible effort to improve the social and economic position of blacks and other minority groups. Others feel that the government should not make any special effort to help minorities because they should help themselves.

J8. We hear a lot of talk these days about liberals and conservatives. I'm going to show you a seven-point scale on which the political views that people hold are arranged from extremely liberal to extremely conservative.

NOTES

1. It is no accident that "rationalism" is associated with formalism. Some form of rationality postulate is ordinarily necessary for deductive inference from the formal models of electoral choice.

2. The Johnson-Goldwater contest of 1964 runs a close second in this regard and might have been more ideological had not the salience of Goldwater's "itchy trigger finger" vastly exceeded that of his conservative domestic program (Converse, Clausen, and Miller, 1965).

3. Each variable was standardized to contribute equal variance to the index. Marquette (1972) notes the hazards of this technique, and Levine (1973) its safety.

4. Neither measure is, however, optimal. Years of formal education are not as good a measure of the ability to manipulate concepts as, for example, I.Q. And the need for objectively "right" answers makes the political information items constitutional and legalistic rather than attuned to current and controversial issues in the political sphere.

5. A tenth item, a tax reform scale, was not used because it suffers from ambiguity—the same kind of ambiguity that stifles popular discussion of the issue. The item (see Appendix) refers to tax rates, ignoring important controversies about what constitutes taxable income. Respondents could choose between "have the same tax rate for everyone" (i.e., lower total tax payments for the wealthy than the current progressive rate system) or "increase the tax rate for high income." The question does not address what is likely to have been on respondents' minds: who should pay more tax and who less. It seems likely that the 30% who responded on the "same tax rate" pole of the scale meant something like everyone should pay his fair share—meaning that the wealthy should pay more—which was just the opposite of the change they were apparently endorsing.

6. The one exception is that the lowest ability group actually responded to fewer items on the average. Some inflation of the appearance of structure in their responses is to be expected.

7. The inclusion of the liberal-conservative scale does affect the factor structure derived for the lowest ability group (but not the number of factors or their explanatory power). This structure is so unstable that virtually any small change affects it dramatically. Since the instability itself is the most salient characteristic of the derived "structure" of beliefs for this group, we are not particularly concerned about those changes.

8. Its best loadings are .40 and .41 on factors 1 and 2, respectively.

9. Marcus et al. (1974) used INDSCAL analysis of paired comparisons of abstract political concepts to show that those of higher cognitive ability (by indicators analogous to ours) used more dimensions to structure their responses than those of lesser ability, and that the number of dimensions used, called cognitive complexity, was an indicator of sophistication of political beliefs. Our analysis (available on request) of responses to political slogans—another data set from the same study—finds patterns similar to the 1972 sample; those of higher ability use fewer dimensions to structure their responses to the slogans than do their low ability counterparts. The INDSCAL analysis of responses to abstract stimuli seems to measure respondents' capability of articulating relational concepts or dimensions used to structure responses to more concrete stimuli. The joint finding: those who are capable of articulating the most dimensions actually use the fewest. "Complexity" and "constraint," which seem logically to be polar opposites, empirically are found together. Those who have the most complex view of the political world develop the most parsimonious structure of beliefs.

REFERENCES

Bennett, Stephen. 1973. "Consistency among the Public's Social Welfare Attitudes in the 1960s," *American Journal of Political Science*, August 1973, pp. 544–570.

Campbell, Angus; Converse, Philip; Miller, Warren; and Stokes, Donald. 1960. *The American Voter*. New York: John Wiley and Sons.

Converse, Philip. 1964. "The Nature of Belief Systems in Mass Publics," in David Apter, ed., *Ideology and Discontent*. New York: The Free Press, pp. 206–261.

Converse, Philip; Clausen, Aage; and Miller, Warren. 1965. "Electoral Myth and Reality: The 1964 Election," *American Political Science Review*, June 1965, pp. 321–326.

Diesing, Paul. 1971. *Patterns of Discovery in the Social Sciences*. Chicago: Aldine-Atherton.

Levine, Mark S. 1973. "Standard Scores as Indices: The Pitfalls of Not Thinking It Through," *American Journal of Political Science*, May 1973, pp. 431–440.

Marcus, George; Tabb, David; and Sullivan, John L. 1974. "The Application of Individual Differences Scaling to the Measurement of Political Ideologies," *American Journal of Political Science*, May 1974, pp. 405–420.

Marquette, Jesse F. 1972. "Standard Scores as Indices: The Pitfalls of Doing Things the Easy Way," *Midwest Journal of Political Science*, May 1972, pp. 278–286.

Nie, Norman H., with Kristi Andersen. 1974. "Mass Belief Systems Revisited: Political Change and Attitude Structure," *Journal of Politics*, August 1974.

Stokes, Donald E. 1966. "Some Dynamic Elements in Contests for the Presidency," *American Political Science Review*, March 1966, pp. 19–28.

Weisberg, Herbert, and Rusk, Jerrold. 1970. "Dimensions of Candidate Evaluation," *American Political Science Review*, December 1970, pp. 1167–1185.

Wilker, Harry, and Milbrath, Lester. 1970. "Political Belief Systems and Political Behavior," *Social Science Quarterly*, December 1970, pp. 477–493.

_____ PERSONAL ACCOUNT

2B. Pursuing Belief Structure: A Research Narrative*

JAMES A. STIMSON

This is a narrative about a fairly normal piece of research. "Belief Systems" needs to be seen in its proper context. It is a contribution to the resolution of problems most scholars in the field considered important, and it left me with the satisfaction of having solved a puzzle. I am proud of it, but it is not a great

*The writing of this narrative was supported by the National Science Foundation under grant SOC-7907543. The original research was supported in part by the State University of New York Foundation. I add a special note of warm appreciation for Donald R. Matthews, from whom I took a nine-year course in the research experience.

discovery. Its importance is small in contrast to the original work on belief structure by Converse. It is not the most important work I have ever done.

Narratives about research are not common. Those that I have read are about great discoveries, breakthroughs so important that autobiographical accounts are useful for the history of science. This is a more humble endeavor. If it has value, it may be as a corrective; it is an account of a typical research experience in political science. If they are to be honest, narratives must be personal, filled with accounts of what the narrator did, thought, and experienced. What I did, thought, and experienced may not strike the reader as important matters to know. They are not. But there is no other way to tell the story.

SATISFYING RESEARCH

Scratch a satisfied researcher and you are likely to uncover bemused guilt. "If this work is so much fun," he asks, "why is someone paying me to do it? Should I enjoy it less or come clean and admit that I have been accepting salary under a false pretense of work?"[1] For what we do, when it is satisfying, is what sensible people experience when they read or watch detective thrillers. And they—in truth, we—lay out cash for the experience.

Authors can't pronounce upon the quality of their work; that is properly left to others. But authors know better than others whether a particular piece of research was satisfying. "Belief Systems" was satisfying research. All the time I played with it, guilt warned me that someone might notice how much time I was devoting to it, when I really should be working.

Satisfying research has a puzzle-like quality. As Kuhn (1962) has pointed out, exciting research and good puzzles have two attributes in common. They must offer considerable challenge to the ingenuity, for easy problems quickly become boring. But they must also hold out the prospect that solution is possible, for serious puzzle-solving activity is difficult to sustain in the face of doubts about whether the problem is ultimately tractable.[2] We are as unlikely to persist in research that might lead only to hopeless confusion as to attempt a difficult jigsaw puzzle with the foreknowledge that pieces might be missing.

If puzzle solving were our only motive, we would put down puzzle-like research and turn to actual crosswords and jigsaw puzzles. But research offers a prospect that puzzles lack; the solution might matter. Research is more than a game (if just as much fun) because its end product might be worthwhile. I must add quickly that I am not talking about Improving the Quality of the World—that is the Madison Avenue sales image of science—but simply about contributing to the state of knowledge. There is satisfaction to be had from clarifying theoretical accounts of the political world, and that satisfaction increases in proportion to the importance of the theories.

"Belief Structure" was a prize puzzle. The fact that serious scholars were spending a good deal of energy contradicting one another attests to its challenge. The fact that the contradictory positions could not *both* be right assured some kind of ultimate solution. And understanding the belief-structure question lay square in the path of empirical democratic theory. In short, it was fun. But no one decides upon a line of research by this kind of reasoning—at least before the fact. Why scholars choose to do what they do is not understood in the general case. And, in truth, I'm not sure that I know what goes into even my own research decisions. But I do remember the sequence of events that led to "Belief Systems." I digress.

A Collaboration That Never Was, A Theory Never Tested

"Belief Systems" is an article about measuring belief structure in the context of the 1972 presidential election. To explain why it evolved into the shape it took I begin by pointing out (1) that it was not intended to be an article, (2) that it was not intended to focus on measuring belief structure, and (3) that the 1972 Center for Political Studies (CPS) study was not the intended data base. Otherwise everything went according to expectations.

The article on its face is part of a public scientific dialogue about the proper way to conceptualize belief structuring. It is what it seems to be, but its origin—and the explanation for many of its embedded research decisions—lies in an unpublished dialogue between potential collaborators, John L. Sullivan and myself.[3] The dialogue started with a grand theory of the causes of belief structuring, progressed to discourse on research design, and then turned into a friendly feud about the meaning of belief structure that led directly to "Belief Systems."

In the beginning there was Philip Converse. His participation in the "levels of conceptualization" analysis in *The American Voter* (1960) and subsequent essay on "The Nature of Belief Systems in Mass Publics" (1964) left political scientists with a bad case of intellectual indigestion. Converse's work suggested that mass political attitudes were so loosely held, so casually picked up and discarded, so randomly arranged, that cherished theories of representative democracy were hopelessly inept descriptions of the reality of political life in the United States. After generations of organizing political thought and action around the notion of a left-right ideological continuum, Converse told us that the mass of American voters was not liberal, not moderate, not conservative, but "none of the above." It was disquieting. To accept Converse's conclusions required the abandonment of generally accepted assumptions about mass behavior that brought neatness and order to politics.

Converse's conclusion that tightly woven structures of political belief are atypical of mass publics was—and is—one of the most important and controverial assertions of modern political science.[4] Much early reaction to Converse was intuitive and largely negative. While my own was positive, it was also intuitive. I read the levels of conceptualization analysis for the first time after a summer on the road, full time, in a congressional campaign. As yet I was neither a scholar nor a particularly perceptive observer, but the experience of talking to thousands of ordinary American voters had not failed to leave a strong impression. Although there was a vast discrepancy between popular accounts of voting behavior and the experience I had lived, I had managed (sadly) to be consciously unaware of that fact, to keep politics and political science in separate mental compartments. Reading Converse destroyed those compartments. What Converse extracted from survey protocols was what I had experienced. "That's the way it is," was my reaction. Such a revelation is dubious grounds for confirming a proposition by conventional scientific criteria, but it is powerful psychology.[5]

Professional politicians do exhibit integrated structures of political belief; that is not a matter of controversy.[6] The question naturally arises, why are politicians' views structured when mass publics are not? That was the beginning of my yet unfinished collaboration with Sullivan. The answer arose naturally from a shared interest in Downs's (1957) economic formulation of politics and from the coincidence that the economy of choice for professional politicians was my "serious" research at the time (Matthews and Stimson, 1975). The answer was obvious:

> Ideology is a strategy of reducing decision costs when large numbers of decisions must be made. It evolves when it serves this function. . . .
> Thus, infrequency of political decision-making is the explanation for the observed low levels of conceptualization in mass publics. (Stimson and Sullivan, 1970)

What we then called a functional explanation of ideology borrowed directly from Downs the notion that ideology could economize decision making: a one-time investment in ideological positioning could save the voter innumerable information-gathering and processing costs for a long string of later decisions on new and different issues, candidates, and so forth. The new wrinkle of our approach was to assert why this process would not occur for typical voters. For them political decisions would be infrequent, intermittent, and casually taken. Ideological thinking would not evolve because its "cost" in intellectual energy was greater than its value for those whose need to make political decisions was neither urgent nor frequent.

Frequency of political decision making was the key. It obviously discriminates between the professional politician and the citizen. We thought it would discriminate among citizens as well. Those who engage in the life of political ideas—people, for example, who cared enough to talk back to the television set—would find ideology a useful decision aid and would invest in its further development. The more passive would make no such investment, and they would be rational in doing so.

And there the matter lies. The theory has never been tested.[7] Both collaborators had other research obligations in the short term. In the longer term the collaboration foundered from disagreement about the very essence of the problem, what belief structure was and how it could be measured. That friendly disagreement explains why "Belief Systems" was started in the first place and accounts for a good many decisions along the way.

Complexity or Constraint?

Belief structure became for me a favorite lecture topic, but I did no original research while my efforts were focused on congressional decision making. Sullivan continued work in the area. An early product was a fifteen-page proposal on "Levels of Conceptualization" (Stimson and Sullivan, 1971),[8] which incorporated the earlier ideas and added a good bit of new material. That document reflected our early (and easy) consensus on the question of belief structure; it was the end of that road.

Through the Psychology and Politics program at Yale, Sullivan formed a good working relationship with George Marcus (and through him, David Tabb). From an intellectual brew I did not witness the three of them produced a series of papers on a strikingly different tack. Abandoning Converse altogether, they argued that different individuals structured their beliefs along different dimensions, that the more sophisticated used multiple—not single— organizing dimensions, and most importantly, that virtually all citizens were ideologues. Called "cognitive complexity," their measure of belief structure was very nearly the opposite of the simple, economical structure Converse called "constraint."

Asked by Sullivan to read and comment on an early paper, I unleashed a seven-page diatribe questioning theory, data, method, and parenthood. The criticism was ferocious because I like to argue (and one can pull all the stops with a friend; there is no need to be politic) and because I thought the cognitive complexity notion of structure misguided. And, the grand theory still in my mind, there was an obvious problem when one collaborator was trying to explain why structured political beliefs were infrequent and the other why they were universal!

The beginnings of the complexity versus constraint dialogue lie in that criticism and a more temperate response from Sullivan. It went beyond argument and opinion when Marcus, Tabb, and Sullivan acquired a newer larger data set of high school juniors and seniors in Connecticut and Minnesota, which allowed them to validate the complexity measure. Their next effort reported that the complexity measure was positively correlated with measures of student I.Q. and level of political information. This is the sort of feat that distinguishes scientific argument from mere difference of opinion. If complexity characterized the more sophisticated respondents, it should have been associated with variables like I.Q. and information, and it was. I was impressed by the demonstration, almost a critical test of complexity versus constraint. But it still did not square with Converse. And it did not fit my campaign experience, however disreputable that claim on truth.

Wanting to resolve the question—whether for pure curiosity or serious research I no longer recall—I asked for the high school data. It was willingly given. It is an incident that I recall whenever I hear cynical talk about careerism and closed-mindedness as dominant forces in research. Although their work had not yet appeared in print, Marcus, Tabb, and Sullivan gave me their data, knowing that if I used it, it would be not to praise them. It is the sort of everyday behavior that gives meaning to the "science" part of political science.

The Analysis

This narrative is supposed to be an example of secondary analysis, the reanalysis of data sets produced by other scholars, usually for other purposes. The question arises, why did I choose to do secondary analysis? To that there are two answers: (1) The most direct criticism of an idea can be made by using exactly the same data that produced it, and (2) I never seriously thought about an alternative research strategy.[9]

I have deliberately written at length about the events that preceded my analysis because they determined the shape of what was to come. The twin measures of cognitive ability used by Marcus, Tabb, and Sullivan to validate the complexity measure were obvious candidates to challenge that validation. To stratify their sample by cognitive ability, they used an index composed of both measures because it was the most direct comparison. When I later turned to the 1972 study, I chose the most similar measures I could get. The whole idea of stratifying was a response to the Marcus, Tabb, and Sullivan validation. Principal components analysis was again a direct response to the Marcus, Tabb, and Sullivan focus on dimensionality; this technique was explicitly designed as a tool for examining dimensionality.[10]

The complexity measure used by Marcus, Tabb, and Sullivan was applicable to individuals. Because constraint is measured by correlations across a group of individuals, it can only be assigned at the group level. My first research task was to examine whether the Marcus, Tabb, and Sullivan validation of complexity would work at the group level. Lacking the ability to correlate a (group-level) measure of constraint with individual measures of political sophistication, I had to shift levels of analysis in order to make comparisons. I stratified the high school sample into high, medium, and low levels of sophistication to see whether the complexity measure would also be validated at the group level. It was. By any reasonable criterion the more sophisticated respondents used more dimensions to structure response to abstract political concepts than did the less sophisticated groups. This validation of the Marcus, Tabb, and Sullivan validation was important because it meant that switching to the group level of analysis did not by itself undercut their original findings.

In a second step I used principal components analysis to examine the constraint between responses to political slogans for the same three groups. As in the 1972 analysis, *fewer* structuring dimensions were used by the more sophisticated than by the less sophisticated. Although buried in a footnote (number 9), that analysis produced what was for me the most interesting finding. It was a solution to the puzzle that was the driving force of the research.

There were two theories, both reasonable and in open conflict. Converse and others argued that a powerful belief structure would subsume a wide variety of specific beliefs and issue positions under an overarching set of abstract principles—orientations toward politics, society, and change so general that they would cross all the boundaries of issue content. That sort of structure seemed to be exemplified in the behavior of politicians, party activists in the electorate, and in those who reported and commented upon politics.

Starting with the reasonable presumption that the world is a complicated place, Marcus, Tabb and Sullivan argued that political conflict is multifaceted, not capable of simple organization because it was inherently complex. It follows that sophisticated observers of politics would deal with complexity by developing appropriately complex structures of belief. Their data showed that to be the case.

Converse had argued plausibly that simple structure would be found among the most sophisticated and demonstrated that it was so. Marcus, Tabb, and Sullivan argued plausibly for complex structure among the sophisticated and demonstrated that it was so. They couldn't both be right. That was the puzzle. The solution to the puzzle is that they were both right. But they were right at different aspects of the structuring question. Marcus, Tabb, and Sullivan asked respondents to make similarity judgments about abstract concepts (Dissent, Private Property, Patriotism, Tolerance, Law, Violence, and so on) and found that those of higher capabilities used more dimensions to structure their responses. They were capable of painting a more complex picture of the political world. But responding to the more concrete slogans of everyday politics, the pattern reversed; these same sophisticated respondents used simpler structure, fewer dimensions.

The problem had a neat resolution. What seemed to be one question with two contradictory answers turned out instead to be two questions. Cognitive psychology suggested complexity. The economy of choice dictated simplicity. When asked to make difficult judgments of the similarity of abstract concepts, the cognitively capable displayed complex structuring principles. Responding to everyday politics, they showed simple powerful structure. There was no contradiction.

Although it remains only in a subtitle and a lengthy footnote, resolving the complexity-constraint puzzle was the essence of "Belief Systems." The rest of the article is a research experience as well, but of a different kind.

"On the Origin of Articles": Charles Darwin and the 1972 Election

"Belief Systems" seems to be an article about the 1972 presidential election. It was not intended to be. Although the pen did not move against my will, the research I started and the article I wrote are two different species. Because this is an obvious case of evolution, something that started out to be one thing and ended up another, the concepts appropriate for that sort of explanation will be employed. Because, as President Reagan has noted, evolution is "only a theory," the tender-minded should not put too much stock in this account.

Evolution occurs when a new trait arises, perhaps by accident, and is "selected" for survival because it is well fit to any of a host of dangers or opportunities in the environment.[11] The individual carrying the trait survives, reproduces, and we all know the rest. From this simplistic account we can focus on (1) the preexisting species, (2) the accident, (3) the selective advantage, (4) reproduction, and (5) the new species.

The preexisting species was research about complexity and constraint. Although its results were satisfying, the findings were clear but not strong. The sample was small and nonrandom in a field dominated by large almost random national cross sections.

The accident was that I was intimately familiar with the 1972 study from an undergraduate honors thesis I was supervising. The data were therefore easily at hand.

The selective advantages of the 1972 data were many. They were new; there was as yet no published account of the election. Therefore, it was topical. Because 1972 had been an unusually ideological election, it was an interesting counterpoint to the dull elections that had been the focus of earlier work on belief structure. It was a nice addition to the central focus on the Marcus, Tabb, Sullivan high school data. Its weakness was that it included no measure of cognitive complexity, the central focus of the research.

The reproductive process was revision. Each draft of an article breeds a new generation. Traits that have a selective advantage become increasingly prominent in each generation; weaknesses are whittled away. As in the evolution of species, this produces not a "better" species, but one better suited to its environment. Each revision in this case produced lengthier commentaries on 1972, less on complexity and constraint. The "predators" in this system are editors and anonymous journal referees. Almost as heartless as their biological counterparts, they make a quick meal of any weakness offered. That led in the end to the extinction of the analysis of the Marcus, Tabb, and Sullivan data; it was pronounced a digression from the main line of argument and remains only a vestigial skeleton in footnote 9. The *new species* is "Belief Systems."

REFLECTIONS

So that is how "Belief Systems" came to be. I have perhaps over-emphasized the capriciousness of the research experience. There were ideas. There were plans for research. There was a design. I certainly do not advocate "unintended consequences" as a starting design for research. That path always leads to failure. Without expectation, there is no joy in discovery.

I have written this account as if it began in 1970 and ended four years later. That probably looks long and unproductive to the student who must begin and complete within the same academic term. "Real" research is different from student research in duration and intensity. Student work is short and intense. Ideas are developed, tested, and written in weeks—not infrequently, in days. Professional research is typically long and shallow. That gives it a very different feel from textbook research. It is, as the texts all say, the interplay of theory, literature, design, and analysis. But that interplay typically occurs on and off over months and years, an experience much more complicated, much more personal than "step 1, step 2, step 3 . . ." My involvement in mass belief structure is considerably longer than even this narrative suggests. It began in 1964 with an undergraduate term paper on the levels of conceptualization analysis in *The American Voter*,[12] and it has not yet ended. That little undergraduate project put belief structure on my agenda of interesting unresolved questions. My interest was completely dormant until 1970 and largely so after that. Most of the work I put into "theory," "design," and "literature" occurred when I was not consciously working. Often, toying around with research ideas is a digression from what seems to be real work.

Playing around with research ideas, one typically does not anticipate a final product—a paper, article, or whatever. There is a kind of natural selection of ideas in my work. Playing around leads to many "neat little ideas." In sober experience most turn out to be truly little but falsely neat. They lead to research blind alleys, tests that are impossible, findings that are uninteresting, theories that are just wrong. They are piled one atop another in a research junkyard. Because it is more play than work, ideas that fail cause little remorse.[13] And occasionally one works.

I have taken up these questions of style and habit because they cannot be experienced by the student of research. No text can systematize those unsystematic experiences. No classroom can simulate them. But they are real and probably fairly typical.

Mistakes are also typical. Most are weeded out along the way, but some inevitably survive publication, at which point they can no longer be fixed. "Belief Systems" has fewer than my normal quota, but there are two I would fix if I could. One is the creation of the "rationalists" as a group with a common position on belief structure questions. It seemed reasonable at the time to combine the Rochester school of rational choice theorists with Marcus, Tabb, and Sullivan. But all they really had in common was that they disagreed with me, Sullivan through the mails, Rochester—in the person of Nancy McGlen—in daily arguments about rationality in politics. The combination didn't work.

The second mistake I would fix is the regression analysis of Table 2.9. Aldrich and Cnudde (1975) have pointed out that it is inappropriate to perform regression on a dichotomous dependent variable. What is galling to me—and must have been noticed with humor by Aldrich and Cnudde—is that their demonstration appeared in the same journal and in the same issue as "Belief Systems." But what really ices the cake is that they used 1972 vote as an illustration of the case. If they had been methodological preachers, the sinner was close at hand.

The Afterbirth

Pure puzzle solving carries an inevitable disappointment. When the puzzle is solved, the challenge is gone, the game over. Research is again more satisfying than the real thing. Like a kind of intellectual breeder reactor, it creates new puzzles more rapidly than it disposes of old ones. "Belief Systems" created a puzzle for me. It went to press with a tidbit of evidence, the apparent centrality of matters of race to the connotation of liberal-conservative, that was not what it should have been. "Race" was not supposed to be central to left-right conceptions of politics, and it was not supposed to have been salient in the 1972 contest, but there it was.

Interesting little questions hinder research; they provoke the imagination but distract attention from the central focus. My personal solution to this common problem is to write a quick and dirty research memo on the distracting questions so that I can feel free to forget about them and get on with the task at hand. This particular memo, sent to that graduate student who had given good advice about factor analysis, proposed a little theory of issue evolution to account for the anomalous tidbit. The research project that followed—still underway as I write—considerably overshadowed the belief structure research. My misspent youth in a small-town pool hall taught me one of the great lessons of life: setting up the second shot is even more satisfying than making the first. Research is like pool.

And what of complexity, constraint, and the unfinished collaboration? After "Belief Systems" had been published, the two collaborators achieved a new consensus on the points (1) that one had made a valuable contribution to the understanding of mass politics, and (2) that the other was a blockhead who refused to see truth though it stared him in the face. Determining who is which has proved a harder question. I could nicely round out the account by saying it didn't matter. But if I believed it didn't matter, the research experience would be no more exciting than accounting, and I would long ago have gone on to a more profitable line of work.

NOTES

1. In truth, not *everything* about research is fun. Writing, although it has its satisfactions, is truly hard work. And the cleanup activities at the end of a project— revision, proofreading, and the like—are work with joy only in the completion.

2. See Judson (1979), Part II (on breaking the genetic code) for an example of puzzle solving at its best. Even natural scientists occasionally throw off their lab coats for the thrill of intellectual chase.

3. It is good operating procedure to cite only published sources, because they are available for others to examine. I will depart from that procedure here because I can't account for why I did things as I did without reference to the private dialogue, a heated (but friendly) skirmish fought through the U.S. mails.

4. The controversy remains. In a tongue-in-cheek complaint at the nuisance of having to read disconfirmations of "The Nature of Belief Systems in Mass Publics"— "better than a half-dozen a year," he estimated—Converse (1980) published a list of suggested strategies for disconfirming Converse to guide the many scholars who are still busy at the task. The piece deserves to be read for its humor.

5. I apologize to the reader for the personal focus of this account. Writing it is uncomfortable, for we are trained to write with cold impersonal logic. But that is a professionally sanctioned fib. The "I" is an important part of the research experience; an honest narrative cannot fail to include it.

6. In a seminar paper with Robert O'Connor, later published as Sullivan and O'Connor (1972), Sullivan himself had determined that congressional candidate positions on a variety of foreign and domestic issues could be reliably scaled on a single liberal-conservative dimension.

7. Sullivan did briefly examine the functional explanation with the "cognitive complexity" measure in Sullivan, Marcus, and Minns, 1975.

8. The title and authorship are as listed on the proposal draft. Sullivan was in fact the sole author.

9. I would not, of course, have offered the second reason in the research design courses that I took, nor would it be tolerated in those I teach.

10. I would not, however, have employed it had it not been for the presence of Ted Carmines, a graduate student. The technique was well suited to the questions asked, but I knew it badly and trusted it not at all. Ted did know it and was on hand to reassure me that I was not committing unknown methodological atrocities.

11. This is but one of many possible evolutionary scenarios. See Dawkins (1976) for a highly readable account of them.

12. For the record: The course was Political Behavior, taught by Bill Flanigan at the University of Minnesota. The grade: "A − "; the " − " part probably kept me from being too smug about the matter. That particular couse over a 4- or 5-year period produced a notable proportion of political behavior analysts of my generation (including Sullivan). That is unusual for any course, but is particularly unlikely for an undergraduate course. And Minnesota was not the center of action in political behavior research.

13. There is a nontrivial corollary to the junkyard thesis: Those who develop facility at menial research tasks, even if a little dull witted, will have more good research ideas, because they can more cheaply reject the bad ones. The scholar who requires a million dollar grant and an army of research assistants will spend his time defending his bad ideas because there is too much at stake to abandon them.

REFERENCES

Aldrich, John, and Cnudde, Charles F. 1975. "Probing the Bounds of Conventional Wisdom: A Comparison of Regression, Probit, and Discriminant Analysis," *American Journal of Political Science* 19:571–608.

Campbell, Angus; Converse, Philip; Miller, Warren; and Stokes, Donald. 1960. *The American Voter*. New York: John Wiley & Sons.

Converse, Philip. 1964. "The Nature of Belief Systems in Mass Publics," in David Apter, ed., *Ideology and Discontent*. New York: The Free Press, pp. 206–61.

———. 1980. "Rejoinder to Judd and Milburn," *American Sociological Review* 45:644–46.

Dawkins, Richard. 1976. *The Selfish Gene*. New York: Oxford University Press.

Downs, Anthony. 1957. *An Economic Theory of Democracy*. New York: Harper & Row.

Judson, Horace Freeland. 1979. *The Eighth Day of Creation: Makers of the Revolution in Biology*. New York: Simon and Schuster.

Kuhn, Thomas S. 1962. *The Structure of Scientific Revolutions*. Chicago: University of Chicago Press.

Marcus, George; Tabb, David; and Sullivan, John L. 1974. "The Application of Individual Differences Scaling to the Measurement of Political Ideologies," *American Journal of Political Science* 18:405–20.

Matthews, Donald R., and Stimson, James A. 1975. *Yeas and Nays: Normal Decision-Making in the U.S. House of Representatives.* New York: Wiley Interscience.

Stimson, James A. 1975. "Belief Systems: Constraint, Complexity and the 1972 Election," *American Journal of Political Science* 19:393–417.

Stimson, James A., and Sullivan, John L. 1970. "A Functional Explanation of Ideology," unpublished research memorandum.

———. 1971. "Levels of Conceptualization," unpublished draft proposal.

Sullivan, John L.; Marcus, George E.; and Minns, Daniel Richard. 1975. "The Development of Political Ideology: Some Empirical Findings," *Youth & Society* 7:148–70.

Sullivan, John L., and O'Connor, Robert E. 1972. "Electoral Choice and Popular Control of Public Policy: The Case of the 1966 House of Elections," *American Political Science Review* 66:1256–68.

CHAPTER THREE

The Feminist and his Father —
A True Detective Story

3. The Feminist and his Father— A True Detective Story

Ball attempts in this paper to provide an answer to a question that has puzzled many scholars—what led John Stuart Mill to become a feminist? In 1869, long before most other men were willing even to consider the feminist position, Mill espoused it strongly in *The Subjection of Women*. What led him to this very early adoption of feminism?

Combining his research report and the description of his research in a single essay, Ball describes his search for an answer as "a true detective story." That is, he sees what he is doing as essentially similar to what Hercule Poirot or Sherlock Holmes would have done on a case: choose a challenging case for investigation, develop various alternative theories for the case, examine those theories in the light of evidence, and finally produce evidence that would convince a judge and jury that the theory he had chosen was the correct one.

Ball compares his research with that of the hero in a detective novel, but he might have just as aptly compared it to so-called "empirical" political research, as exemplified by the Sullivan et al. and Stimson articles you have already seen. There has long been a fruitless tension in political science between students of political philosophy and students of "empirical" political science. What has often been missed in this tension is that while the two types of work address somewhat different sorts of questions, and while evidence introduced in "empirical" work is more likely to be statistical than evidence used in political philosophy, and while there is relatively more attention to values in political philosophy—what has often been missed is that these are differences of emphasis only, and that the underlying structure of argument is the same. Values were certainly involved in the research reported by Sullivan et al. and by Stimson; and as you will see in this article, empirical evidence is important in the development of Ball's argument.

You may be pleased, however, to find that none of the empirical evidence in Ball's article is statistical in nature. This allows me to shorten this introduction, as compared with the first two, since I do not need to introduce you to any statistical techniques.

3. The Feminist and His Father— A True Detective Story

TERENCE BALL*

As an empirical discipline, political science deals with political facts. But political scientists are not mere compilers of facts. Rather, they seek to *explain*—to give a coherent account of—the particular phenomena being studied. Hence they advance provisional hypotheses—conjectures or educated guesses—which can then be tested against the available facts and, accordingly, accepted as true or rejected as false. This procedure is characteristic of *all* controlled inquiry, whether undertaken by a motor mechanic, a coroner, a detective—or a historian of political thought.

The history of political ideas is no less "empirical" than its sister subfields within political science. The historian formulates hypotheses, tests them against the available evidence, and accepts or rejects them accordingly. The task of the historian has often been likened to that of the detective (see Winks, 1969), and the comparison is apt. For the historian, like the detective, is a solver of mysteries. Both seek to unravel and understand human acts, omissions, utterances—"behaviors," in short—that would otherwise appear to be puzzling or even paradoxical.

The history of political ideas harbors more than its fair share of unsolved mysteries. Recently I set myself the task of solving one of these mysteries. Why, I wanted to know, did the English philosopher John Stuart Mill (1806–1873) become the nineteenth century's most ardent and articulate defender of women's rights? Who, or what, inspired and influenced him to risk derision, ridicule and loss of reputation by championing this unpopular

_____

*Every scholar is beholden to his or her benefactors. Mine include the National Endowment for the Humanities, which awarded me a fellowship for individual study and research during the 1978–1979 academic year; the University of Minnesota, which granted me leaves from my teaching duties in 1975 and 1978–1979; and the warden and fellows of Nuffield College, Oxford, who extended their kind hospitality to me in 1978–1979. For all this support, tangible and intangible, I am most grateful.

cause? None of the answers offered by other analysts satisfied me. Some struck me as far-fetched and implausible; others seemed plainly mistaken. So, donning my deerstalker, I set out to see if I could solve this mystery. What follows is the story of that attempt.[1] I shall begin by setting the stage and introducing the main characters in this true detective story.

I

The main character in our story is of course John Stuart Mill. With typical understatement he calls his *Autobiography* "the record of a remarkable education" (1971, p. 1). The young Mill's education was by any standards extraordinary, not to say bizarre. By the time he was two years old he was reading Greek; by age five he was composing Latin verse; by eight he was learned in logic, mathematics, history, and political economy (as the discipline of economics was then called); and by twelve he was a match for the best minds of the day. His sole teacher was his father, James Mill, himself a philosopher, psychologist, journalist, and educational theorist. In undertaking—at home, and with no outside assistance—the education of his eldest son, James Mill was attempting to prove the practicability of his educational theory. John Stuart Mill became a guinea pig in his father's educational experiment. Whatever its faults and excesses, this experiment shaped and sharpened the mind of a remarkable man.

One of the nineteenth century's most formidable intellects, John Stuart Mill was a philosopher, a logician, an economist, a political theorist and, in later life, a practicing politician (he was elected to Parliament in 1865). Like his father and Jeremy Bentham, Mill was a Utilitarian. He held that the principle of utility—"the greatest happiness of the greatest number"—was the standard by which laws and policies should be judged. He was also an active and committed feminist. A modern historian does not exaggerate when she calls Mill "the patron saint of the women's movement" (Williford, 1975, p. 174). His dedication to this movement was lifelong. As a young man Mill was arrested and jailed for distributing birth control information; he strongly supported early attempts to legalize divorce; and many years later, as a member of Parliament, he introduced a bill giving women the right to vote (it was overwhelmingly defeated by unsympathetic colleagues in the House of Commons). But today Mill is remembered as the author of, among many other works, one of the key manifestoes of the modern women's movement, *The Subjection of Women*.

First published in 1869, *The Subjection of Women* was greeted with almost universal contempt. Some reviewers questioned Mill's manliness, while others willfully misread his book or misrepresented his meaning (saying, for example, that he wished to dress men in petticoats and women in trousers).

But, after this fire storm of controversy subsided, the intellectual and political landscape was not quite the same as before. From this point onward the question of women's rights—to own property, to vote, to hold public office, to control their reproductive functions, to divorce cruel or uncaring husbands—would not go away. The question of women's rights was at last up for respectable public discussion—placed on the agenda, as it were, by a thinker of undoubted stature who was, of all things, a man.[2]

II

Why did this man, in particular, openly and articulately defend so unpopular a cause? The easy answer is that he believed the cause to be a just and worthy one. But why did he believe this? Who, or what, inspired John Stuart Mill to champion the cause of women? Several answers have been suggested. Some modern feminists credit Mill's enlightened view of women to his wife, Harriet Taylor Mill. Still others maintain that Mill's feminism derives from his philosophical godfather, Jeremy Bentham (1748–1832). Other commentators claim that Mill's feminism may be traced to the influence of other contemporary writers, and particularly to the English historian Thomas Babington Macaulay. Despite their disagreements, however, all are agreed on one point: John Stuart Mill became a feminist *in spite of*—not because of—his father's influence. It is this scholarly consensus that I wish to challenge.

In making this challenge I shall proceed as follows. I shall begin by examining the evidence offered in support of the claim that James Mill was a shameless male chauvinist and, hence, that he could not possibly have been the source of his son's feminist views. By looking at other, long-neglected evidence I shall show that this is not the simple and settled matter that others have believed it to be. Then I shall examine the evidence (or lack of it) adduced for the hypotheses that Harriet Taylor, Bentham, and Macaulay were Mill's models or mentors. None of these claims, I argue, is credible in the light of some rather decisive counterevidence. And finally, I shall conclude my scholarly sleuthing by disclosing the identity of our Mystery Man.

III

A modern biographer writes that John Stuart Mill's interest in women's rights was "independently acquired as his father cared nothing for it" (Packe, 1954, p. 63). The claim that James Mill was an ardent antifeminist and hence no model for his son is invariably supported by pointing to a particular paragraph in his *Essay on Government*.[3] As a "radical" (i.e., a democrat) James Mill favored a considerable widening of the franchise. He stopped short, however, of enfranchising everyone:

One thing is pretty clear, that all those individuals whose interests are indisputably included in those of other individuals, may be struck off without inconvenience. In this light may be viewed all children, up to a certain age, whose interests are involved in those of their parents. In this light, also, women may be regarded, the interest of almost all of whom is involved either in that of their fathers or in that of their husbands. (Mill, 1828, p. 21)

The anti-feminist tone and implications of this paragraph are patent: politically speaking, a woman is like a child, but with this difference—children (or at least male children) grow up to become fully enfranchised citizens, while women do not. Abandoning his usual understatement, J. S. Mill later termed this paragraph from his father's *Essay* "the worst in point of tendency he ever wrote" (J. S. Mill, 1961, p. 98).

If this single paragraph contained his first and last words on the subject, James Mill would indeed appear to be the ardent antifeminist that his critics have supposed him to be. This harsh judgment may be softened somewhat if we turn from the *Essay* to the work of which he was proudest, his massive *History of British India*. For the views defended in the *History* differ markedly from—indeed contradict—those in the *Essay*. A comparison of these two works may prove revealing.

Mill's multivolume *History* stands in stark contrast to the brief *Essay*. The *Essay*, he remarked, was nothing more than a "comprehensive outline" (Mill, 1820, fol. 354), a sketch or "skeleton map" (1821) in which "the principles of human nature" and their political implications were briefly and boldly exhibited. His *History*, by contrast, was meant to portray in copious detail the operation of these principles (1817a, pp. x–xii). For this reason his *History*, Mill boasted, "makes no bad introduction to the study of civil society in general" (1817b). India was for Mill and his fellow Utilitarians a laboratory in which to conduct experiments in social, legal, and political reform. His is a "critical" or "judging history" in which India's past and present were judged by Utilitarian criteria (1817a, p. x). In criticizing and condemning Indian customs and practices, Mill believed he was helping to pave a path toward a more "progressive" future (Forbes, 1951; Stokes, 1959, pp. 48–57). Interestingly, we find in Mill's criticism and condemnation of Hindu practices an implicit, and even impassioned, defense of the rights of women.

In the *History*, James Mill takes "the condition of women" to be "one of the most decisive criteria of the stage of society at which [a nation has] arrived. Among rude [i.e., backward] people, the women are generally degraded; among civilized people, they are exalted. . . . the history of uncultivated nations uniformly represents the women as in a state of abject slavery, from which they slowly emerge, as civilization advances" (Mill, 1817a, p. 293). James Mill explains moral and social progress in "materialist" terms. The moral "state of society" depends, in his view, upon economic and technological conditions.

In backward or "rude" societies, a premium is placed upon sheer physical strength; the strong are valued over the weak because their physical strength is the society's means of wresting a living from a harsh and unyielding nature. Because women are physically weaker than men, they are subservient to them. Once this subsistence stage is transcended, however, physical strength comes to count for less; other qualities—"qualities of mind"—begin to be recognized and developed. "In proportion as society . . . advances into that state of civilization, in which . . . the qualities of the mind are ranked above the qualities of the body," says Mill, "the condition of the weaker sex is gradually improved, till they associate at last on equal terms with the men, and fill the place of voluntary and useful copartners" (Mill, 1817a, pp. 293–94).

Taking the "condition of women" as a "decisive criterion," Mill passes a harsh judgment on Hindu society. There is, in his view, no more primitive or rude society than that of the Hindus, if we are to judge by their treatment of women: "A state of dependence more strict and humiliating than that which is ordained for the weaker sex among the Hindus cannot easily be conceived" (Mill, 1817a, p. 294). With the arrival of the British and the introduction of advanced Western technology, this mistreatment of women loses, as it were, its material-productive basis and justification and has its source only in archaic Hindu religious beliefs and practices. By way of illustration Mill cites several passages from the Institutes of Menu, the Hindu holy book:

"Day and night," says Menu, "must women be held by their protectors in a state of dependence." Who is meant by their protectors is immediately explained: "Their fathers protect them in childhood; their husbands protect them in their youth, their sons protect them in old age: a woman," it is added, "is never fit for independence. . . . In childhood must a female be dependent on her father; in youth, on her husband; her lord being dead, on her sons: a woman must never seek independence." (quoted in Mill, 1817a, p. 294)

Another Hindu holy text, the *Hetopadesa*, contains a similar commandment: "In infancy the father should guard her, in youth her husband should guard her, and in old age her children should guard her; for at no time is a woman fit to be trusted with liberty" (quoted in Mill, 1817a, p. 295). Such commandments, says James Mill, are outmoded relics of a bygone era, and ought now be discarded. "Nothing," he says, "can exceed the habitual contempt which the Hindus entertain for their women. Hardly are they ever mentioned in their laws, or other books, but as wretches of the most base and vicious inclinations, on whose nature no virtue or useful qualities may be grafted" (Mill, 1817a, p. 295). Worse still, Mill adds, is the Hindus' failure to recognize, much less develop, the moral and religious "qualities of mind" that women share with men. Mill thinks it a mark of "extreme degradation" that women "are not accounted worthy to partake of religious rites but in conjunction with their husband" (Mill, 1817a, p. 296).

Ironically, the trap that James Mill sets to catch the Hindu ensnares him as well. The "decisive criterion" that he applies to Indian society is not applied to English society. It is curious that Mill, who in his *History* thought it a sign of "extreme degradation" that Hindu women "are not accounted worthy to partake of religious rites but in conjunction with their husbands," was nevertheless prepared to exclude Englishwomen from that preeminently political rite—voting—on the ground that their husbands may speak for them (Mill, 1828, p. 21). In identifying a girl's interest with her father's, and a woman's with her husband's, isn't Mill in effect endorsing the Hindu maxim that "Their fathers protect them in childhood; their husbands protect them in youth . . ."? And doesn't this amount to saying, with Menu, that "a woman must never seek independence . . . at no time is a woman proper to be trusted with liberty"? In short, isn't Mill's exclusion of women from the franchise merely an anglicized and politicized version of the very practices for which he condemns the Hindus?

James Mill does indeed appear to stake out and defend two mutually contradictory positions. When prescribing for the Hindu, Mill assumes one position—his missionary position, as it were—but when prescribing for his countrymen, he adopts quite another. The first has pro-feminist implications overlooked by his critics; the second has anti-feminist implications which his critics were quick to seize upon. It is this latter position for which he is today remembered and roundly condemned. Yet this condemnation is less than just, when we take the pro-feminist passages of his *History* into account, as I have attempted to do. In the final analysis James Mill's view of the role and rights of women appears to be an ambivalent one.

His son's views on the political role and rights of women are, by contrast, anything but ambivalent. John Stuart Mill favored the full emancipation of women. Their emancipation could not come about, he believed, until they got the vote: "When that has been gained, everything else will follow" (quoted in Packe, 1954, p. 500). By "everything else" he meant women's right to own property, to practice birth control, to get divorced, and the many other things that modern women now take pretty much for granted. In J. S. Mill's day these things were widely regarded as radical, not to say scandalous. Where, then, did he acquire these radical ideas?

IV

Several feminist writers have suggested that the younger Mill's feminism was inspired by his bright, beautiful, and outspoken wife, Harriet Taylor Mill. Alice Rossi for example, sees Harriet as "a central figure in [J. S.] Mill's intellectual and personal life," and credits her with Mill's conversion to feminism. "It is doubtful that *The Subjection of Women* would ever have been written if it were not for Mill's twenty-eight-year relationship with Harriet Taylor" (Rossi, 1970, p. 6). Certainly Mill himself was extravagant in his praise for Harriet, crediting her with inspiring and influencing much of his later work, especially his *Principles of Political Economy* (1848) and *On Liberty* (1860). But he explicitly denied that his feminist convictions were the product of his relationship with Harriet. As Mill mentions at the beginning of *The Subjection of Women*, his view that women are men's equals is "an opinion which I have held from the very earliest period when I had formed any opinions at all on social or political matters . . ." (1869, p. 1). And as he tells us in his *Autobiography*, these opinions were formed very early indeed. At age twelve his most fundamental opinions were already molded, and at eighteen he was writing articles and essays on political subjects. He did not meet Harriet until 1830, when he was twenty-five and she twenty-three. As he remarks in his *Autobiography*, he was initially attracted to Harriet, and she to him, because both had *already* arrived at similar conclusions on a number of subjects, including the rights of women (Mill, 1971, p. 147, n. 8).[4] Doubtless his subsequent relationship with Harriet deepened and strengthened his feminist convictions, but she was evidently not their original source.

An alternative explanation is that Mill's feminism derives from his philosophical mentor, Jeremy Bentham. "Perhaps the most significant contribution of Bentham to the women's movement," writes Miriam Williford (1975, pp. 174–75), "was his influence on John Stuart Mill." The younger Mill was led by "Bentham's influence . . . to his initial interest in the condition of women." He "took issue with [his father's] *Essay on Government* [and] accepted Bentham's view of women. . . ." Williford's claim that "Bentham was a feminist" is widely shared by, among others, Elie Halevy (1955, p. 20), Mary Mack (1962, p. 112), David Baumgardt (1966, p. 238), and Lea Boralevi (1978), who calls Bentham "the father of feminism."

Is Bentham the Mystery Man for whom we have been looking? Certainly some weighty scholarly opinion suggests that he is. But empirical questions cannot be answered by appealing to authority. We need to look more closely at the arguments and evidence advanced in favor of this hypothesis. The argument, stated syllogistically, amounts to this: *first premise*: Bentham was a feminist. *Second premise*: Mill was a feminist, and Bentham's intellectual heir. *Ergo*: Mill's feminism derives from Bentham. In the section following I shall dispute the conclusion by refuting the first premise.

V

Jeremy Bentham's reputation as a feminist has several sources. One of these was his outspoken criticism of the marriage laws, which did not then permit divorce except on rare occasions. Any legal union from which there is no possibility of escape, Bentham believed, is a kind of "slavery" (1843b, pp. 352–55). Even more important was his supposed defense of women's suffrage. He dissented from James Mill's *Essay on Government*, with its proposal for excluding women from the franchise (Bentham, 1824, folio 302). In *Constitutional Code* he writes: "If a man who calls for the right of suffrage to be given to any one human being, calls for its being refused to any other human being, it lies upon him to give a particular reason for such refusal." If we are to deny anyone right to vote, we must first specify those "disqualifying circumstances" which would tip the balance against the presumption of their being eligible to vote. In the case of children, the balance is easily tipped; they are excluded only temporarily, on the ground that they are "not yet competent to the management of [their] own affairs." But "the exclusion thus put on the ground of age, is not like the exclusion put on the ground of sex," because gender, unlike age, does not change. Why, asks Bentham, "exclude the whole female sex from all participation in the constitutive [i.e., electoral] power?" For surely "On the ground of the greatest happiness principle, the claim of this sex is . . . at least . . . as good as that of the other. The happiness and interest of a person of the female sex, constitutes as large a portion of the universal happiness and interest, as does that of a person of the male sex." There is "no reason . . . why a person of the one sex should as such have less happiness than a person of the other sex" (1843k, p. 108).

Bentham's case for giving women the vote comes to this: Everyone has an equal interest in happiness. But it does not follow from this that women's interests (as James Mill would have it) are wholly "included in" those of their husbands or fathers. On the contrary, a husband's and wife's interests may not only be different, but antithetical. For example, if a man's interest in happiness is served by his regularly beating his wife, it does not follow that her interest in happiness is "included in" that of her husband; on the contrary, her pain being the source of his pleasure, her interest is utterly contrary to his. Women are, moreover, subject to certain kinds of pain—for example, the physical and psychic pain of rape—to which men are not similarly subject. If women are to have a say in the passage of legislation affecting their happiness, it follows, Bentham argues, that they must have a hand in electing legislators. Their enfranchisement is consistent with—indeed, required by— the Utilitarian's greatest-happiness principle (see Bentham, 1843k, pp. 106– 8). Granted that the principle is sound, he asks: "Can [any] practical good . . . [come] from admitting the female sex into a participation of the supreme constitutive power [i.e., the electorate]?" He answers: "Yes. The affording increased probability of the adoption of legislative arrangements, placing sexual intercourse upon a footing less disadvantageous than the present to the weaker sex" (Bentham, 1843k, p. 109). The enfranchisement of women thus appears to be justified in principle and in practice.

Yet the appearance is quite misleading. What Bentham gives with the one hand he takes away with the other. After a lengthy consideration of the reasons for enfranchising women, Bentham nevertheless concludes that they should, after all, be denied the right to vote! He justifies this rather surprising conclusion on grounds of practicality and of principle.

Bentham's "practical" argument for exclusion runs as follows. He does not "think it at present expedient to propose a set of legislative arrangements directed to this end" because "the contest and confusion produced by the proposal of this improvement would entirely engross the public mind, and throw improvement, in all other shapes, to a distance" (Bentham, 1843k, p. 109). Returning to his original question—"Why exclude the whole female sex from all participation in the constitutive power?"—he answers: "Because the prepossession against their admission is at present too general, and too intense, to afford any chance in favour of a proposal for their admission" (Bentham, 1843k, p. 108). Believing this "practical" objection to be decisive, Bentham proceeded to draw up a less-than-radical *Radical Reform Bill* in which women were explicitly excluded from the franchise. There he stipulates that the suffrage must be both "universal" and "equal." But then he adds: "*Universality* we say for shortness, instead of *Virtual Universality*. No man means that children that can but just speak, should vote [nor] that females should vote" (1843h, p. 559). What then of equality? "By equality of suffrage," Bentham explains, "is meant equality . . . between the suffrage of one man and the suffrage of another" (1843h, p. 561). Nor does Bentham mean "man" in the generic sense. The electors include "every male person" who meets residence, literacy, and other requirements (1843h, p. 564).

Bentham's objections to women's suffrage are not, however, exclusively "practical" ones resting upon political expediency. Some of his objections are based explicitly or implicitly upon "principle." Of his scheme for "virtual universality" of suffrage—in which all women are excluded—Bentham says that it is "defensible on principle" (1843i, p. 599). Now when Bentham says "principle" he invariably means the principle of utility. The enfrancisement of women must then somehow contravene this principle. But how, in the light of his argument in *Constitutional Code*, is such a view even conceivable, much less defensible? For the answer we must turn to Bentham's *Introduction to the Principles of Morals and Legislation*, where he draws a distinction between learned and innate differences between the sexes—or, as we would say nowadays, between "nurture" and "nature." Differences of the first sort stem from education and environment; differences of the second, from "primitive modifications of the corporeal [i.e., bodily] frame." The former can at least be modified, through education; the latter, being innate, cannot. But to which category do the *politically* relevant differences between the sexes belong? Bentham answers that they belong, in the main, to unchangeable nature. A woman's nature, he maintains, renders her virtually unable to make rational political judgments—that is, decisions based upon the principle of utility. For "the female is rather more inclined than the male to superstition; that is, to observances not dictated by the principle of utility." This difference between the sexes, he adds, "may be pretty well accounted for" by innate inclinations, that is, by "the primitive modifications of the corporeal frame" that "influence the quantum and bias of sensibility" (1970, p. 64). A woman's "sympathetic biases," Bentham continues, "are in many respects different: for her own off-spring . . . her affection is commonly stronger than that of the male. Her affections are apt to be less enlarged: seldom expanding themselves so much as to take in the welfare of her country in general, much less that of mankind, or the whole sensitive creation: seldom embracing any extensive class or division, even of her own countrymen, unless it be in virtue of her sympathy for some particular individuals that belong to it." Women, in other words, are scarcely capable of thinking about, much less promoting, the greatest happiness of the greatest number; their "sympathetic biases" rarely, if ever, extend beyond an immediate and intimate circle comprised of family and friends. "In general," Bentham concludes, a woman's "antipathetic, as well as sympathetic biases, are apt to be less conformable to the principle of utility than those of the male" (1970, pp. 64–65).

The upshot is both clear and astounding. A Utilitarian polity could not enfranchise women without subverting itself. To permit women to vote would be to open the door to "superstition" and other forces hostile to the principle of utility. Considered in this light, Bentham's justification of "virtual universality" of suffrage as "defensible on principle" comes at last into clearer view. Politically speaking, biology—"primitive modifications of the corporeal frame"—is destiny, and women are destined to be excluded from participation in utilitarian politics. Their exclusion is predicated upon the principle of utility itself.

To the degree that biology is destiny, the education of females must differ from that of males. This view, which is implicit in Bentham's *Introduction to the Principles of Morals and Legislation*, is quite explicit in his treaties on education, the *Chrestomathia*. Although "female children" are to be admitted to Bentham's model "Chrestomathic" School, they—unlike the boys—are to receive instruction in "needle-work" and other aspects of "domestic economy" (1843j, p. 56). In any case, to instruct young women in the political arts would be a waste of precious pedagogical resources. For, Bentham holds, not only should women be excluded from the franchise; they should also be excluded from serving on juries (1843c, p. 127), holding public office (1843k, p. 108), and even from attending parliamentary debates (1843e, p. 327)!

In proposing to deny to women any distinctively political rights and roles, Bentham considerably outdistances James Mill. Mill, as his son later remarked (1971, p. 63), merely suggested that women could be excluded from the franchise, not that they *should* be. Bentham would deny them not only the right to vote, but to serve on juries, to hold public office, and even to attend parliamentary debates. Women are consigned by Bentham to perpetual political unemployment. Women's natural sphere centers on home and hearth. And yet, when we inquire into his views concerning the familial microcosm, we find that women fare little better there than they do in the wider political macrocosm.

There is, says Bentham, a "fundamental law, which subjects the wife to the authority of the husband" (1843b, p. 356). This fundamental law, upon inspection, turns out to be the law of the stronger:

Between the wishes of two persons who pass their life together, there may at every moment be a contradiction. The benefit of peace renders it desirable that a pre-eminence should be established, which should prevent or terminate these contests. But why is the man to be the governor? Because he is the stronger. In his hands power sustains itself. Place the authority in the hands of the wife, every moment will be marked by revolt on the part of the husband. (1843b, p. 355)

If James Mill believes that husband and wife might one day be equals, Bentham does not. "Master of the wife as to what regards his own interests," the husband, Bentham says, "ought to be guardian of the wife as to what regards her interests" (1843b, 355). The husband alone has the "aptitude" for judging his wife's interests and the "authority" to enforce his judgments. "This being the case, it is manifest," says Bentham, "that the legal relation which the husband will bear to the wife will be a complex one: compounded of that of master and that of guardian." Therefore, "the condition of a husband," he adds, "stands upon the same footing as that of a parent," but with one difference: a husband is empowered to command "certain reciprocal services" of a sexual nature which a parent may not command from a child (1970, p. 255). Between husband and wife "there subsists a legal obligation for the purpose of . . . a sexual intercourse to be carried on between them," in addition to "the indiscriminate train of services at large which the husband in his character of master is impowered [sic] to exact" (1970, pp. 254–55). Even so, Bentham admonishes,

. . . it is not proper to make the man a tyrant, and to reduce to a state of passive slavery the sex which, by its weakness and gentleness, has the greatest need of protection. The interests of females have too often been neglected.

From this history of neglect Bentham derives a moral: Men should not cease to be masters but should strive to be better masters. We should at all costs avoid the "dangerous snare" of "absolute equality" between the sexes:

. . . those who, from some vague notion of justice and of generosity, would bestow upon females an absolute equality, would only spread a dangerous snare for them. To set them free, as much as it is possible for the laws so to do, from the necessity of pleasing their husbands, would be, in a moral point of view, to weaken instead of strengthen their empire. (1843b, p. 355)

These arguments against "women's liberation" have a remarkably familiar ring. Even more remarkable is the fact that they are advanced by the erstwhile "father of feminism" (Boralevi, 1978).

It therefore seems doubtful that J. S. Mill, whose views on these matters are so different, could have been led by "Bentham's influence . . . to his initial interest in the condition of women" or that he could have "accepted Bentham's view of women" (Williford, 1975, pp. 174–75). Clearly, then, Bentham is not our Mystery Man.

VI

Having thus eliminated the first two suspects—Harriet Taylor Mill and Jeremy Bentham—let us turn now to our third candidate, Thomas Babington Macaulay. A left-of-center Whig and political moderate, Macaulay feared the "radicalism" of James Mill. The too-rapid expansion of the franchise would, he believed, bring social instability in its wake. In the political debate preceding the Reform Bill of 1832 Macaulay felt it necessary to criticize James Mill's oft-reprinted and still influential *Essay on Government*. Macaulay, a consummate stylist and political essayist, wished to beat James Mill and the radicals at their own game. So, in 1860 he launched a savage and satirical attack against the elder Mill's *Essay*. He criticized James Mill's methods, his premises, and his conclusions; he tried, with some success, to turn Mill's own logic against itself. The single paragraph about women came in for special censure.

"Mr. Mill," wrote Macaulay, "recommends that all males of mature age, rich and poor, educated and ignorant, shall have votes. But why not the women too? This question has often been asked in parliamentary debate, and has never, to our knowledge, received a plausible answer." Nor does Mill supply an answer: "Mr. Mill escapes from it as fast as he can." Pausing "to dwell a little on the words of the oracle," Macaulay quotes the notorious paragraph from Mill's *Essay*. Then he continues:

Without adducing one fact, without taking the trouble to perplex the question by one sophism, he placidly dogmatizes away the interest of one half of the human race. If there be a word of truth in history, women have always been, and still are, over the greater part of the globe, humble companions, playthings, captives, menials, beasts of burden. Except in a few happy and highly civilized communities, they are strictly in a state of personal slavery. Even in those countries where they are best treated, the laws are generally unfavourable to them, with respect to almost all the points in which they are most deeply interested. (Macaulay, 1860, p. 407)

He then goes on to question Mill's identity-of-interest thesis:

Mr. Mill is not legislating for England or the United States; but for mankind. Is then the interest of a Turk the same with that of the girls who compose his harem? Is the interest of a Chinese the same with that of the woman whom he harnesses to his plough? Is the interest of an Italian the same with that of the daughter whom he devotes to God?

Clearly not, Macaulay believes. But he then proceeds to *agree* with Mill's exclusionist position:

The interest of a respectable Englishman may be said, without any impropriety, to be identical with that of his wife. But why is it so? Because human nature is *not* what Mr. Mill conceives it to be; because civilized men, pursuing their own happiness in a social state, are not Yahoos fighting for carrion; because there is a pleasure in being loved and esteemed, as well as in being feared and servilely obeyed. Why does not a gentleman restrict his wife to the bare maintenance which the law would compel him to allow her, that he may have more to spend on his personal pleasures? Because, if he loves her, he has pleasure in seeing her pleased; and because, even if he dislikes her, he is unwilling that the whole neighborhood should cry shame on his meanness and ill-nature. Why does not the legislature, altogether composed of males, pass a law to deprive women of all civil privileges whatever, and reduce them to the state of slaves? By passing such a law, they would gratify what Mr. Mill tells us is an inseparable part of human nature, the desire to possess unlimited power of inflicting pain upon others. That they do not pass such a law, though they have the power to pass it, and that no man in England wishes to see such a law passed, proves that the desire to possess unlimited power of inflicting pain is not inseparable from human nature. (1860, p. 408)

The "identity of interest between the two sexes" in England, says Macaulay, arises from the Englishman's "pleasure of being loved, and of communicating happiness" (1860, p. 408). The Englishman's character and his institutions combine to make him a breed apart from other, lesser men. The upshot of Macaulay's whiggish reasoning is "chauvinistic" in both the older, nationalist and the newer, sexual senses of the term. The exemplary behavior of Englishmen, he concludes, falsifies Mill's "law" even as it justifies his exclusionist position. This rather self-congratulatory conclusion differs markedly from the position taken by J. S. Mill in *The Subjection of Women*.

J. S. Mill writes in his *Autobiography* that Macaulay's "famous attack" on his father's *Essay* "gave me much to think about" (J. S. Mill, 1961, p. 134). But the thoughts inspired by Macaulay were about epistemological and methodological matters and *not* about the position of women. Packe is apparently mistaken, therefore, in suggesting that, of all the many remarkable passages in Macaulay's critique,

The passage about the position of women struck [J. S. Mill] particularly hard: throughout his life, that question was so much a passion with him that he often made it the final issue, the test on which depended his acceptance or rejection of a philosophic system. In this case, it was the means of doubling the gap between his father and himself; and . . . he incorporated unconsciously and without acknowledgement [Macaulay's] two striking concepts—that the interests of women were no more identical with that of their husbands than the interests of subjects with their kings, and that the denial of rights to women was the enslavement of one half of the human race—almost word for word into the groundwork of all his future dissertations. (Packe, 1954, p. 90)

Packe's attribution of influence is mistaken in several respects. First, John Stuart Mill was struck particularly hard not by the passage about women's rights (which he never mentions) but by Macaulay's methodological critique of the elder Mill's *Essay* (1961, pp. 134–36). Secondly, the younger Mill's making "the position of women" a "test on which depended his acceptance or rejection of a philosophic system" was inspired not by Macaulay's attack but—as we shall see—by his father's *History*. Thus, third, it cannot be true that J. S. Mill's criterion of acceptability "was the means of doubling the gap between his father and himself"; on the contrary, it was, if anything, a means of *narrowing* the gap between them. Fourth, Packe attributes to Macaulay "two striking concepts" which, as we have just seen, he took great pains to *deny*: his critique is anything but a feminist tract.

The conventional view about the sources of John Stuart Mill's feminism appears to be mistaken. He owes little, if anything, to Bentham, still less to Macaulay, and rather a lot to an heretofore unsuspected source—James Mill's *History*.

VII

In good Holmesian fashion I have now eliminated our main suspects. I have turned the spotlight, not on the butler, but on the father—the one person whom no one suspected. It is time to tie up the loose ends and to close the case.

Earlier I tried to show that the elder Mill was not the unabashed anti-feminist he is reputed to be. His unsavory reputation rests entirely upon one paragraph in his *Essay on Government* and is undercut (if not contradicted) by his discussion of women in the *History of British India*. His son's feminism was no doubt grounded in part in his reaction against his father's *Essay*. But to stop here is to overlook the possibility that the son's feminist perspective owes something to his father's other writings. Let us briefly compare the son's *Subjection* to the father's *History*.

In *The Subjection of Women* John Stuart Mill maintains that "the principle which regulates the existing social relations between the two sexes—the legal subordination of one sex to the other—is wrong in itself, and now one of the chief hindrances to human improvement; and that it ought to be replaced by a principle of perfect equality, admitting no power or privilege on the one side, nor disability on the other." This, he adds, is "an opinion which I have held from the very earliest period when I had formed any opinions at all on social or political matters" (1849, p. 1). As readers of his *Autobiography* will recall, his opinions on social and political matters were formed at an early age, under his father's stern tutelage. J. S. Mill and the *History of British India* were conceived in the same year (1806) and quite literally grew up together. "Almost as soon as I could hold a pen," he writes, "I [wanted to] write a history of India too" (1961, p. 43). For twelve years James Mill toiled over his *History* as his son, seated beside him, labored over lessons in Latin, Greek, and political economy. That experience, and the end result—*The History of British India*—had a profound and formative influence upon the younger Mill:

A book which contributed very much to my education was my father's History of India. . . . During the year [preceding its publication] I used to read . . . the manu-script to him while he corrected the proofs. The number of new ideas which I received from this remarkable book, and the impulse and stimulus as well as guidance given to my thoughts by its criticisms and disquisitions on society and civilization in the Hindoo [sic] part . . . made my early familiarity with this book eminently useful to my subsequent progress. And though I can perceive deficiencies in it now as compared with a perfect standard, I still think it the most instructive history ever yet written, and one of the books from which most benefit may be derived by a mind in the course of making up its opinions. (J. S. Mill, 1961, p. 50)

Unfortunately John Stuart Mill does not tell us exactly how his mind "benefit[ed] . . . in the course of making up its opinions." But one possibility immediately suggests itself. Among his father's "criticisms and disquisitions on society and civilization in the Hindoo part" was—as we have seen already—an historical explanation and moral critique of the debasement of women (see again Mill, 1817a, pp. 293–95). In particular, James Mill takes a society's treatment of women as a "decisive criterion" for judging its level of material and moral development (1817a, p. 293). Turning to *The Subjection of Women* we find his son likewise taking the "elevation or debasement [of women] as on the whole the surest and most correct measure of the civilization of a people or an age" (J. S. Mill, 1869, p. 38). The elder Mill envisions sexual equality not merely as an ideal but as a genuine historical possibility (1817a, pp. 293–94). So, too, does the younger Mill: "Through all the progressive period of human history, the condition of women has been approaching nearer to equality with men. This does not of itself prove that the assimilation must go on to complete equality; but it assuredly affords some presumption that such is the case" (J. S. Mill, 1869, p. 38). No less striking is James Mill's stress upon the "qualities of mind," shared by men and women alike, that are recognized and rewarded in "advanced" societies (1817a, p. 294). This emphasis is equally apparent in his son's *Subjection of Women* (1869, chap. 3). Moreover, just as the elder Mill criticizes the Hindus' debasement of women as a historical anachronism, so his son likewise contends that "The social subordination of women . . . stands out as an isolated fact in modern social institutions; a solitary breach of what has become their fundamental law; a single relic of an old world of thought and practice exploded in everything else, but retained in the one thing of most universal interest" (J. S. Mill, 1869, p. 36). Finally, James Mill's criticism of exclusionist *religious* practices is extended by his son in a distinctly *political* direction. The elder Mill, it will be recalled, thought it a sign of "extreme degradation" that Hindu women "are not accounted worthy to partake of religious rites but in conjunction with their husbands" (1817a, p. 296). So too the younger Mill thought it degrading that women were excluded from sharing the rights and participating in the rites of political life (1869, pp. 95–97; 1961, pp. 98–99). Upon the right to vote, said J. S. Mill, everything else depends: "When that has been gained, everything else will follow" (quoted in Packe, 1954, p. 500). And on this final matter the author of the *Essay* parted company with his son. What is striking, however, is not this well-publicized difference between them, but the many remarkable similarities between the view of women advanced in James Mill's *History* and his son's *Subjection of Women*.

On the basis of some rather strong circumstantial and textual evidence I therefore conclude, dear Watson, that our Mystery Man is none other than James Mill. As they say, old chap: like father, like son.

NOTES

1. For a fuller account of my scholarly sleuthing, see Ball (1980a, 1980b). Portions of the present chapter draw heavily upon these previously published articles.

2. The importance of this fact should not be underestimated. Mary Wollstonecraft's *Vindication of the Rights of Woman*, published in 1792—seventy-seven years before Mill's *Subjection of Women*—was dismissed outright as the hysterical ravings of a "mannish" madwoman. On the opposition to feminism in the history of political thought, see Okin (1979). Schneir (1972) is a particularly useful anthology.

3. First published in the Supplement to the Fourth Edition of the *Encyclopaedia Britannica*, Mill's *Essay on Government* was subsequently serialized in *The Traveller Evening Paper* (April 24–28, 1821), issued as a pamphlet (May 1821), and reprinted in 1823, 1825, and 1828 in collections of Mill's essays (see Fenn [1971, vol. II, pp. 80–84, 297–300] for further details). I mention this merely to show how widely the *Essay on Government* circulated. On its critics' reception see Ball, 1980a.

4. Rossi (1970, p. 20) acknowledges—and then dismisses as "curious"—J. S. Mill's denial of Harriet's influence upon his feminist views.

REFERENCES

Ball, Terence. 1980a. "Utilitarianism, Feminism and the Franchise: James Mill and his Critics," *History of Political Thought* 1 (Spring): 91–115.

———. 1980b. "Was Bentham a Feminist?" *The Bentham Newsletter* (University College London) 4 (May): 25–32.

———. 1980c. "Bentham No Feminist: A Reply to Boralevi [1980]." *The Bentham Newsletter* 4 (May): 47–48.

Baumgardt, David. 1966. *Bentham and the Ethics of Today*. Princeton, N.J.: Princeton University Press.

Bentham, Jeremy. 1824. [Critical Notes on James Mill's *Essay*]. Bentham MSS., U.C.L., Box 34, Folder 12, folios 302–303.

———. 1843a. *The Influence of Time and Place in Matters of Legislation*. In *Works*, ed. John Bowring. London: Simpkin, Marshall, & Co. Vol. I, pp. 169–94.

———. 1843b. *Principles of the Civil Code*. In *Works*, I: 297-364.

———. 1843c. *Principles of Judicial Procedure*. In *Works*, II: 1–188.

———. 1843d. *The Rationale of Reward*. In *Works*, II: 189–266.

———. 1843e. *Essay on Political Tactics*. *Works*, II: 299–373.

———. 1843f. *The Book of Fallacies*. *Works*, II: 375–487.

———. 1843g. *Plan of Parliamentary Reform*. *Works*, III: 433–557.

———. 1843h. *Radical Reform Bill*. *Works*, III: 558–95.

———. 1843i. *Radicalism Not Dangerous*. *Works*, III: 599–622.

———. 1843j. *Chrestomathia*. *Works*, VIII: 1–191.

———. 1843k. *Constitutional Code*. *Works*, IX: 1–622.

———. 1970. *An Introduction to the Principles of Morals and Legislation*, ed. J. H. Burns and H.L.A. Hart. London: Athlone Press.

Boralevi, Lea Campos. 1978. "Bentham: Father of Feminism," paper read at the Annual Joint Seminar, European Consortium for Political Research, Grenoble, April 1978.

———. 1980. "In Defense of a Myth." (A critique of Ball [1980b]). *The Bentham Newsletter* 4 (May): 33–46.

Forbes, Duncan. 1951. "James Mill and India." *Cambridge Journal* 5 (October): 19–33

Halevy, Elie. 1955. *The Growth of Philosophic Radicalism*, trans. Mary Morris. Boston: Beacon Press.

Macaulay, Thomas Babington. 1860. "Mill on Government." In *Miscellaneous Writings*. London.

Mack, Mary P. 1962. *Jeremy Bentham*. London: Heinemann.

Mill, James. 1817a. *The History of British India*. London: Baldwin. Vol. I.

———. 1817b. Mill to David Ricardo, 19 October. In Piero Sraffa, ed., *Works and Correspondence of David Ricardo*, VII: 195–96. Cambridge: Cambridge University Press, 1962.

———. 1819. Mill to Macvey Napier, 10 September. British Museum Additional MSS. 34612, fols. 287–88.

———. 1820. Mill to Napier, 11 May. B.M. Add. MSS. 34612, fol. 354.

———. 1821. Mill to Etienne Dumont, 8 June. In MSS Dumont, Bibliothèque Publique et Universitaire de Genève, MS. 76, fol. 21.

———. 1828. *Government*. In *Essays*. London: J. Innes.

Mill, John Stuart. 1869. *The Subjection of Women*. London: Longman, Green.

———. 1961. *The Early Draft of John Stuart Mill's Autobiography*, ed. Jack Stillinger. Urbana: University of Illinois Press.

———. 1971. *Autobiography*. Oxford and London: Oxford University Press.

Okin, Susan Moller. 1979. *Women in Western Political Thought*. Princeton, N.J.: Princeton University Press.

Packe, Michael St. John. 1954. *The Life of John Stuart Mill*. London: Secker and Warburg.

Rossi, Alice, ed. 1970. "Introduction" to John Stuart Mill and Harriet Taylor Mill, *Essays on Sex Equality*. Chicago: University of Chicago Press.

Schneir, Miriam, ed. 1972. *Feminism: The Essential Historical Writings*. New York: Vintage Books.

Stokes, Eric. 1959. *The English Utilitarians and India*. Oxford: Oxford University Press.

Williford, Miriam. 1975. "Bentham on the Rights of Women." *Journal of the History of Ideas* 36 (January–March): 167–76.

Winks, Robin W., ed. 1969. *The Historian as Detective: Essays on Evidence*. New York: Harper & Row.

CHAPTER FOUR

The Institution and Maintenance of Representation in West Germany

4. The Institution and Maintenance of Representation in West Germany

Farah wished to assess the extent to which members of the West German parliament act like (1) "delegates" instructed by the electorate as to how they should vote in parliament, (2) independent "trustees" who use their own best judgment on votes irrespective of what their constituents might rightly or wrongly think was best, or (3) members of a party "team" who subordinate both their own and their constituents' judgment to the collective judgment of the party they represent in parliament.

There are no new technical terms to which you need to be introduced before reading this piece. Correlations are the main statistics used, and you have seen these in the Stimson article.

Once again, it is worthwhile to point out the basic unity of method in all political science research. Note how similar the underlying logical structures of this and Ball's piece are, even though one is a "behavioral" examination of parliamentary behavior and the other is "political theory." In both cases, the problem is one of explanation: "Why was Mill a feminist?" "Why do members of parliament vote as they do?" Different kinds of evidence are used, but the underlying structure of argument is the same.

Note especially in this article the grave problem of how to measure legislators' votes on bills, and the necessarily approximate measure that Farah had to use for roll-call votes.

_____ RESEARCH ARTICLE

4A. The Institution and Maintenance of Representation in West Germany

BARBARA G. FARAH

A central concern of political practitioners and scholars is the representative nature of the democratic political system. Indeed, the popularity of the theme in these societies is reflected in the volumes written on the subject.[1] While the normative prescriptions have outlined how the representational relationship *ought* to function, the more recent genre of scholarly works have focused on how well democratic politics have measured up to some of these ideals. The study of representation in West Germany, emerging from the empirical tradition of Warren Miller and Donald Stokes, is the topic of this work.

Much of the relevant normative discourse has centered on the two polar types represented by the mandate-independence controversy that Edmund Burke provoked in his classic "Speech to the Electors of Bristol" in 1774. According to the supporters of the mandate form of representation, the representative was a deputy of the district and enjoined to do its bidding. His sole purpose was to represent the interests and opinions of the constituents who had elected him.[2] Edmund Burke challenged this interpretation by questioning the logic of having legislators "bound blindly and implicitly to obey, to vote, and to argue for, though contrary to the clearest convictions of his judgment and conscience" the opinions of his constituents.[3] For Burke, a representative owes to his electors no more than "his unbiased opinion, his mature judgment, his enlightened conscience."

More than a century later, with the evolution of clear-cut legislative and electoral parties out of a looser factionalism characterizing any deliberative body, a distinct third type, championing the supremacy of party responsibility as the main representative obligation, found its way into the normative discussion as well. The responsible party model has provided a third alternative to the normative debate on the representational relationship.[4]

Miller and Stokes, in their classic 1958 study of representation in the American Congress,[5] created a causal model to depict the process of representation that flows from constituency influence to legislative behavior. The paths in their model, which is represented by the diamond-shaped configuration shown in Figure 4.1, capture in a parsimonious fashion the relationships between the represented and the representatives that had been posited by the two ideal types, trustee and mandate, with the former occupying the upper half of the model and the latter dominating the lower half. If the only important causal paths are those in the upper half of the model, for instance, representation is of the "trustee" sort—constituents' attitudes affecting the representative's own attitude (if only because he or she has been selected from among those constituents and probably shares many of their attitudes), and it is the representative's own attitude that then determines how he or she votes on roll calls. If the only important causal paths are those in the bottom half of the diagram, on the other hand, by the same sort of reasoning, representation must be of the "mandate" sort. Although not explicitly diagrammed, the responsible party model can also be examined in the Miller-Stokes model. A basic assumption here, however, is that constituents' attitudes and the representatives' attitudes are linked by the political parties on the basis of shared policy preferences that have been carefully nurtured by the party system.

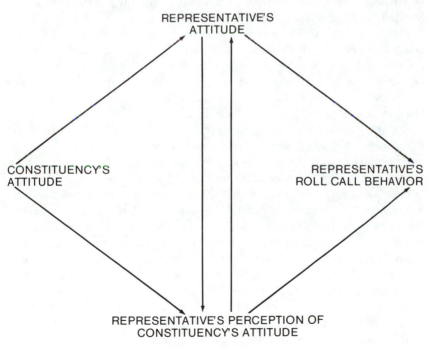

FIGURE 4.1
Miller-Stokes Model

To address the question of issue linkage, Miller and Stokes used both a sample of congressional district constituents and a corresponding sample of representatives and nonincumbents. Roll-call votes of the legislators were also included to examine the behavioral consequences of the representational linkages.

Miller and Stokes found that in the American system representation assumes multiple forms, which are largely dependent upon the issue area under consideration. On the civil rights issue the path by which the constituents exert control over the actions of their representatives is through the "mandate channel." In the area of foreign affairs, the "independent delegate," applauded by Edmund Burke, dominates. Finally, on policies of social welfare the responsible party model seems to hold sway.

Since Miller and Stokes designed their model to be a diagnostic tool, it is not too surprising that their study design was replicated in a half dozen Western democratic societies, including West Germany.[6] The studies, conducted in the late 1960s and early 1970s, share the same conceptual schema and sample design. By examining the components of the representational relationship from a comparative perspective, it was anticipated that it would be possible to determine the types of constraints, institutional and normative, that influence the relationship in a particular polity.

The West German setting provides an interesting contrast to all the other countries where the Miller-Stokes paradigm was employed. Aside from the rather tumultuous development of a democratic system of government in Germany, which sets this nation apart from most of the other Western democracies, there are other, rather unique structural features that make the German case an interesting one to explore.

A striking feature of the *Basic Laws* (the constitution of West Germany) is the clear delineation of the role and responsibilities of the key actors in the representative process: the citizens and the representatives. The constitutional framers placed great weight on the prevailing normative theories of representation in defining these roles. Article 20 of the *Basic Laws* establishes the authority of the people in the Federal Republic: "All state authority emanates from the people. It shall be exercised by the people by means of elections and voting and by separate legislative, executive and judicial organs." Certainly this is a clarion call for mandated representation. It is apparent, however, that the framers did not have complete trust—or at least confidence—in the German people, because they also established the autonomy of the legislators in the *Basic Laws*. Article 38 states: "[The deputies] shall be representatives of the whole people, not bound to orders and instructions and subject only to their conscience." This is pure Burkean terminology. According to this formulation the autonomy of the individual legislator is preserved in order to insulate the legislative elites from the whims and passions of a mass public.

If fear of too much citizen control prompted the constitutional framers to institutionalize a trusteeship representational relationship, at least some concern was also expressed about the representatives having too much independence of action. This factor was particularly relevant in the context of the German situation where a parliamentary system of government was being designed. Unless the governing parties or party had tight control over its members, the stability of the system would be seriously jeopardized. This led the framers to include Article 21 in the *Basic Laws*: "The political parties shall participate in forming the political will of the people." While not necessarily contradictory to the Burkean interpretation of the representative's role, the prominent position given the political parties at least creates a dyadic relationship between the legislator, on the one hand, and the parliamentary party, on the other hand. The legislators are psychologically and politically bound to the party of their choice and have an obligation to support the policy guidelines set down by the party.

The tension among all three models of representation is manifested in the electoral system as well as in the legislative decision-making process. A large portion of the theoretical literature dealing with democratic representation stresses the importance of the electoral system in shaping the nature of the linkages between the represented and the representatives.[7] Proponents of the single-member district system, often associated with the classical theories of representation, contend that majority rule is secured under this electoral arrangement. The elected representatives identify with a particular geographical unit and the majority of voters within these borders. Further, the elites are held personally responsible for acting in the interests of their constituency. In Germany this discussion was largely framed in terms of whether a majority would result, thereby alleviating the problem of the proliferation of splinter parties that emerged under the Weimar electoral configuration. Opponents of this system argue that the majority rules at the expense of the rights of the minority. To redress this shortcoming and to maximize the representativeness of the political system, this latter group advocates a system of proportional representation that preserves the heterogeneity of opinions and ideological perspectives present in a nation. The representatives under this system are not necessarily associated with particular geographic areas but rather are identified as members of political parties.

The German electoral system is a hybrid form of proportional representation and single-member district representation. The simple contours of a rather complicated accounting system provide that half the members of the Bundestag (Parliament) are directly elected representatives and an equivalent number are party-list representatives. Perhaps unintentionally, the creation of the hybrid electoral system provides an opportunity for half of the legislators to display more independence from the state or national party and rely instead on local support, whether it comes from the constituents as a whole or from the local party organization.

One further feature of the electoral system that might have some impact on the representational relationship should be noted here. In a majority of cases, deputies appear on both sides of the ballot as both single-member district candidates and list candidates. Moreover, a decidedly large proportion of the candidates who are defeated in the majority-rule contest nevertheless win admission to the Bundestag through their position on the party list. The West German legislative body, therefore, is alone among Western democratic nations in having both "winners" and "losers" in the Bundestag.[8]

It would appear from the above discussion that the constitutional framers were deliberate in their efforts to insure that all three normative forms of representation would find some expression in Germany. Indeed, we might be tempted to conclude without empirical proof, that no one form of representation dominates in contemporary West Germany. Instead we might anticipate that a constant tension exists among these three modes of representation. The actual consequences of the constitutional and electoral arrangements on the representational relationship are examined below.

SETTING, DESIGN AND MEASURES

This study slices into the early period of the first *Machtwechsel*—change in government—in German postwar history. The national election of 1969 ended twenty years of domination of the Christian Democrats (CDU/CSU) and ushered in the coalition of Social Democrats (SPD) and Free Democrats (FDP). Unlike the preceding period, which was dominated by the Grand Coalition (the partnership between the CDU/CSU and the SPD), the SPD-FDP coalition, under the chancellorship of Willy Brandt, had only a bare majority. Only a few voting deviations from the government's position would seriously impair the survival of the Brandt administration. This meant that party discipline was carefully reinforced and that party voting was the rule, not the exception. Only the FDP did not always conform to this pattern. A few members, who were closer ideologically to the old leadership and to the CDU, manifested their disagreement with their party's coalition with the SPD either by defecting to the CDU/CSU or by voting against the government's position on major policy matters. These "renegades" were not numerous enough to impair the effectiveness of the SPD-FDP coalition, but they did show the FDP to be a partner that had to be watched carefully.

The data for this study come from two separate populations: voters and elected representatives. The voter sample is based on a 1969 postelection survey conducted by INFAS, a commercial polling firm in Bonn. A total of 3,819 respondents were interviewed in this multistaged, stratified, random sample of citizens of voting age living in the Federal Republic, excluding Berlin. The elite study consists of a sample of members of the Bundestag that could be linked to the election study by means of the electoral districts (*Wahlkreise*). A total of 143 deputies were interviewed from the two leading parties, the Social Democrats (SPD) and the Christian Democrats (CDU/CSU), with fifteen additional interviews coming from Free Democratic deputies (FDP). (See following narrative for a description of the sample of deputies.)

Unlike the Miller and Stokes study, which focused on three issue domains and had multiple measures for each issue to test the representation model in the United States, a series of questions on issue positions and a series of questions on agenda priorities each represented by six items were all that were available in the German survey. Both sets were used to unravel the question of constituency control but from different angles. The issue items, expressed in terms of agree-disagree statements, covered the major policy cleavages in German society: income, education, foreign policy, values, trade unions, and capitalism. These issue questions tapped the broad contours of the political debate that shaped German partisan politics in the postwar years. The items were chosen because of their centrality to the concerns of the two major parties. The second series of six questions dealt with the policy priorities in Germany. In contrast to the first battery, the agenda items identified the importance that both the voters and their elected officials placed on such policy matters as: a stable government, a stable economy, equitable distribution of income, *Ostpolitik* (foreign relations with the Eastern bloc nations), improved educational opportunities, and the preservation of national interests. The agenda priorities were not as clearly "partisan" in nature as were the issue cleavage items. Indeed, there were several items, namely stable government, stable economy, and preservation of national interests, that were universally applauded as important by both major parties and their supporters. What we would anticipate, however, is a high level of consensus on these agenda measures, a situation that would decrease their importance in differentiating among deputies in their agreement or disagreement with constituents.[9]

Only the agenda series contains all the elements necessary to examine the three normative theories of representation; the issue series can only be used to evaluate the independence and responsible party theories. We will begin our empirical evaluation of the representational ties with the truncated version of the model, that dealing with the issue cleavages, but only after we comment on the measure of roll-call votes and the problems of small sample size.

A critical aspect of the Miller-Stokes model is policy outputs, which were operationally defined as the legislators' roll-call votes. In the German setting it is virtually impossible to obtain information on the roll-call votes of an individual deputy. Most votes are cast as a mere "show of hands" or are subject to a secret ballot. Although there is a provision in the legislative decision-making process for roll calls by name (*Namentliche Abstimmungen*), this form of voting has been virtually abandoned.[10] The rare occurrences of this latter form of legislative voting, which is essential for the testing of the Miller-Stokes model, led us to conclude that we had to find an alternative measure which would still capture the roll-call intention of the deputies without seriously distorting the substantive meaning of the vote.

Our solution was to assign a party code to the issue items and to the agenda priorities. That is, we have assigned all CDU/CSU members a score of "0" and the SPD members a score of "1," correspondingly. We felt we could take this form of action because of the nature of legislative decision making during the 1969–1972 period. As stated above, the minimal ruling coalition condition that prevailed necessitated that strict party unity be maintained. Only the FDP seemed to deviate from this norm on occasion. Indeed, approximately half of the FDP members in our sample seem to favor a leftist position on the issues and the other half supported a rightist position. After contemplating what type of scoring to assign to the FDP, we decided that the least distortion would result if we scored all FDP elites midway between the two other parties, giving them a score of "0.5." In assigning the scores, we had to key all the issue agenda items accordingly.

Following the Miller and Stokes lead, we confined our interest in the representational relationship to establishing the *strength* of the various linkages in the model. We achieved this by comparing the deputy's score with the mean score of his district and reporting correlation coefficients (Pearsonian r), which measure the degree of correspondence between deputies' scores and their districts' scores. Since we are using the average scores for the districts, it is critical to know whether the voter sample estimates are accurate measures of the district population as a whole. Indeed, if the sample estimates were exact replications of the population parameters, we would expect to find perfect congruity between the two values—or a correlation of 1.0. In most instances, however, the match between the sample estimates and the true district characteristics falls short of unity. One major explanation for this "lack of fit" or measurement error is attributed to "noise." "Noise" stems largely from inaccurate or incomplete reporting on the survey instrument and is difficult, if not impossible, to eliminate completely. We assume, however, that following good survey research techniques in the interviewing, coding, and subsequent data processing, the impact of this form of measurement error would be held to a minimum.

A more troublesome source of error, beyond "noise," is related to small sample size. According to sampling theory, the fewer the cases in the sample, the greater is the error margin associated with these estimates and, consequently, the further the correlation will fall short of unity. Knowing the inherent limits of small samples, we are able to calculate the exact amount of "erosion" or attenuation that can be expected in a correlation that is directly attributed to limited sampling and then make the appropriate correction to the correlation. It should be emphasized that in most instances there is no way to verify empirically the accuracy of the theoretically derived attenuation effect. After all, having a complete enumeration of the views of the district population on such things as political issues defeats the primary purpose of a sample survey, which is to obtain information not available on a population at relatively low cost. The soundness of the theory, however, remains strong assurance that these estimates are appropriate corrections for a given sample.

We know, due to the nature of the German sample, that we are faced with the problem of small sample attentuation of estimates. As we mentioned above, the district estimates are based on few cases relative to the actual number of registered voters in each district (100,000 to 200,000). Moreover, since the original study design did not have the representation model in mind, the number of respondents in the survey are unevenly distributed across the 94 *Wahlkreise* (voting districts). This means that in several districts only a handful of cases must represent the views of their constituency (see the following narrative for description of the sample frame).

By estimating the attenuation correction for each correlation and then applying this correction to the correlation, we can present an adjusted version of the correlations.[11] While it might be assumed that one single factor may serve as the correction on all raw correlations where small-sample district estimates are involved, this is decidedly not the case. Indeed, the attenuation correction is a function not only of sampling size but also of the geographical maldistribution of the variable in question. Even though the number of cases in the district remains constant across the variables, the total observed variance changes according to how the particular attributes for each variable are distributed across the districts. The appropriate correction factor, therefore, has to be variable-specific.[12] Another reason why the attenuation correction has to change is that some of the analyses will be based on subgroups of cases. In this instance the error variance increases further, and consequently the attenuation factor will be affected.

Yet another issue to be addressed pertains to when the attenuation factor is to be used. Since our major concern in this study is centered on linking the attitudes of the constituency to the opinions and behavior of the elected representative from the district, we will be matching district-level estimates to individual-level responses. We already know that small-sampling error affects the district estimates, since a few dozen cases are expected to represent thousands of opinions. In the case of the other half of the pair—the representative—there is no need to correct for sample size because we are not "sampling" at all; we are simply observing the deputy.

THE APPLICATION OF THE MILLER-STOKES MODEL IN GERMANY

In order for the Burkean form of representation to emerge in the German setting, there must be high congruence between the deputies' opinion and roll-call intention (B→D). This, after all, would confirm that the deputies' conscience is directing the legislative voting process. Yet, according to the Miller-Stokes formulation, which places a premium on citizen control of the representational-legislative process, there must also be some, albeit modest, congruence between the opinions of the district as a whole and the opinions expressed by the elected representatives (A→B).

When we look at the linkages between district opinion and deputies' attitude (see Figure 4.2), we find little evidence to suggest that the constituents and their deputies are like-minded. Indeed, on five of the six issues the relationship hovers around zero, and even more distressingly the correlations are consistently negative across all six items. Whereas a null relationship might suggest that the representatives are totally independent of the wishes of their constituency, the persistence of the negative correlations across all items is an indicator that there is actually a slight tendency for these elected officials to *mis*represent the policy preferences of their constituents.

One possible explanation for these negative correlations is that a subset of party representatives is more out of touch with the wishes of their district than another set of party representatives. In testing for the impact of partisanship on this linkage, we compute partial correlations controlling for the effects of the party. In so doing we find virtually no change in the magnitudes of the coefficients across the six issues. On five of the items the partials remain negative; in the case of the sixth, trade unionism, the sign is reversed but the magnitude of the coefficient is very close to zero.[13]

Although we are left to puzzle over the genesis of these negative relationships at this point, we are able to find confirmation of the Burkean form of representation, if we are willing to assume that district congruence is not essential. Looking at the linkage between the deputies' attitudes and the roll-call intention we find that, with the exception of the Western bias in foreign policy issue, there is a moderate to strong correlation on this link. Another way of stating this relationship is to assume that perfect agreement with the party position would yield a correlation of 1.00. The low correlation of the foreign policy item, .11, is something we expected, given the new direction in foreign policy under the leadership of the SPD. There was some expectation that an SPD electoral victory would mean that the ties with the Eastern bloc would be cultivated, and thereby diminish the Western bias in German foreign policy.

Even though the level of agreement on the linkage between deputy's attitude and roll-call intention is not perfect for any item, it is high enough to

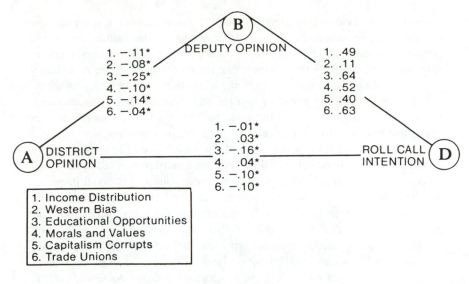

FIGURE 4.2
Issue Cleavages

suggest that the trustee form of representation finds some level of support in the German system. Since legislative voting is party-bound, these results also indicate the degree to which the views of the deputies are compatible with those of their party.

We have already noted that the deputies' attitudes are not linked to constituency opinion. Yet we know that the political parties exert control over the representatives' voting behavior. This latter factor would suggest that perhaps the representational relationship is independent of specific elites or elite opinion and is more directly linked to the party and its policy platform. In this instance the party serves as a mechanism through which the interests of the citizens are articulated. In voting for a particular party, then, the constituents assume some control over the behavior of their deputies. For this form of representation to manifest itself it is necessary for the constituents to be aware of the issues and also to be able to identify them with the policy directives of particular parties. If the party form of representation were indeed present in Germany, we would expect to find at least moderate issue agreement between the district opinion and the roll-call intention, depicted in the direct path (A→D).

The data do not bear out these expectations of the responsible party model. In almost every instance the correlations are very close to zero, and on the majority of issues the correlations are once again disturbingly negative. There seems to be no evidence to support a direct linkage between district opinion on any of these salient issues and party voting in the Bundestag. These negative findings, in fact, confound the nature of the representational relationship, since substantively they suggest that the representatives are more likely to act against the expressed wishes of their constituents than to act for them.

When we turn to the agenda priorities and examine the representational linkages that were explored in the issue battery, we find the same patterns emerging once again (see Figure 4.3). That is, in examining the linkages depicting the trustee relationship we find the persistence of low and negative correlations on the bond between district opinion and deputies' attitudes. Only on two issues, income maldistribution and preservation of national interests, are the correlations positive and modest, .28* and .19*, respectively. The congruence on these two items is encouraging for constituency control, particularly since the agenda priorities are not expected to yield strong correlations. It is also somewhat surprising to find a positive correlation surfacing on the income maldistribution item in light of the negative correlation that emerged on a similar issue in the cleavage battery. We would assume that the discrepancy on this item between the two series is in part a reflection of the different foci of the two series: the issue cleavages tap the directionality and the ideological preferences while the agenda priorities measure the importance of an issue regardless of its partisan nature.

When we controlled for the effects of the political parties, as we did with the issue battery, we once again found practically no changes in the correlations (not shown).

The linkage between the deputies' attitude and the roll-call intention (B→D) shows correlations that are for the most part lower than those found for the issue battery, averaging around .27, which is something we had anticipated. What is important to emphasize is that the general direction of the relationship upholds the pattern established in the issue battery.

Looking next at the responsible party model, which is depicted in the linkage between district opinion and the roll-call intention (A→D), the results are no different from those uncovered in the earlier series. The persistence of these negative and null relationships across two independent series simply confirms that we are faced with an intriguing problem that was not encountered in the American study of representation.

Before pursuing this line of inquiry further, we still have to address the last theory of representation—the mandate form—that is present in the agenda priorities series. In terms of our model, the mandate form of representation, like the Burkean formulation, is represented by indirect paths, in this case, those occupying the lower half of the diagram. Since constituency control over the actions of the elected representatives is so central to the mandate view of representation, we would expect to find at least moderate congruence between district opinion and the deputies' perception of district sentiment

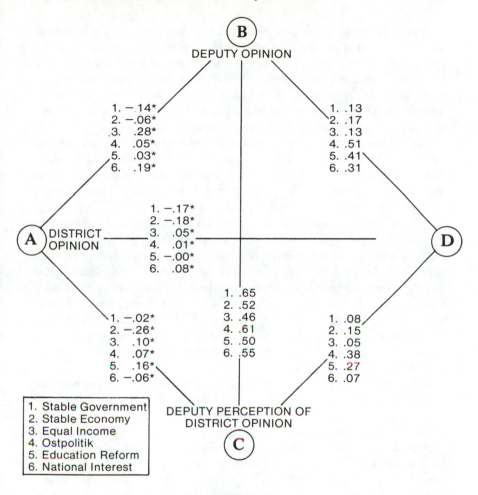

FIGURE 4.3
Agenda Priorities

(A→C). For the mandate model to emerge we would also expect to find high congruence between the deputies' perception of district opinion and legislative action (C→D).

The results indicate that there is very little basis for believing that district opinion is being considered by the deputies when a roll-call vote is being contemplated. The mandate paths closely parallel the results found for the Burkean model, but appear to be weaker. Even the linkage between the deputies' perception of the voters' attitude and the roll-call intention is in all cases weaker than the case represented by the trustee model. The weakness in this latter path is even more sobering when we realize that a considerable amount of the deputies' perception of district opinion is merely a projection of their own position on these agenda items. While the average zero-order correlations for this linkage is .17, it drops to practically nothing (.02) once the deputies' own opinion is removed. This finding lends further confirmation to the fact that the mandate version of representation does not seem to be operative in Germany. The perceptual linkages are weak at both the constituency end and the roll-call-intention end of the diamond.

Thus far the evidence we have mounted in examining the representational linkages in West Germany might be evaluated in two ways: methodologically and substantively. Had the German case been the first empirical test of the leading normative theories of representation, some of these findings might have been attributed to methodological problems of design. That is, the largely null correlations, coupled with the systematic negative relationships on some of the linkages, namely that between constituency opinion and both deputies' attitude and roll-call intention, are findings that might not have been anticipated given the basic assumptions of the model. Yet we already know that the model has yielded substantively meaningful results in the United States. Moreover, the subsequent use of the model in France largely follows the contours of the earlier American findings.[14] We, therefore, would reject the methodological argument and suggest instead that the German case provides a counterpoint to the other two countries in which this model has been analyzed.

In searching for possible substantive reasons for the null and negative relationships, it is necessary to take a critical look at some of the basic assumptions made about the political system and evaluate them in terms of the German setting. The notion of representational congruence is premised on the likelihood that the majority sentiment (district mean) will be mirrored by the winning candidate. What happens to the relationship, however, when a vast majority of the districts have both "winning" and "losing" candidates represented in the Bundestag? This curious consequence of the two-ballot electoral system may be a major contributor to the perplexing results that we have obtained thus far in our analyses. The uniqueness of the German case provides a rare opportunity to examine the consequences of the two leading electoral configurations, majority rule and proportional representation, on the representational process in a single country.

ELECTORAL CANDIDATE TYPES AND REPRESENTATION

Although once in the Bundestag there are virtually no distinctions made between the directly elected and the list deputies (who are "indirectly" elected via proportional representation) in terms of positions they are likely to hold or the responsibilities assigned to them, there are some intrinsic differences

TABLE 4.1
Linkage on Issue Cleavages Between Constituents and Deputies
(Directly Elected and List Deputies)

	A→B		B→D		A→D	
	Directly Elected	List	Directly Elected	List	Directly Elected	List
Income Distribution	−.16*	−.05*	.56	.40	−.04*	.04*
Western Bias	.01*	−.18*	.12	.09	.11*	−.05*
Educational Opportunities	−.12*	−.47*	.72	.54	−.24*	−.03*
Morals and Values	.01*	−.24*	.45	.61	.19*	−.20*
Capitalism Corrupts	.06*	−.49*	.44	.35	.06*	−.38*
Trade Unionism	.05*	−.14*	.73	.50	.18*	−.55*
N	(79)	(80)				

*Attenuation Correction

separating directly elected representatives from the party-list representatives that affect the nature of the bonds between the electors and the elected. Directly elected deputies, for example, consistently outdistance the list members in terms of time spent on district matters, whether the Bundestag is in session or in recess. Moreover, district members spend more time in the home district than their list member counterparts. From indicators of this sort, we might expect to find district deputies to be more conscientious and cognizant of district needs with respect to policy matters than the list members. We can examine the data once again, this time distinguishing between the directly elected deputies and the list deputies. From this we will be able to determine whether the electoral arrangements exert an impact on the representational linkages in West Germany.

Looking first at the issue cleavage battery and the Burkean paths among the two electoral types of deputies for all voters in the district (Table 4.1), we are immediately struck both by the continuity in the overall pattern and also by some of the changes that emerge as a result of this differentiation by representative type. The most significant finding is the persistence of the largely low agreement across all issue domains for the direct and indirect linkages from the constituency (A→B and A→D). However, this should not negate the fact that differences do appear in the correlations when we separate the directly elected from the list deputies, differences that are notable and substantively meaningful.

Illustratively, the linkage between district opinion and the deputies' attitude (A→B) indicates that, with the single exception of the income distribution issue, the directly elected members' opinions are more congruent with constituency sentiment than are the list representatives' views. The correlations between the district viewpoint and the directly elected deputies' opinion are, with this one exception, always an improvement on the correlations in the original model, while the same relationships involving the list deputies emerge in a much poorer light than before. The differences in level of congruence on this linkage between the directly elected and the list members ranges from .11* to .38*, or an average of .27*. These differences provide striking evidence of the way in which electoral constraints exert an impact on the nature of the representational linkages.

The same pattern emerges when we look at the direct linkage involving constituency control, that between district opinion and roll-call intention (A→D). Like the first linkage described, the strength of the original relationships between district attitudes and both deputy opinions and behavior has been suppressed by virtue of including a group of "losing" candidates into the linkage constellation. Indeed, the mystery of the largely negative correlations in the original model seems to be attributable to the list members, who happen to be very much in disagreement with the sample of voters in their constituency, while the "winning" district candidates show more issue agreement with their partisan voters.

Switching to the last linkage in the issue cleavage mdoel, that between the deputies' own attitudes and their roll-call intention (B→D), we find there is a higher level of agreement with the party position for the directly elected deputies than for the list deputies on all issues except one, moral and value decay. It is suggestive to note that these findings reconcile neatly with the results of an earlier work done on CDU deviancy in the Bundestag,[15] in which list members were shown to deviate from the party position on the roll-call votes. The explanation offered for this was that list members were representatives of special interest groups and differed from the party in order to be responsive and responsible to the interests they represented. Curiously, both our findings and those from this earlier work are not what we might have anticipated from the literature on proportional representation. Party dominance is supposed to prevail in such electoral systems.

In drawing this distinction between the district deputies and the list members, it is important to reiterate at this point that the deviance we are now noting is in the attitudes of the list deputies rather than the actual voting behavior. Insofar as the attitudes of the list members seem less neatly bound to the party position, it is most likely a reflection of their dual status as both an interest group representative and a party member and the potential conflict that might surface as a consequence.

What is apparent, however, is that the list members do not see a tension between themselves and the constituency in which they actively seek to be elected. The foci of representation for the list members, rather than being the single-member district, seems to be more clearly the state, since it is the state party organization that establishes the ordering of deputies on the list. Indeed, when we look at the congruence between the list deputies and the voters of their state, on every issue there is a substantial improvement in issue agreement (table not shown). We would conclude from this finding that the electoral distinction made between the two deputy types manifests itself as well in the geographical foci of representation with the district deputies being more in tune with the wishes of the local constituents while the list members are more likely to reflect the sentiments of the state's voters.

The results of the agenda priorities confirm what has just been presented for the issue cleavages. The patterns established in the issue cleavage battery surface as well in this independent test, with the distinction between the directly elected and list deputies being sharply visible (table not shown). Although the distinction between the district deputies and the list deputies is upheld when we look at the mandate linkages, there is no improvement in the correlations on this dimension. Consequently, our basic conclusion about this path to representation remains unchanged.

Perhaps one final difference that should be pointed out pertains to the linkage between the deputies' own attitudes and their perception of district opinion (B→C). On five out of six of the agenda items there is more agreement between the attitudes and perceptions of district sentiment for the directly elected deputies, the district winners, than for the list members, the losers of the single-member district competition. We cannot help but speculate that the perceptions might be influenced by a "winning effect."[16] That is, the "winners" of the majority rule contest are most likely to feel that they are better informed about the interests of the district by virtue of their electoral victory. The "losing" candidates, in contrast, seem to dissociate themselves from the district in terms of acknowledging that a great gap exists between their own policy priorities and those of the constituents who failed to elect them in the single-member district contest.

The comparison of the "winning" and "losing" deputies in the representation model provides persuasive evidence that the hybrid electoral system has a measurable impact on the quality of the linkages between the constituents and their representatives in a geographic sense. Despite the striking differences between the directly elected and the list deputies, however, the basic weakness in the issue positions connecting the constituents to the elected officials remains. We have yet to determine the source of the weak relationship across all issue domains. We focus on this problem in the final section.

THE PARTY MODEL AND PARTISAN SUPPORTERS

Throughout this study the main assumption being made about the linkages between the represented and the representatives is that they are constituency-based. Indeed, the two leading normative theories of representation, mandate and independence, were formulated with a majority-rule electoral system in mind and the notion that district voters elect individuals who act out the district's will, whether as instructed delegates or trustees. Yet the third normative theory of representation, the responsible party model, is premised on another set of assumptions. In contrast to the other two theories, this twentieth-century formulation of the representational relationship relies on the attachment of the electorate to the political parties and their policies and programs rather than to individuals who are identified with local interests. According to this theory the parties are responsible to a subset of voters, the partisan supporters, and not necessarily to any one constituency as a whole.

We have argued that the party model has relevance for district-level representation insofar as the parties are involved in electoral politics and have to rely upon consensus building that extends beyond their group of supporters. Partisan representatives, hoping to win additional votes from nonparty identifiers, may, therefore, perceive electoral responsibility to the constituency as a whole. From this situation we expected to find at least some congruence between the district opinion of the winning candidates and the party measure of roll-call intention. Our assumptions were not borne out by the data, however. In our initial testing of the party linkage we found that whatever inroads the German parties have made into the support groups of their electoral rivals, they do not seem to be manifested in constituency-based politics.

What remains to be explored in terms of the Miller-Stokes model is the relationship between the partisan supporters and the party representatives. Since the German electoral system distinguishes between two sets of representatives, those who represent the majority of voters in the district and those who are identified with the minority opinion, a distinction that has been found to be meaningful, we will continue to treat these two groups separately in our subsequent analysis. This will also give us a better chance to view the role of the list deputies from the perspective of electoral "winners" rather than principally as district "losers."

The analysis of partisan subgroups will entail looking at four sets of linkages: the relationship between the district representatives and both their supporters and nonsupporters and the party list members and their supporters and nonsupporters. Partisan supporters are defined as citizens who voted for either the SPD or the CDU/CSU on the first ballot in the 1969 federal election and the nonsupporters as all other citizens who voted for a different party in that same electoral contest.[17]

In testing the party model with the supporters and nonsupporters, we are essentially interested in two sets of linkages in the Miller-Stokes model: the indirect linkage between the partisan voters' opinions and the attitudes of the party representatives (A→B) and the direct path leading from partisan

TABLE 4.2
*Linkage on Issue Cleavages Between Partisan Supporters and Nonsupporters for
Directly Elected Deputies*

	A→B		B→D	A→D	
	Supporters	Non-supporters		Supporters	Non-supporters
Income Distribution	−.12*	−.29*	.56	.46*	−.54*
Western Bias	.15*	−.14*	.12	.33*	−.33*
Educational Opportunities	.51*	−.37*	.72	.39*	−.49*
Morals and Values	.16*	−.11*	.45	.47*	−.15*
Capitalism Corrupts	.10*	−.14*	.44	.38*	−.35*
Trade Unionism	.20*	−.41*	.73	.52*	−.50*

*Attenuation Correction

TABLE 4.3
*Linkage on Issue Cleavages Between Supporters and Nonsupporters
for List Deputies*

	A→B		B→D	A→D	
	Supporters	Non-supporters		Supporters	Non-supporters
Income Distribution	.16*	−.19*	.43	.53*	−.45*
Western Bias	−.28*	−.15*	.10	.28*	−.22*
Educational Opportunities	−.27*	−.56*	.57	.06*	−.21*
Morals and Values	.11*	−.21*	.64	.15*	−.42*
Capitalism Corrupts	−.33*	−.37*	.37	.53*	−.76*
Trade Unionism	.42*	−.45*	.52	.42*	−.74*

*Attenuation Correction

supporters to the roll-call-intention meausre (A→D). Should the issue congruence between the supporters and the party vote be strong, we would conclude that citizens are identifying with a party label and by their votes exert some control over the actions of the political parties. In this instance the representational relationship is not linked to a particular geographical area but is defined in terms of a national constituency.

The comparison of the linkages for the supporters and nonsupporters in the issue cleavage series for both sets of deputies is shown in Tables 4.2 and 4.3. Looking first at the indirect path, between constitutency opinion and deputies' attitude (A→B), we find a consistent pattern across the two elite groups: there is closer agreement between the supporters and their representatives than between the nonsupporters and these same representatives. Despite some lingering disagreement on certain issues between the supporters and their deputies, policy agreement seems to dominate, especially if the relationship being targeted is with the district deputies. In contrast, there is only disagreement between the deputies and their nonsupporters for all six items, a divergence in opinion that ranges in magnitude from $-.11^*$ to $-.56^*$ across the two elite groups. Perhaps what is most striking is the sharp polarization between the correlations of the supporters and representatives on the one hand, and the nonsupporters and these same representatives on the other hand. The average difference between the correlations of the supporters and nonsupporters is $.40^*$ for the directly elected members' constituencies and $.29^*$ for the list deputies' districts. Indeed, on some issues the differences are as great as $.87^*$ and $.88^*$ (trade unionism and educational opportunities, respectively).

When we compare the patterns for the two sets of elites, it seems that there is more consistency and congruence between the attitudes held by the directly elected deputies and their supporters than between the opinions expressed by the list representatives and their supporters. We note, for example, that while the district representatives reach a healthy level of agreement on the educational question with their supporters ($.51^*$), the list deputies are much more likely to take a position that is contrary to the expressed wishes of their partisan supporters ($-.27^*$). This is not meant to suggest, however, that the list deputies are totally removed from their supporters. On the contrary, these deputies seem to be aware that they are assuming the role of "shadow" representative for their district supporters, at least on the issues of trade unionism, income distribution, and moral value decay. These results would seem to indicate that a certain level of political expression and control is insured to minority opinion not only through the institutionalization of the proportional representation system but also through the additional safeguard of linking a large portion of the list deputies to their party voters.

Despite the overall improvement in the correlations between the representatives' constituency supporters and the representatives' own opinions, with very few exceptions, the issue linkages are weaker than we would have expected for a confirmation of the party model through the indirect path. The notable exceptions are the issues of educational opportunities and trade unionism for the directly elected members and their supporters, and trade unionism for the list members and their supporters. In all three instances the agreement between the representatives' opinion and their roll-call intention is substantial: the correlations between the partisan deputies' own attitudes and the expected party vote in the Bundestag for these issues are .72, .73, and .52, respectively. Only with respect to these issues can we say that the deputies' legislative actions are based in part on the sentiments expressed by their district supporters. One possible explanation for the high level of agreement on the issues of trade unionism and educational opportunities may be that these policies have long-standing ties with the Social Democrats. Trade unionism had been synonymous with the SPD since its inception; educational reform, while a more recent issue, nevertheless was a major plank in the SPD campaign of 1969.

Aside from the two issues mentioned, however, the congruence between the representatives' opinions and their roll-call intention is what dominated the indirect paths in this partisan model, a situation that adds further support to the Burkean formulation of the representative relationship.

In light of these results, we might ask whether partisan voters have any other recourse by which they might influence the actions of the political parties. We have already indicated that control over the political parties could come about directly, through the agreement between the policy views of the partisan supporters and the actions of the legislative elites. When we look at the direct linkage (A→D) we find sufficient evidence to support the party model in Germany. In every instance the correlations between the party voters and the partisan roll-call intention are moderate to high, ranging between .33* and .52* for the directly elected subgroup and between .06* and .53* for the list members. Even though the relationship is weaker for the list deputies on a couple of issues, the basic pattern receives some confirmation from both groups.

The strength of the relationship between the partisan supporters and legislative action stands in sharp relief to the strong disagreement that prevails between the attitudes of the representatives' nonsupporters and their own legislative behavior, the magnitudes of which are almost a complete mirror image of the supporter side of the model. We might reflect for a moment on the consequences that these strong negative correlations might have for political systems that do not have some institutional corrective for the representation of minority opinion. Dissenting opinions that are articulated through partisan politics often do not find expression in legislative action as they do in Germany.

The further unfolding of the agenda priorities model into partisan supporters and nonsupporters for both the list deputies and the directly elected representative subsets conforms to the basic pattern already unveiled in the previous iteration of the data and need not be repeated here. Perhaps the one difference in the findings between the two series concerns the uniformly higher agreement between the supporters and the directly elected deputies than between the supporters and the list members on the issue cleavages, and the mixed pattern that emerges on the agenda series. In the case of the latter, however, there does not seem to be any discernible pattern in the pairing of the agenda priorities. We are left with no ready explanation for this occurrence.

CONCLUSION

In terms of the normative theories of representation that were being tested, only two received some empirical verification, namely the trustee and responsible party model. The mandate theory does not appear to find any expression in the German political system, at least not in terms of our model. The strongest confirmation came from the Burkean formulation insofar as the congruence between the deputies' own attitudes and the legislative voting intention was, in most cases, exceptionally high. What did not emerge from this trustee interpretation was any link back to the constituency. Indeed, to the extent that we are interested in the question of citizen control and, consequently in elite responsiveness at the district level, the data provide little evidence to support such notions. What we might be led to conclude from this is that the district representatives and their "shadow" counterparts are not at all influenced by district sentiment in executing their legislative responsibility.

The linkage between the partisan voters and legislative action across the various issue domains, both domestic and foreign, was strong enough to confirm that the party model is operative in Germany. By structuring policy preferences along partisan lines for a polity that is not well informed, the political parties insure that the political system remains responsive to its citizens. Maintaining this tension between party responsibility and the representatives' legislative autonomy works to insure that no one group holds a virtual monopoly on the German political system.

APPENDIX A

Issue Cleavages*

(Response categories: Agree–Disagree)
1. The distribution of income is unjust for the workers.
2. The foreign policy of the Federal Republic is too much oriented toward the West.
3. Our educational system offers almost no opportunities for social betterment to the children of the lower classes.
4. It is deplorable that our morals and values degenerate more and more.
5. Capitalism corrupts our democracy.
6. The trade unions have too much power in Germany.

---

*All issue items were keyed so that agree = liberal position and disagree = conservative position.

Agenda Priorities

(Response categories: Very important, less important, unimportant)
1. A stable government
2. A stable economy
3. A more equitable distribution of the national income among social strata of the population
4. Improved relations with the countries of the Eastern bloc
5. Improved opportunities for education for all groups of the population
6. Preservation of our national interests

NOTES

1. For a critical discussion of the evolution of the concept of representation see Hanna Pitkin, *The Concept of Representation* (Berkeley: University of California Press, 1972).

2. A. H. Birch, *Representation* (London: St. Martin's 1971); Jeane J. Kirkpatrick, *The New Presidential Elite* (New York: Basic Books, 1976), chap. 10.

3. *The Works of the Right Honorable Edmund Burke*, 8 vols. (Boston: Wells and Lilly, 1826), 2: 10.

4. Austin Ranney, *The Doctrine of Responsible Party Government* (Urbana, Ill.: University of Illinois Press, 1962); E. E. Schattschneider, *Party Government* (New York: Rinehart, 1942); A. H. Birch, *Representative and Responsible Government* (London: George Allen and Unwin, 1964).

5. Miller and Stokes present their central thesis of representation in three articles: Warren E. Miller and Donald E. Stokes, "Constituency Influence in Congress," *American Political Science Review* 57 (1963): 45–56; Donald E. Stokes and Warren E. Miller, "Party Government and the Saliency of Congress," *Public Opinion Quarterly* 26 (1962): 531–46; Warren E. Miller, "Majority Rule and the Representative System of Government," in E. Allardt and Y. Littunen, eds., *Cleavages, Ideologies and Party Systems* (Helsinki: Transactions of the Westernmarck Society, 1964), pp. 343–76.

6. The other nations to replicate the Miller-Stokes research design are: France, Italy, the Netherlands, Sweden, Great Britain, Brazil, Japan, Australia, and New Zealand.

7. For a good review of the literature dealing with the impact of the electoral system on the style of representation see Douglas Rae, *The Political Consequences of Electoral Laws* (New Haven, Conn.: Yale University Press, 1967).

8. For a good description of the German electoral system, see Gerhard Loewenberg, *Parliament in the German Political System* (Ithaca, N.Y.: Cornell University Press, 1967), pp. 64–65.

9. See the Appendix for a complete listing of the issue and agenda questions.

10. Loewenberg, *Parliament in the German Political System*, pp. 354–61.

11. The procedure used to estimate the attenuation factor is one first formulated by Donald E. Stokes for the American representation study and was later modified by Philip E. Converse. Our procedure is adopted from the latter. The formula for the attenuation correction is: $\alpha = \sqrt{1 - \text{MSSW/MSSB}}$ where MSSW = mean sum of squares within groups (districts), and MSSB = mean sum of squares between groups.

12. All subsequent analyses will use this attenuation correction factor and will be designated by an asterisk (*).

13. The partial correlations for the six items, in the order that they appear in the listing are: $-.12^*$, $-.08^*$, $-.20^*$, $-.14^*$, $-.11^*$, $+.03^*$.

14. Philip E. Converse and Roy Pierce, *Political Representation in France* (forthcoming).

15. George L. Rueckert and Wilder Crane, "CDU Deviancy in the German Bundestag," in Herbert Hirsch and M. Donald Hancock, eds., *Comparative Legislative Systems* (New York: The Free Press, 1971), pp. 392–99.

16. Kingdon develops this concept in his study of Wisconsin state legislators. See John W. Kingdon, *Candidates for Office* (New York: Random House, 1968).

17. The FDP leaders and supporters have been deleted from this analysis because the number of supporters of this party in the sample is too small to allow for meaningful comparisons.

PERSONAL ACCOUNT

4B.   The Research Process: A Personal View

BARBARA G. FARAH

I cannot claim that I began my research on political representation after years of contemplation on the subject. Instead, my dissertation research happened mainly by chance, because I was at the right place at the right time. The place was Bonn, West Germany, and the time was 1968–1970. I had gone to Germany in the fall of 1968 to gather information on a local party organization, the Christian Democrats (CDU), to be used for my dissertation on party membership, recruitment, and incentives. When I left for Germany I did not have my topic well thought through, nor did I have the blessings of my department. Instead, several faculty members cautioned me against just going off to Germany without any funding or faculty sponsorship. Despite most of the advice to the contrary, I felt that I needed the practical experience of being and living in a foreign country, so that I could gain an understanding of the political and social climate of the country. Initially I had planned to be away only one year.

The period of adjustment to living in a foreign country took much longer than I had anticipated. I spent the first couple of months at a German language institute, trying to get my conversation skills up to an acceptable level. It took another couple of months to relocate to a permanent living site, in this case Cologne, and to find a part-time job in computer programming at the University of Cologne. I did contact the local party organization of the CDU early in 1969 and was given permission to go through their membership files.

My advisor visited Germany in the spring of 1969 to consult on a collaborative project with a German political scientist, who was also the director of INFAS, a political polling firm in Bonn. During his brief visit we met and talked about my progress and timetable. Our discussion centered on progress rather than on substantive issues. What had become perfectly clear to me before my advisor arrived was that my slow progress on the dissertation made it necessary for me to remain in Germany another year to complete my data gathering. I talked about finding another job, one that would pay a little more than the job I presently held; I had been considering making enquiries at INFAS.

When my advisor returned to Germany in November to do further work on his collaborative project, I had already obtained a job at INFAS and had been working there for several months. During my advisor's week-long visit, we had several opportunities to talk about my research progress. Since I had made some strides in my study of the local party organization, my advisor was somewhat hesitant about asking me to switch my dissertation topic to the study of representation. Quite unknown to me, the director of INFAS had agreed to add several issue questions to his postelection study survey—the consequence of my advisor's spring visit to Germany. The questions were compatible with some of the issue items asked in other European representation studies that had been inspired by Warren E. Miller's and Donald E. Stokes's work on the American Congress and constituency representation. Although a representation study had *not* been contemplated at that time, mainly because there was neither the money nor the personnel available for such a project, my presence in Germany, and more exactly my work at INFAS, made the prospects of doing the elite counterpart study feasible.

The Center for Political Studies at the University of Michigan, under the directorship of Warren Miller, had agreed to put up what amounted to "pocket money" to insure that interviewers would be paid and that basic administrative costs of the study, such as postage, correspondence, and the duplication of the interview schedule, would be covered. What remained was my consent.

I had very little difficulty making up my mind to accept this offer, although I must confess that at the time I had very little idea of what the project would entail. I knew that it would be challenging and would allow me to learn more about the research process than the project I was doing on my own. Moreover, I had a basic interest in the question of representation and was assured that I would be able to develop some of my own research interests in this study.

The pace at which I worked escalated as a result of my decision to work on the representation study. I knew that I had to complete the data-collection phase of the study by June 1970, so that I could return to the United States in time for the fall semester at the University of Michigan. This meant that I had to become familiar with the Miller-Stokes sample design and with the questionnaires that had been used in other countries, and then decide what modifications I would have to make in the original American model to suit the German situation. My major innovation with respect to the latter concerned the unique electoral system in Germany (described in the previous chapter). Since Germany had a mixed electoral system, which combined proportional representation and single-member district majority rule, we had a unique opportunity to examine the impact of these two electoral systems on the representational relationship.

The two major aspects of the data-collection phase for most survey projects are sampling and interviewing. Questionnaire construction can also require considerable time, but in the case of this study most of the questions were replicated from previous representation studies. Some changes were made in the survey instrument to insure issue compatability with the German situation, but beyond these minor revisions the interview schedule was largely decided upon. It is worth going into some detail about the two aspects of the study that did consume the next six months of my life in Germany, sampling and interviewing, mainly because they are so vital to an understanding of survey research as a whole, and they lend insights into the larger comparative project of political representation.

SAMPLE DESIGN

As indicated in the previous chapter, the study of representation as conceptualized by Miller and Stokes draws upon data from two separate populations: the voters and the elected representatives. The German voter sample was based on a 1969 postelection survey, funded and conducted by INFAS, which included the universe of citizens of voting age living in the Federal Republic, excluding West Berlin, who were registered in the community central registry of inhabitants (*Einwohnermeldekartei*). A sampling procedure was used in the selection of respondents that resulted in a voter sample that was representative of each state (*Land*) and of the nation as a whole.[1] A total of 3,819 respondents were interviewed in the INFAS election study. The response rate was high and compared favorably to previous election studies in the INFAS series. A shortcoming of the voter survey, which had implications for the elite sample, was that the sampling units were based on administrative subunits (*Gemeinde*) rather than electoral districts (*Wahlkreise*). This meant that we did not have a voter sample that was stratified by electoral districts, a necessary condition for a study of constituency-based representation.

Our willingness to grapple with the various problems associated with the electoral survey sample design was based largely upon the success of a similar operation that had been performed on the original American representation study. Like the German case, the American electoral sample used for the Miller-Stokes study was not based on congressional districts. The experience with the parent study was ample proof that many of the sampling problems could be surmounted without impairing the validity of the findings.[2]

The first concern was to find out how many of the 248 *Wahlkreise* had been included in the voter study. After assigning the 3,819 respondents to their electoral districts, we found that 194 constituencies were represented in the election survey. Although one option for the elite study would have been to include all 194 constituencies in our survey, the high cost of elite interviewing precluded this possibility and dictated instead that we draw a sample for the deputy component. In designing this sample we were concerned about two constituency characteristics: (1) the number of voter respondents in each electoral district, and (2) the number of candidates from a district who were elected to the Bundestag.

If the voter survey had been constructed as part of a linkage study, we could have employed a sample design to produce a uniform number of respondents in each constituency. This would have insured that the estimates of constituency opinion were based on approximately the same number of sampled respondents in each district. Unfortunately the reality of the situation was otherwise. The number of respondents actually contained in each *Wahlkreise* touched by the national sample ranged between four and sixty-one people. Our problem was to limit the inefficiencies of estimation associated with districts producing only a handful of interviews. One way of alleviating this difficulty was to maximize the selection of constituencies that had large numbers of respondents from the election study. In order to do this we divided the constituencies into three groups: small, or those containing four to nine respondents; medium, ten to fourteen respondents; and large, fifteen or more respondents. The distribution of constituencies among these three categories was far from equal. There were 123 districts eligible for the "large" category, while 35 and 36 constituencies were classified as "medium" and "small," respectively. Our objective in classifying the constituencies in this manner was to establish a probability ranking that would run from low to high to correspond to the "small" to "large" ordering of the constituencies.

A second criterion that was used to shape the elite sample was not related to the problem of the voter study sample but rather addressed the theoretical question concerning possible constraints imposed by the electoral system. One of the consequences of the German mixed electoral system is that the district candidates and ("proportionally" elected) list candidates are not mutually exclusive. It is quite common to find candidates represented on both sides of the ballot. While this double placement does not guarantee seats in the Bundestag for all candidates, it has allowed a considerable number of "losers" in the district contest to enter the Bundestag by way of the party list. For example, in 126 of the 194 *Wahlkreise* in our sample universe, both the "winners" and "losers" of the single-member district contest became members of the Bundestag after the 1969 federal election.

We decided to maximize the selection of constituencies having both the "winning" and "losing" single-member district contest candidates. More specifically, we wanted to oversample the districts that had the district "losers" elected to the Bundestag by means of the second ballot, the party list. In our sample universe there is almost a two-to-one ratio between the two-deputy district and the one-deputy district. The second criterion in our elite sample, then, was to rank the constituencies in terms of whether they had one or two deputies from the single-member district competition elected to the Bundestag.

It might have been worthwhile to include in our sample deputies who were on the party list but who did not enter the single-member district competition, because we would have had an independent sample of list candidates and not just district candidates who happened to be on the state list as well. This latter option was impossible because of budgetary constraints. Another possibility for our sample design would have been to include candidates who were not successful in their electoral bid for office. Indeed, the original Miller-Stokes study included a group of unsuccessful candidates. Since interviews with the defeated candidates meant that we would have had to travel to the home district, a cost that the budget could not afford, we did not include this group in our sample design either.

We decided that 200 interviews would suit our budgetary considerations and would provide us with a sufficient number of elites for subgroup analyses. A sixfold table was created to reflect the two sampling criteria and then the 194 constituencies were assigned to their appropriate cells (see Table 4.4). Given our concerns, we established a sampling design that would insure a greater selection rate among the electoral districts having both the largest number of voter respondents and also two-deputy representation (the upper right corner cell) and at the same time would minimize the selection of the constituencies having very few voter respondents and only one deputy (the lower left corner cell). This was done by allotting differential sampling rates

TABLE 4.4
Sample Design of Parameters for German Elite Study

Sampling Information	Number of Respondents		
	Small (4–9)	Medium (10–14)	Large (15–61)
Districts With Two Deputies			
Total Number of Districts	23	19	84
Probability of Selection	.2	.4	.8
Number of Districts Selected	5	8	67
Number of Interviews	10	16	134
Districts With One Deputy			
Total Number of Districts	13	16	39
Probability of Selection	.1	.2	.4
Number of Districts Selected	1	3	16
Number of Interviews	1	3	16

to each cell. These rates were constrained by both the joint distribution of these characteristics and also the desired sample size. In order to maximize the difference in the selection rate between the two extreme cells, 80 percent of the districts having the largest number of voter respondents and two deputies were to be selected as compared to only 10 percent of the constituencies with a low number of voter respondents and one deputy. In the latter case a sampling fraction of 0.1 was assigned to insure at least minimal representation of this cell type. Once these two extremes were set, weights were assigned to the remaining four cells along a connecting gradient. A 0.4 probability of selection was allotted to the constituencies occupying the cells adjacent to the main category while a 0.2 probability was assigned to the cells adjacent to the minimal representation cell. The main cell, containing both the largest number of voter respondents and two deputies, received a weighted probability of 0.8.

Once these sampling fractions were established, we were able to determine how many constituencies were to be chosen from each cell for our sample. This was done by multiplying the total number of electoral districts in each of the six cells by the appropriate sample rate. By this procedure we arrived at a sample size of 100 constituencies and 180 interviews.

Our interest in examining the impact of the political parties on mass-elite linkages encouraged us to pay special attention to the representatives from the minor party, the FDP. Although there were only thirty FDP candidates elected to the Bundestag in the 1969 election, all from the party list contest, they nevertheless reflected the views of a small but powerful segment of the electorate. Because of the scarcity of these members in the Bundestag on the one hand, and our need to conduct interviews with a sufficient number of them to make our analyses meaningful on the other hand, we randomly selected one out of every two FDP deputies for our sample. With these fifteen additional interviews we brought our total sample size up to 195 elite interviews.

INTERVIEWING

Once the sample was drawn, we were ready to begin in the interviewing phase of the project. To keep the expenses of the study to a minimum, it was necessary to limit the interview site to the Bonn area. This meant that we would have to conduct the interviews during a period when the Bundestag was in session, since most of the deputies returned to their *Wahlkreise* during the recesses. With this consideration in mind the fieldwork was scheduled to begin after the Easter vacation, at the end of April 1970, and to terminate in July when the Bundestag recessed for the summer. We had to contend with several two-week parliamentary recesses scheduled during this period. Although we did not anticipate being able to interview any deputies during the recesses, we found that for at least some of the Bundestag members who were obligated to remain in Bonn to attend special party meetings, these periods were more convenient for them.

We had been forewarned that the German parliamentary elites were among the most interviewed members of the international community of legislators and, consequently, we would encounter some difficulty in gaining access to them. Indeed, a large number of German deputies had been interviewed for a study conducted by a team of German political scientists just a few months before our own fieldwork began. Further, a Canadian-sponsored survey project was to begin at the same time as our own.

A letter from the Institute for Social Research in Ann Arbor, Michigan, was sent to every deputy who was selected to be in our survey to inform them of their selection, of the basic objectives of the study, and of the interviewing timetable. (The letter was in German). A postcard was also included for them to fill out the time they wanted to set for the interview. We had also indicated that the respondent would be contacted by the study director, me, or one of the interviewers to confirm the appointment.

We had counted on the uniqueness of the study—the focus on the linkages between the representatives and their constituency—and also the sponsorship—an American research institute—to get the deputies to participate. Indeed, during the course of the interviewing most German representatives expressed a keen interest in the topic. One deputy candidly exclaimed: "My relationship with my constituency? What an interesting topic. . . . I haven't really thought much about that." This latter comment gave me pause to think just how relevant an empirical study of representation in Germany really was.

It was only in the latter phases of the interviewing that we had good reason to believe that some interviews were granted to assuage a certain curiosity about a study being handled exclusively by women. It became apparent that the introductory letter had revealed not only that the study director was a woman, but also that all the assistants (*Assistentinnen*) who were also conducting interviews were women. Repeated comments from the deputies to all eight interviewers about the composition of the study staff led us to conclude that having a young, all-female team worked inadvertently to our advantage.

Whatever the reason that may have prompted the Bundestag members to participate in our study, the response rate was gratifyingly high. Out of 195 Bundestag members targeted to be interviewed, 158 actual interviews were taken, for an overall response rate of 81 percent. These figures included the special sample of FDP members, where all fifteen granted interviews. In the regular sample population of 180 Bundestag members from the SPD and CDU/CSU 143 interviews were taken, for an overall response rate of 79 percent. The noninterviews were most heavily concentrated among party notables and government officials, both ex-officio (CDU) and the incumbent SPD members. In addition, two elected Bundestag members died in office and one resigned during the interview period and had not been replaced by others.

When we tallied the deputies who were interviewed by party, the response rate was fairly close: 83 percent of the CDU deputies (seventy-three out of eighty-eight in the sample) as compared to 76 percent of the SPD deputies (seventy out of ninety-two in the sample) had been surveyed. Looking at the basic two-party sample in terms of electoral paths to office, we again found that the response rate for the directly elected candidates matched that of the party list candidates reasonably well. Out of a possible one hundred directly elected representatives sampled, seventy-seven members participated in the survey while sixty-six list candidates from a sample of eighty members responded, for completion rates of 77 percent and 82 percent, respectively. Shifting to the sampled subset of "winners" and "losers" in the majority-rule contest, fifty pairs of interviews from twenty-five districts out of a potential eighty pairs were completed, for a response rate of 63 percent.

The 143 SPD and CDU deputies interviewed in the sample represented ninety-four constituencies. Changing the focus from the individual deputies to constituency characteristics, we made some comparisons between the population as a whole, all 248 *Wahlkreise*, and the population subgroup, the ninety-four districts, along occupational, economic, religious, and political dimensions (Table 4.5). At the aggregate level we found that in every instance except one the sampled constituency population matched the total population almost exactly. The difference between the two groups never exceeded 1 percent on the political, occupational, and economic measures. Only with respect to religion did the sampled group diverge noticeably from the total population statistics: the Catholics in the sampled districts were underrepresented in our study by 4.8 percent.

We also made extensive comparisons between the 2,090 respondents from the INFAS voting study who represented the sampled population from the ninety-four constituencies and the 3,819 voters from the same original study. Table 4.6 presents a summary of the major comparisons that included sex, marital status, income, employment status, church attendance, and union membership, as well as political interest, voting behavior, and party preference. In all instances the differences between the original survey population and the subset matched to the elite sample were only 2 percent or less.

On the basis of these elaborate checks I was reassured that our newly drawn sample had no detectable biases and that I could return to the United States with both data sets in hand, to begin the remaining phases of the project.

FINAL PHASES OF THE PROJECT

Once the data are collected, the major obstacles in a research project are supposed to be over. Although I would agree wholeheartedly with this assessment, my own situation would suggest just the opposite. My return to the United States, to begin a graduate student role once again, required at least as great an adjustment as did my initial trip to Germany. Since I had taken a job as a research assistant at the Center for Political Studies, both to pay my way and also to utilize some of my newly learned skills, work on my own data was done in my "spare time." I spent several months coding the elite data, not an easy task because many of the questions were asked in an open-ended format. (That is, instead of asking respondents to check off one or another answer—"Yes," "No," "None of the above"—they were asked such "open-ended" questions as "What jobs do you perform for your constituents?") This meant that code categories had to be developed and the responses had to be translated into English. I also had to link the issue measures from the mass survey to the elite survey, a task that had to be done largely by hand, because the sophisticated programs that specialize in hierarchical dataset files were not available at that time.

TABLE 4.5
Comparison Between the 248 Wahlkreise *and the 94* Wahlkreise *along Economic, Religious, and Political Dimensions*

	248 *Wahlkreise*	94 *Wahlkreise*
% Pop. in Agriculture	8.3	8.1
% Pop. in Industry	42.4	42.7
% Pop. in Services	28.9	28.8
% Self-Employed	22.7	22.5
% Civil Servants	26.3	25.9
% Skilled and Semiskilled Workers	45.6	46.2
% Catholics	45.5	40.7
% CDU/CSU Vote in 1969	46.1	45.4
% SPD Vote in 1969	42.7	43.3
% FDP Vote in 1969	5.8	5.8

TABLE 4.6
Comparison Between the INFAS Survey and the INFAS Sample Subset along Demographic and Political Dimensions

Respondent Characteristic	INFAS Survey	INFAS Subset
% Male	49.6	49.9
% Married	76.7	77.3
% Employed	55.0	54.2
% Living in Same Community since Birth	39.3	38.9
% Attend Church Regularly	73.5	71.4
% Lower- or Working-Class Self-Identification	41.0	42.5
% Monthly Family Income < 1001 DM	49.7	50.4
% Trade Union Member	26.6	26.6
% Voted in 1969 General Election	89.8	89.9
% Voted SPD in 1969 General Election (2nd Vote)	50.5	50.5
% SPD Identifiers	51.3	50.7
TOTAL *N*	3,819	2,090

My data files were ready for analysis within a year of my return to the United States. The many years of delay between the data-processing phase and the data analysis and dissertation-writing phases were due mainly to my involvement in other survey projects at the center. When I finally decided to finish the dissertation, the analysis and writing took very little time. I was pleasantly surprised to find intriguing twists and puzzles emerging from the analyses. The story line became an interesting one and added several new wrinkles to the empirical study of representation.

In terms of time committed to a project, and especially to a Ph.D., my experience is at least two standard deviations away from the mean. It took much too long. Aside from this factor, however, I felt that I was rewarded and I benefited from every phase of this project. My experience should not frighten off some would-be Ph.D. candidates who want to do "primary research" but rather should encourage them to pursue this course. The rewards of survey research are plentiful.

NOTES

1. A stratified, multistage, random sampling procedure was used.

2. Some of the details of the sample design are presented in Warren E. Miller and Donald E. Stokes, "Constituency Influence in Congress," *American Political Science Review* 57 (1963): 45–56.

CHAPTER FIVE

Strategic Contingencies, Dependence and Power

5. Strategic Contingencies, Dependence, and Power

Politics does not only happen in Congress and the White House. Politics may be defined reasonably as *the use of power to make public choices*, where "public" is understood to mean "on behalf of a group of people." This might then refer to Congress and the president, who make choices on behalf of the United States citizenry, but it might also refer to a factory, where managers and labor leaders make choices on behalf of the workers and shareholders, or to a classroom where a professor makes choices (what shall we need? when and how shall we be tested?) on behalf of the class.

Brudney examines here some theories of how public choices are made in organizations generally. In so doing, he taps into the broad field of organizational theory, which spans several disciplines—political science, sociology, economics, and others.

This paper is particularly interesting for its explicit addressing of theories and for the problems of measurement that arose as Brudney went out and began to interview organization officers.

5A.   Strategic Contingencies, Dependence, and Power*

JEFFREY L. BRUDNEY

The study of power in organizations has generally focused on power from the hierarchical or "vertical" perspective, the archetypical example being the relationship between supervisor and subordinate (Mowday, 1978). A growing body of literature, however, has challenged the adequacy of the hierarchical model as a basis for understanding power in organizations. Critics point out that this model cannot account for differences in power possessed by officials who hold comparable positions in the hierarchy of an organization, a phenomenon noted by several observers (Dalton, 1959; Woodward, 1965: 126–27; Perrow, 1970: 59–60). Nor can the hierarchical model provide an explanation for the surprisingly great power sometimes wielded by "lower participants in complex organizations" (Mechanic, 1962). The vertical perspective is also disputed by "coalitional" or "political" models of power which challenge the assumption that all parts of the organization share the same goals (e.g., March, 1962; Cyert & March, 1963).

As a result of these critiques, a number of theorists have turned away from the vertical approach to examine instead the distribution of power among functional groups, or subunits, at the same level of the organizational hierarchy—a study which Landsberger (1961) christened the "horizontal dimension." This research has yielded two primary perspectives on the determinants of organizational power. The first derives from sociology and is premised on the notion of social exchange (Emerson, 1962; Blau, 1964, 1968). Imbalance in exchange relationships gives rise to dependence of some subunits on others, which, in turn, is a source of power for those that are less dependent. This conception is incorporated in numerous studies of in-

*This article is adapted from the author's unpublished doctoral dissertation, *An Exchange Approach to Intraorganizational Power* (Ann Arbor, Mich.: University of Michigan, 1978). The National Science Foundation and the Horace H. Rackham School of Graduate Studies of the University of Michigan provided support for this research.

traorganizational power dependencies (e.g., Mechanic, 1962; Dubin, 1963; Lodahl, 1973; Cotton, 1976).

The second model is identified as "strategic contingencies" (Hickson, Lee, Schenck, & Pennings, 1971; Hinings, Hickson, Pennings, and Schenck, 1974). According to this view, power is considered a function of the critical environmental uncertainties facing an organization. The greater the ability of a subunit to resolve such problems, and the more exclusive its ability to do so, the greater its anticipated power. This explanation has venerable roots in classic studies by Crozier (1964) and Thompson (1967), which concluded that the ability of a subunit to cope with uncertainty is an important source of power.

This article demonstrates the conceptual similarity between the exchange and strategic contingencies formulations of intraorganizational power. A model based on the exchange perspective is developed, which also examines the impact on power of subunit size and leadership. Data collected from the subunits of six organizations provide the basis for an empirical test.

Strategic Contingencies and Dependence

The prevailing explanation of the horizontal distribution of power in organizations is the strategic contingencies theory. Developed by Hickson et al. (1971) and tested empirically shortly thereafter by Hinings et al. (1974), the theory posits that power is a function of a subunit's control of strategic contingencies, a construct consisting of three variables: (1) the ability of a subunit to cope with environmental uncertainty for the other subunits, (2) the degree to which its activities are interconnected with those of the rest of the organization ("centrality of workflows"), and (3) the availability of alternative mechanisms for coping ("substitutability").

Exchange views of organizational power—the main alternative to strategic contingency theories—are predicated on analyses of the conditions of power and dependence presented by Emerson (1962) and Blau (1964, 1968). This approach posits that power arises from asymmetries in the exchange of resources, that is, from dependence relationships. As Emerson (1962: 32) succinctly put it, "*power* resides implicitly in the other's dependency" (emphasis in original). He stipulated that the dependence of one actor on a second is related positively to the motivational investments of the first in goals mediated by the second, and inversely to the availability of these goals to the first from some source other than the second. That is, A is dependent on B to the extent that B can provide things A wants, and that dependence is less if the things can also be acquired by A other than through B.

Although the terminology employed in the two theories is different, the thrust is very much the same. In fact, Hickson et al. (1971: 217–23), in presenting the strategic contingencies theory, acknowledge their strong intellectual debt to Emerson. Building upon his treatment of power-dependence relations, they argue that the critical issue for the explanation of subunit power is the determination of intraorganizational dependence, or control of contingencies: "Control of contingencies . . . represents organizational interdependence; subunits control contingencies for one another's activities and draw power from the dependencies thereby created" (Hickson et al., 1971: 222).

The parallels between the strategic contingencies and exchange models of dependence can be elucidated. The first of the strategic contingencies concepts, coping with uncertainty, is derived from the pioneering work of Thompson (1967) and Crozier (1964), who recognized the pivotal role played by uncertainty and its resolution in modern organizations. Since "the central problem for complex organizations is one of coping with uncertainty" (Thompson, 1967: 13), those subunits that deal most effectively with most uncertainty provide a resource in great demand by the other subunits. This idea is analogous to motivational investments for goal achievement in Emerson's model of dependence, which refers to an actor's control over access to resources desired by other actors. In fact, a resource can be defined as that which reduces uncertainty. As Hickson et al. (1971: 220) argue, a subunit that copes with organizational uncertainties provides "pseudo-certainty" for the other subunits and garners power from this state of dependence.

The second concept in the strategic contingencies theory, centrality of work flows, consists of two elements: *pervasiveness* (the degree of task interconnection between subunits) and *immediacy* (the speed and severity with which the work flows of a subunit affect the final outputs of the organization). Centrality is intended to assess "the importance of the coping to the outputs of the rest of the organization" (Hinings et al., 1974; 22; cf. Salancik & Pfeffer, 1974: 455; Pfeffer 1977: 256), a further indicator of the desirability of the resources provided by a subunit.

The final strategic contingencies concept, substitutability, taps the second component in Emerson's dependence model, the availability of alternatives. The greater the number of alternative suppliers for a desired service or resource, the less the hypothesized dependence on any one of them. These three "independent variables . . . together . . . determine the variation in interdependence between subunits" (Hickson et al., 1971: 222).

Thus, the strategic contingencies and the exchange formulations of the dependence-power relationship are similar. This presents an opportunity to evaluate the strategic contingencies theory from an alternative perspective. The theory focuses on the sources of uncertainty and the mechanisms by which it is resolved in complex organizations. Exchange theory is predicated on inter-subunit dependencies for services and resources, transactions that ultimately have the same impact (uncertainty reduction) for the subunits. Thus, examination of the distribution of subunit dependencies provides insight into the extent to which subunits control contingencies for the activities of one another. According to both theories, then, it may be hypothesized that the greater the dependence of the other subunits on a given subunit, the greater its anticipated power in organizational affairs. Conversely, the greater its dependence on the other subunits, the less the predicted power.

Based on Emerson's (1962) interpretation of the dependence relationship, these hypotheses are tested empirically below. Also investigated is the role in subunit power of two additional variables frequently overlooked in this connection: subunit leadership and size.

Reacting to a literature that they consider dominated by individual and social-psychological approaches to the study of power in organizations, analyses of the distribution of horizontal power by Perrow (1970), Hickson et al. (1971), and Hinings et al. (1974) concentrate on structural sources and are not concerned with individual characteristics of organizational members. Nevertheless, Dalton (1959) emphasized the importance of the individual dimension, and major theories of power in bureaucratic organizations (Rourke, 1976; Meier, 1979) explicitly incorporate leadership into the model. Moreover, theorists of power have long recognized the problematic nature of the conversion into actual influence of power resources such as wealth, armaments, and structural dependence (e.g., Van Doorn, 1962; March, 1966; Wrong, 1968; Bell, Edwards, & Wagner, 1969; Nagel, 1975; Caporaso, 1978). Some managers may be more skillful than others in this conversion process. By virtue of qualities of leadership such as drive and charisma, they may be better able to increase dependence upon their subunits, to minimize their dependence upon other subunits, and to use the configuration of structural dependencies as a point of leverage in organizational affairs. From this point of view, managerial leadership can be expected to enhance dependence on the subunit, reduce dependence on other subunits, and augment the power of the manager.

The size of a subunit may contribute to organizational power, but only indirectly. Larger subunits are likely to be advantaged over their smaller counterparts in specialization, expertise, variety of functions performed, and of course, personnel. While these are distinct advantages, they can be expected to exert an impact on power only to the degree that other subunits depend upon the services and resources they are used to generate. Thus, it is hypothesized that the effect of size will not be direct but will be mediated by dependence upon the subunit. Even though it might be anticipated that subunit size will reduce the *external* dependence of a subunit on the others, this linkage will be less strong, for the division of labor in organizations virtually assures that regardless of size, a subunit will still require services and resources provided by other subunits.

DATA

Empirical research on the horizontal distribution of power has tended to focus on a narrow range of organizational types. For example, in their empirical tests of the strategic contingencies theory, Hinings et al. (1974) examined five breweries and one container company. Lodahl (1973), Salancik and Pfeffer (1974), and Cotton (1976) concentrated on academic departments of universities.

The sample of organizations in the present study is more heterogeneous, consisting of six organizations, public and private, profit and nonprofit. These include a public transportation authority providing both bus and commuter rail operations; a private corporation manufacturing several lines of programmable computer terminals; the engineering and research center of a large, diverse manufacturing concern; a public utility corporation supplying gas and electric service; the corporate headquarters of a multifactory company; and a nonprofit data processing and analysis organization, which prepares statistical papers and reports for subscribing organizations.

In each of these organizations, data were collected pertaining to the two highest levels of the organizational hierarchy. The first level of horizontal division of labor and responsibility in the organization is divided into subunits which we shall call the *divisions*. These subunits constitute the primary units of analysis. Divisions are further subdivided into *departments*. Structurally, divisions are composed of departments, each responsible for the performance of one or more of the major functions of the division.[1] To illustrate, a typical manufacturing firm might consist of four divisions—finance and administration, sales and marketing, research and development, and production—and the first of these divisions might include the personnel, control, and purchasing departments.

This two-level design was necessary because fieldwork interviews in the sample of organizations indicated that the heads of the divisions, or *vice-presidents,* possessed different types of knowledge from the heads, or *managers,* of the departments. These interviews left no doubt that the division vice-presidents wielded considerable power in the organization. Not only did these officials enjoy virtual autonomy within their divisions, but also they met on a standing basis collectively, and usually individually as well, with the president of the organization, and participated regularly with him in decision making in areas with profound consequences for the organization.

While the vice-presidents were thus able to provide reliable information concerning the critical dependent variable in this study—power—they were not able to provide reliable information with respect to the key independent variable—dependence. The major problem encountered in fieldwork interviews was that the division was too broad and diverse to allow the vice-presidents to discriminate and summarize readily their relative dependence upon the other divisions. For this reason, this information was obtained from *department managers*, who evaluated the dependence of their department upon each of the other departments in the organization. The managers were naturally responsible for a much more circumscribed set of operations than the vice-presidents, and were therefore able to provide a more variegated and reliable assessment of structural dependence. Because the tasks of the division are divided among the constituent departments, the dependence of one division upon another can be derived as a function of the departments of the one upon the departments of the other (see below).

The organizations in the sample displayed comparable horizontal structure, ranging from four to nine divisions, and from sixteen to twenty-four departments. Structured interviews were conducted with the president, the vice-presidents of the divisions, the department managers, and where applicable the executive assistant to the president in each organization. These data constitute complete samples of the divisions and departments in the six organizations. In all, data were collected from the 6 presidents, 38 division vice-presidents, and 115 department managers in these organizations. These data provide the basis for operationalization and empirical analysis.

OPERATIONALIZATION

Dependence

In accordance with Emerson's (1962) conceptualization, subunit dependence is defined as a function of two components: (1) need for services or resources provided by other departments, and (2) the availability of alternative sources for their provision.

Need for Services and Resources

The first component of dependence encompasses any felt need or requirement that one department might have for the services or resources of a second department. Operationally, department managers were asked to rate on a seven-point scale the extent to which their department was "directly dependent upon each of the other departments to do their work." Managers gave a distinct rating with respect to each of the other departments in the organization. The breadth of the item was intended to encourage a comprehensive assessment of interdepartmental needs for services and resources. The complete text of this and all other items may be found in the Appendix.

Availability of Alternatives

For each department for which they had indicated a need for the services or resources provided, department managers were asked to consider whether in the event that these inputs could not be acquired from the customary supplier they could be obtained from alternative sources.[2] Three types of alternatives were examined. The first two of these are *other subunits* capable of supplying the needed services or resources and *other organizations* from which they might be obtained. Third, commensurate with Blau's (1964, 1968) analysis of the conditions of dependence, managers indicated whether if necessary their department might be able to *provide for itself* the services or resources normally received from a given subunit.

Blau's argument fails to take into account the cost and practicality of alternatives. In addition, it ignores organizational regulations, rules, and norms surrounding the exchange of activities among subunits. Other than to remind department managers to evaluate possible alternatives "realistically" and to report only those "feasible for your department" (see Appendix), the indicator of alternative sources employed here is also subject to these criticisms.

Nevertheless, fieldwork and standardized interviews indicated that use of alternatives for the provision of needed services and resources normally supplied by another department was not simply a hypothetical issue to department managers, but a viable response to a dependence relationship which a number of them had contemplated and employed. Managers re-counted instances in which they had turned to alternative sources both inside and outside the organization for the satisfaction of departmental needs. For example, the manager of customer service in one organization, skeptical of the glowing monthly statements prepared by the marketing department con-cerning customer feedback, had established a working relationship with the field engineering department (responsible for organizational field offices) as a more reliable source of information. A second manager was able to persuade one of the production departments in his organization (each responsible for related product lines) to construct the component he required after the others had refused. The manager of sales in a rapidly expanding organization had resolved his dependence on the organization's heavily understaffed advertis-ing department by contracting with an outside advertising firm. Rather than rely on the personnel department of her own organization, another manager insisted on a professional placement service to fill key positions vacated in her department. One organization routinely permitted the use of outside legal firms, even though it maintained a legal staff in-house.

In addition to using other departments and other organizations as alternative sources, department managers proved remarkably resourceful in developing the capability within their department to provide for themselves inputs or contributions formerly supplied (unsatisfactorily) by other subunits. For example, rather than tolerate the impersonality and poor quality of work she had found in the organization's clerical services department, one manager terminated the association of her department with clerical services. Eventually, she was able to hire a stenographer to attend to the needs of her department for secretarial services. Faced with an analogous situation with respect to the organization's centralized maintenance department, another manager withdrew his department from the unsatisfactory relationship and was able to secure maintenance personnel attached exclusively to his own department. Other managers reported that they had striven to acquire broad expertise among their staff in order to provide for future periods in which their relationships with other departments might deteriorate. In the most dramatic case encountered of a department moving to satisfy its needs internally, a research and development unit, frustrated by the consistently low priority assigned to its requests for computer services by the organization's computing center, ultimately was able to convince top management to acquire for the department its own computing facilities.

While the interviews conducted with the department managers in the sample do not warrant a conception of the subunits in an organization as an unrestricted "free market," they do suggest that managers seriously consider and sometimes use alternatives to present exchanges. The three types of alternative sources mentioned most frequently are other subunits, outside organizations, and internal provision.

A Multiplicative Model of Dependence

Operational definitions have been presented for the two components of dependence. It remains to consider the functional form by which these components may be appropriately combined to form measures of departmental dependence. While Emerson's (1962) discussion offers little guidance in this effort,[3] Blau's (1964, 1968) analysis is more helpful. Equating A's dependence on B with B's power over A, Blau maintains:

Finally, if they are not able or willing to choose *any of these alternatives,* they have no other choice but to comply with his wishes, since he can make continued supply of the needed service contingent on their compliance.

. . . To achieve power over others with his resources, a person must prevent others from choosing *any of the . . . alternatives*, thereby compelling them to comply with his directives as a condition for obtaining the needed benefits at his command. (Blau, 1964: 119, 121, emphasis added)

Blau's argument suggests that A remains dependent on B for services or resources unless A has access to *any* alternative, in which case dependence is alleviated or broken completely. This conceptualization of dependence can be modeled well as a multiplicative function in which A's need for services or resources supplied by B is multiplied by the availability to A of alternative sources for these services or resources, the latter component transformed to indicate the presence or absence of alternatives.

More specifically, if department A is dependent upon department B for services or resources and has *no* alternative source for them, then A's dependence upon B is considered equal to A's need for these services or resources. However, if department A has access to *any* of the alternative sources discussed above (other departments, outside organizations, or internal provision), then A's dependence upon B is considered dissipated and, hence, takes the value zero. In the multiplicative model, this interpretation of dependence is accomplished by scoring the availability of alternatives component as 1 if no alternative source is available, and as 0 if any alternative is available.

Dependence is assessed between organizational *departments*, the first level of horizontal differentiation below the divisions. However, the *divisions* are the units of analysis in this study, and in order to derive measures of dependence at this level, the department-based assessments must be aggregated for the division as a whole. Since the departments in a division are responsible for its major functions and work flows, division dependence is operationalized as the *average of the dependencies of its constituent departments*. In this manner, four measures of dependence at the division level are constructed and examined.

Dependence-in is an indicator of the functional dependence of the other divisions in an organization on a given division. The measure is defined as the mean dependence of the departments outside of the division upon the departments constituting the division, where departmental dependence is conceived as a multiplicative function of need for the services of resources provided by a department and the availability of alternatives.

Dependence-out is an indicator of the functional dependence of a given division on the other divisions in the organization. It is defined as the mean dependence of the departments constituting a section on the other departments in the organization, where again departmental dependence is conceived as a multiplicative function of needs and alternatives.

Need-in and need-out. In order to evaluate the explanatory performance of the dependence measures in empirical analysis, two analogous variables are introduced: the need-in and the need-out of a division. These eliminate the availability of alternatives component from the respective dependence measures and are based solely on division need for the services and resources provided by other divisions. Thus, need-in is defined as the mean need of the other departments for the services or resources provided by the departments constituting a given division. Conversely, need-out is considered the mean need of the departments constituting a division for the services or resources provided by the departments outside the division. While the analyses of dependence by Emerson and Blau leave no question of the importance of alternatives in the creation of dependence, comparison of the performance of dependence and need indicators yields insight into the contribution of the availability of alternatives to the explanation of subunit power.

Influence in Decision Making

Vice-presidential power is defined as influence in the resolution of important organizational issues. Exploratory interviews with the president, executive assistant, division vice-presidents, and several department managers in each organization in the sample yielded lists of twelve or thirteen (depending upon the organization) significant organizational issue and problem areas. A careful effort was made to retain in these lists the diversity of concerns voiced across the different divisions. The measure of power used in this study is the average level of influence attributed to the vice-president of each division in decision making across the list of important issues by the president, executive assistant, and the other vice-presidents in the organization. Because fieldwork interviews indicated that department managers did not participate in major organizational decision making, nor did they have influence comparable to these other officials, they were excluded from consideration on this variable.

Leadership

Leadership is intended to tap the personal sources of the power of the vice-presidents. The measure is based on an open-ended item which asks respondents (the president, executive assistant, vice-presidents, and managers) to name the "three people in this organization who have greatest ability to get things done through personal leadership." The indicator employed here is the number of nominations given to a vice-president by the department managers in the organization.

Leadership is an intensely difficult concept to operationalize, and the present measure is vulnerable to at least two challenges. First, it may be argued that vice-presidents of larger divisions will receive more nominations simply because their sections include more departments, and hence, a greater number of managers. However, the item solicited nominations of three officials, and therefore, managers were required to spread their attributions of leadership beyond the vice-president of their section.

Second, although theories of power in bureaucratic organizations contend that power and leadership are distinct concepts (Rourke, 1976; Meier, 1979), it was feared that respondents might equate the two. That is, because a vice-president has influence across a series of important organizational issues, he or she *must* be a good leader. For this reason, care was taken to divorce the assessment of vice-presidential leadership as much as possible from the measurement of influence. First, these variables are derived from different groups of respondents. As explained above, those most knowledgeable regarding organizational decision processes, the president, executive assistant, and vice-presidents, provided the information concerning vice-presidential power, while department managers were the exclusive source of nominations of leadership. Moreover, the types of items utilized are quite different. Power is based on a set of highly circumscribed items soliciting ratings of vice-presidential influence in decision making across a list of concrete issues—a domain in which managers demonstrated little or no knowledge in fieldwork interviews. In contrast, the assessment of leadership is predicated on completely open-ended nominations. This distinction corresponds to the specificity of influence in decision making and the generality of organizational leadership. These precautions help to avert possible contamination of the leadership measure.

Size of Division

Four measures are available for the size of division: number of personnel, percent of personnel in the division relative to the total number in the organization, number of departments in the division, and number of officials reporting directly to the vice-president of the division. Because the first of these indicators contained large outliers, the log of personnel is employed, rather than the simple number of personnel. The four variables are highly related to each other, as shown in Table 5.1 below. Since they were so similar, they were combined into a single measure by the technique of factor analysis.[4]

FINDINGS

Dependence and Power

Applied to organizational subunits, the exchange model of power leads to the hypotheses that dependence upon a division leads to an increase in the power of its vice-president, while the outward dependence of the division upon the other divisions leads to a decrease in vice-presidential power. As elaborated above, these terms are referred to as "dependence-in" and "dependence-out" respectively.

TABLE 5.1
Inter-Correlations of Size Variables
N = 36

	Log Personnel	Percent Personnel	Number Departments	Number Reporting
Log Personnel	—			
Percent Personnel	.64	—		
Number Departments	.50	.58	—	
Number Reporting	.54	.39	.45	—

TABLE 5.2
Regression Analysis of Vice-Presidential Influence in Decision Making[a]
N = 36

Dependent Variable	Explanatory Variables	R^2
Influence in Decision Making	= .49 Dependence-in** − .25 Dependence-out* (.14) (.14)	.32** (0.14)
Influence in Decision Making	= .12 Need-in − .09 Need-out (.17) (.17)	.03 (0.17)

*Statistically significant at $p < .10$
**Statistically significant at $p < .01$
[a]Table reports standardized regression coefficients (beta weights) and multiple correlation coefficients with appropriate standard errors beneath them in parentheses.

The exchange hypotheses are investigated empirically in Table 5.2. The table reports the results of the regression analysis of vice-presidential influence in decision making with predictor variables the inward and outward dependence of the division. In order to serve as a baseline for evaluating the explanatory performance of these measures, Table 5.2 also displays the results of the regression of vice-presidential influence on "need-in"—the need of the other divisions for the services or resources provided by a given division—and "need-out"—the reciprocal need of the division for the services or resources of the other divisions. As explained above, the need measures are analogous to dependence-in and dependence-out, except that they omit the availability of alternatives component of dependence.

Two major findings emerge from the regression analysis. First, the regression equations offer support for the exchange model of power: Both dependence upon a division and need for the services or resources it provides are associated with an increase in the power of the vice-president. The reciprocal dependence and reciprocal need of the division on other divisions are found to decrease vice-presidential power.

Second, the performance of the regression model based on dependence clearly surpasses that of the model based simply on need for services or resources. The regression statistics attest to this conclusion: Neither need-in nor need-out manifests a statistically significant impact on vice-presidential influence, and the "need model" as a whole can account for just 3 percent of the variation in power. In contrast, the effects of both dependence upon a division and its dependence upon others attain statistical significance (minimally) at the .10 level, and the "dependence model" can account for nearly one-third (32 percent) of the variation in vice-presidential influence. Thus, the introduction of the availability of alternatives into the assessment of dependence yields a definite improvement in the explanation of power over the "baseline" need model. For these reasons, the need measures will not be considered in further analysis.

Size, Dependence, Leadership, and Power

Several hypotheses were advanced above regarding the explanation of vice-presidential influence in decision making. In addition to the exchange propositions, which receive strong empirical support in Table 5.2, it was hypothesized that vice-presidents who possess greater skills as leaders would be better able to cultivate dependence on their divisions, to avoid dependence on other divisions, and to achieve greater influence in organizational decision making. It was also suggested that the size of a division would increase the dependence of the other divisions upon it, but that size would have less impact on the external dependence of the division on its counterparts in the organization. Finally, it was anticipated that division size would affect vice-presidential influence only indirectly through the resulting dependencies on the division.

Based on the techniques of path analysis (Land, 1969; Asher, 1976), these relationships are estimated in Table 5.3. The resulting model is displayed graphically in Figure 5.1.

Table 5.3 indicates that all of the estimated coefficients in the model are in the predicted direction, and that the model is more successful in accounting for vice-presidential influence than the configuration of division dependencies alone (Table 5.2). The first two equations show the larger divisions have greater dependence upon them than do smaller ones, and that they are slightly less dependent on other divisions. However, contrary to expectation, leadership is virtually unrelated to either dependence-in or dependence-out. Thus, size appears to be the major determinant of division dependencies, regardless of the leadership skills of the heads of these subunits.[5]

Equations 3 and 4 examine the effects of the hypothesized determinants of vice-presidential influence: dependence-in, dependence-out, and leadership.

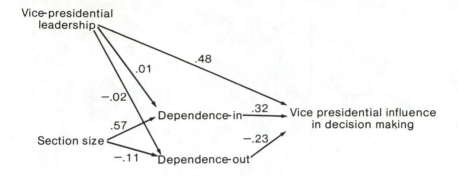

FIGURE 5.1
Estimated Model of Vice-Presidential Influence in Decision-Making

In order to test the impact of size of division, equation 4 also includes this variable. These equations demonstrate three important results. First, as found in Table 5.2, dependence upon a division is related positively and the outward dependence of a division negatively to the influence of its vice-president; the associated coefficients attain statistical significance minimally at the .10 level. These effects again provide support for the exchange model of power. Second, leadership also enhances the influence of the vice-president. This finding attests to the existence of individual sources of organizational power. Finally, equation 4 shows that size of division has only marginal impact on vice-presidential influence. Its effect on power appears to be mediated through division dependencies, primarily dependence on the division.[6]

DISCUSSION AND IMPLICATIONS

The results of this study provide firm support for the exchange model of subunit power. As hypothesized, dependence upon the division is found to increase the power of the vice-president, while its dependence upon the other divisions leads to a decrease in power. These effects persist even when the impact of vice-presidential leadership is taken into account. In addition, this study substantiates the conceptualization of dependence developed by Emerson (1962) and Blau (1964, 1968): its incorporation of the availability of alternatives into the measurement of dependence yields dramatic improvement in explanation over the baseline model predicated on the need component of dependence alone.

These findings are also fully consistent with the predictions of the theory of strategic contingencies. The exchange of services and resources among

TABLE 5.3
Regression Analysis of Model of Vice-Presidential Influence in Decision Making[a]
N = 36

Equation	Dependent Variable		Explanatory Variables	R^2
(1)	Dependence-in	=	.01 Leadership + .57 Size*** (.16) (.18)	.34*** (0.20)
(2)	Dependence-out	=	−.02 Leadership − .11 Size (.21) (.21)	.01 (1.24)
(3)	Influence in Decision Making	=	.32 Dependence-in** − .23 Dependence-out* + .48 Leadership**** (.13) (.12) (.13)	.53**** (0.12)
(4)	Influence in Decision Making	=	.27 Dependence-in* − .22 Dependence-out* + .43 Leadership*** + .12 Size (.15) (.12) (.15) (.26)	.54*** (0.66)

*Statistically significant at $p < .10$
**Statistically significant at $p < .05$
***Statistically significant at $p < .01$
****Statistically significant at $p < .001$
[a]Table reports standardized regression coefficients (beta weights) and multiple correlation coefficients with appropriate standard errors beneath them in parentheses.

subunits helps them to cope with the critical uncertainties confronting them. Asymmetries in these exchanges lead to subunit interdependencies—or control of strategic contingencies. Subunits which mediate the uncertainties of others through dependence relationships were found to enjoy greater power in organizational affairs.

In contrast to traditional approaches which conceive of intraorganizational power exclusively as an hierarchical phenomenon (what we have called "vertical" power), a primary implication of the present research is that horizontal relationships between subunits have consequences for power. Considerations of leadership aside, simply as a result of their positions in a network of work flow exchange relationships, some subunits are more advantaged than others with respect to power. This finding helps to explain the common empirical observation that subunits at the same level of the organizational hierarchy may nevertheless differ in power.

A second major implication of this analysis is that both structural characteristics and individual actors must be included in the explanation of intraorganizational power.

The findings of the present study suggest that models of intraorganizational power incorporating structural and individual sources merit increased development and consideration. Significant strides in this direction have been taken by Salancik and Pfeffer (1977) and Pfeffer (1977). In addition, while this inquiry has pointed to important factors in organizational power, further research is needed to explicate the processes of power—how, when, where, and why organizational vice-presidents (and other members) choose to exert influence. Research that attempts to explain these processes systematically, such as that by Mowday (1978) pertaining to "upward" influence in the organization, is rarely encountered. According to the results of this examination, a model of power based on social exchange offers a promising point of departure.

APPENDIX: VARIABLES

Need for Services and Resources

Departments in organizations can mesh in different ways. Some departments may be able to do their work *regardless* of what happens in other departments. On the other hand, some departments may be *dependent* upon what goes on in other departments in order to do their work. Here is a list of the departments in this organization. Please rate the extent to which your department is *directly* dependent upon each of the other departments to do your work.

Seven-point scale: Not at all . . . to . . . a great extent.
[List of departments in organization follows]

Availability of Alternatives

Now I would like to ask you something a little bit different. Suppose that a *work stoppage* occurred in a department which provides inputs or contributions to your department (For Example: you might imagine that a critical piece of equipment broke down in the department, or that the employees of the department went on strike, etc.). The consequence is that your department could *not* obtain from this department the inputs or contributions it normally provides to you. In that case, your department would have three alternatives:

1. Provide the same or similar inputs or contributions *yourself*.
2. Obtain the same or similar inputs or contributions from *another department(s)* in the organization.
3. Obtain the same or similar inputs or contributions from *another organization(s)*.

If there were a work stoppage in a department that provides inputs or contributions to your department, realistically, would any of these alternatives be *feasible* for your department?

[List of departments in organizations follows]

Influence in Decision Making

Here is a list of issues dealt with by this organization, which was compiled from interviews with several high-ranking organizational officials. Could you please rank the divisions (i.e., vice-presidents) of this organization in order according to their actual influence in decision making on this issue and check the appropriate position on the accompanying scale.

Seven-point scale: No influence at all . . . to . . . Very great influence
[List of important organizational issues follows]

Leadership

Not counting yourself or the president, which three people in this organization have greatest ability to get things done through personal leadership?

Size of Division

Number of personnel in division
Percent of personnel in division relative to total number in organization
Number of departments in division
Number of officials reporting directly to vice-president of division

NOTES

1. Some smaller divisions in the sample of organizations consist of a single department. Typically, these are subunits responsible for highly specialized staff functions (e.g., legal) which lack sufficient personnel to warrant further departmentalization.

2. The alternatives items were restricted to those departments for which the manager had given a rating of at least 3 on the seven-point scale assessing the need of the department for the services or resources provided. Initially, the attempt was made to collect data regarding alternative sources across the entire range of departmental need. However, this procedure was terminated shortly after administration of standardized interviews began for two major reasons: First, little seemed to be gained from the procedure. For very low levels of departmental need (that is, points 1 and 2 on a seven-point scale), managers consistently indicated that outside alternative sources—other departments and organizations—were "irrelevant," and that "we could get by without them" (the department in question), or "we could do it ourselves." Second, the procedure tended to irritate some respondents, who considered the alternatives items "pointless," " a waste of time," when "there is not enough interaction between us and this department to worry about," or "we just don't need them that much." Since the standardized interview schedule was long, and the alternatives items in particular were time-consuming and complex, the decision was made not to jeopardize rapport with respondents for the sake of a procedure that elicited some irritation and little information.

3. Emerson left this issue as an "empirical question." See p. 32 of the discussion, Emerson reference.

4. The factor analysis yielded a unidimensional solution, which accounted for 64 percent of the variance among the indicators. All variables loaded positively on the dimension, with loadings ranging between .61 and .80. Factor scores were computed and serve as the measure of the size of division in empirical analysis.

5. Part of the reason for this finding may be statistical. Analysis of bivariate correlations indicates that, as expected, vice-presidential leadership is related positively to dependence-in ($r = .35$) and negatively to dependence-out ($r = -.08$). However, division size and leadership are themselves highly correlated ($r = .59$); division vice-presidents recognized as better leaders tend to be responsible for larger divisions, although the direction of this relationship is problematic. (These variables are treated as exogenous in the model.) As a result, it can be difficult to distinguish the separate effects of these variables. Nevertheless, statistical theory assures that under this condition, estimates of model parameters remain unbiased (Johnston, 1972).

6. Interestingly, various interactive models that were tried failed to add greatly to the explanatory power of this model. This is striking, because one might surely have expected that the effect of dependency on power would be mediated by the leadership skills the vice-president showed in converting the dependence into power for his or her unit.

REFERENCES

Asher, Herbert B. 1976. *Causal Modeling*. Beverly Hills, Calif.: Sage Publications.

Bell, Roderick; Edwards, David V.; and Wagner, R. Harrison; eds. 1969. *Political Power: A Reader in Theory and Research*. New York: Free Press.

Blalock, Hubert M. 1972. *Social Statistics*, 2d ed. New York: McGraw-Hill.

Blau, Peter. 1964. *Exchange and Power in Social Life*. New York: John Wiley & Sons.

————. 1968. "Interaction, IV: Social Exchange," in *International Encyclopedia of the Social Sciences*, ed. David L. Sills. Glencoe, Ill.: Macmillan Free Press, 7:425–58.

Caporaso, James A. 1978. "Dependence, Dependency, and Power in the Global System: A Structural and Behavioral Analysis," *International Organization* 32:13–43.

Clark, Terry N., ed. 1968. *Community Structure and Decision-Making: Comparative Analysis*. San Francisco: Chandler.

Cotton, Chester C. 1976. "Measurement of Power-Balancing Styles and Some of Their Correlates." *Administrative Science Quarterly* 21: 307–19.

Crozier, Michel. 1964. *The Bureaucratic Phenomenon*. Chicago: University of Chicago Press.

Cyert, Richard M., and March, James G. 1963. *A Behavioral Theory of the Firm*. Englewood Cliffs, N.J.: Prentice-Hall.

Dalton, Melville. 1959. *Men Who Manage*. New York: John Wiley & Sons.

Dubin, Robert. 1963. "Power, Function, and Organization." *Pacific Sociological Review* 6: 16–24.

Emerson, Richard M. 1962. "Power-Dependence Relations." *American Sociological Review* 27: 31–41.

Enderud, Harald. 1976. "The Perception of Power," *Ambiguity and Choice in Organizations,* ed. James G. March and Johan P. Olsen. Bergen, Norway: Harald Lyche, pp. 386–96.

Hickson, D. J.; Hinings, C. R.; Lee, C. A.; Schenck, R. E.; and Pennings, J. M. 1971. "A Strategic Contingencies Theory of Intraorganizational Power," *Administrative Science Quarterly* 16: 216–29.

Hinings, C. R.; Hickson, D. J.; Pennings, J. M.; and Schenck, R. E. 1974. "Structural Conditions of Intraorganizational Power," *Administrative Science Quarterly* 19:22–24.

Johnston, J. 1972. *Econometric Methods*, 2d ed. New York: McGraw-Hill.

Kenny, David A. 1979. *Correlation and Causality*. New York: John Wiley & Sons.

Keohane, Robert O., and Nye, Joseph S. 1977. *Power and Interdependence: World Politics in Transition*. Boston: Little, Brown and Company.

Land, Kenneth C. 1969. "Principles of Path Analysis," in *Sociological Methodology,* ed. Edgar Borgatta. San Francisco: Jossey-Bass, pp. 3–37.

Landsberger, Henry A. 1961. "The Horizontal Dimension in Bureaucracy," *Administrative Science Quarterly* 6: 299–322.

Lodahl, Janice Beyer. 1973. "Power Dependencies and the Structure of University Departments." Ph.D. dissertation, Cornell University.

March, James G. 1962. "The Business Firm As a Political Coalition," *Journal of Politics* 24: 662–78.

———. 1966. "The Power of Power," in *Varieties of Political Theory*, ed. David Easton. Englewood Cliffs, N.J.: Prentice-Hall, pp. 39–70.

Mechanic, David. 1962. "Sources of Power of Lower Participants in Complex Organizations." *Administrative Science Quarterly* 7: 349–64.

Meier, Kenneth J. 1979. *Politics and Bureaucracy: Policymaking in the Fourth Branch of Government*. North Scituate, Mass.: Duxbury Press.

Mowday, Richard T. 1978. "The Exercise of Upward Influence in Organizations," *Administrative Science Quarterly* 23: 137–56.

Nagel, Jack H. 1975. *The Descriptive Analysis of Power*. New Haven, Conn.: Yale University Press.

Perrow, Charles. 1970. "Departmental Power and Perspective in Industrial Firms," in *Power in Organizations*, ed. Mayer N. Zald. Nashville, Tenn.: Vanderbilt University Press, pp. 59–89.

Pfeffer, Jeffrey. 1977. "Power and Resource Allocation in Organization," in *New Directions in Organizational Behavior*, ed. Barry M. Staw and Gerald R. Salancik. Chicago: St. Clair Press, pp. 235–66.

——— and Salancik, Gerald R. 1974. "Organizational Decision Making As a Political Process: The Case of a University Budget," *Administrative Science Quarterly* 19: 135–51.

——— 1978. *The External Control of Organizations: A Resource Dependence Perspective*. New York: Harper & Row.

Rourke, Francis E. 1976. *Bureaucracy, Politics, and Public Policy*. Boston: Little, Brown and Company.

Salancik, Gerald R., and Pfeffer, Jeffrey. 1974. "The Bases and Use of Power in Organizational Decision-Making: The Case of a University," *Administrative Science Quarterly* 19: 453–73.

——— 1977. "Who Gets Power—and How They Hold on to It: A Strategic-Contingency Model of Power," *Organizational Dynamics* 5: 3–21.

Tannenbaum, Arnold S. 1968. *Control in Organizations*. New York: McGraw-Hill.

Thompson, James D. 1967. *Organizations in Action*. New York: McGraw-Hill.

Van Doorn, J.A.A. 1962. "Sociology and the Problem of Power," *Sociologica Neerlandica* 1: 3–47.

Woodward, Joan. 1965. *Industrial Organization: Theory and Practice*. London: Oxford University Press.

Wrong, Dennis H. 1968. "Some Problems in Defining Social Power," *American Journal of Sociology* 73: 673–81.

5B. Research in Complex Organizations: A Personal Essay

JEFFREY L. BRUDNEY

"Congratulations, *doctor,*" the members of my dissertation committee welcomed me back to the hearing room with the traditional greeting extended to anxious students who have successfully defended their dissertations and thus navigated the often circuitous path through graduate school. It marked the first time that I had had the pleasure of this appellation (except in my own wishful thinking), and I could not help but reflect on how long I had labored for the honor. I had entered graduate school nearly six years before, and for the last three of these I had done little besides devote my energies to the doctoral research. I reflected, too, on how different the completed dissertation seemed from the one my committee and I had envisioned at the start of the project. What had happened to the original plan?

I could easily recall the defense of the dissertation prospectus, in which this vision was conceived. In a seminar in organization theory early in my graduate education, I was struck by the inconclusiveness of the research treating power in organizations; I filed this stimulating tidbit away for future use. When the time came to undertake doctoral research, I decided to pursue this broad topic and assembled a dissertation committee both knowledgeable and interested in the area. At the defense of my proposal, then, it came as no surprise that the committee members endorsed the subject of organizational power and the theoretical framework I had developed as worthy of doctoral study. What came as a surprise, however, were the prescient comments and suggestions they offered concerning the *actual conduct of the research*.

Basically, the dissertation proposed to investigate the relationship between dependence and power in organizations. Sociologists had elaborated the idea that dependence is the obverse of power in order to understand a variety of power situations in social life: To the extent that one actor is dependent on a second, the second is thought to have power over the first. The members of the committee considered this a fertile notion for explaining past research results in organizations and making more systematic the study of organizational power, but they questioned the manner in which the necessary sample of organizations and consequent data for empirical analysis were to be obtained.

As a graduate student at the University of Michigan, the home of the most extensive collection of social science data in the world (the Interuniversity Consortium for Political and Social Research, or ICPSR), I had labored under the natural—but, unfortunately, mistaken—impression that surely *one* data set from these vast holdings would satisfy the empirical needs of the dissertation. However, my dissertation committee argued cogently that precisely because I intended to investigate the topic of organizational power from a novel perspective, the appropriate data would *not* be available. This hard fact left two avenues for proceeding with the inquiry: First, I could search the archives of the ICPSR for a usable data set, albeit imperfect for the purposes of the research, yet close enough to its aims to allow "secondary" analysis. The committee expressed skepticism regarding the availability of even such second-best data, and moreover, given the status of the project as a doctoral dissertation, were loath to allow such compromises in the research. Second, I could collect data first-hand, thereby perfectly suited to the study. Clearly, this was the choice of the committee members, and two options had been reduced irrevocably to one. How this preference ultimately resulted in the completed dissertation is the subject of this essay.

OBTAINING FUNDING: WRITING A GRANT PROPOSAL

The prospects of first-hand data collection opened up a myriad of unanticipated problems: What organizations would be used for analysis? How many were necessary? What methods of data collection were appropriate? How would access to designated organizations be secured? And so on.

Underlying these issues was a nagging practical concern: the cost of collecting data in organizations is not trivial, and the question of financial support imposed an immediate and serious obstacle to the research. The dissertation committee recommended that I investigate sources of funding and prepare a grant proposal. The best opportunity for assistance appeared to be the National Science Foundation (NSF), which sponsors a grant program dedicated to doctoral research in the social sciences, especially for that requiring travel.

The NSF grant application solicited an array of information that at the time seemed bewildering. The application requested an explicit statement of the hypotheses guiding the research, the goals of the study, its potential contribution to the literature, and the anticipated findings and their significance. In addition to these academically oriented items, it sought the procedural and administrative details of the project including a timetable for starting and completing each phase of the study; the requirements of the project for personnel, travel, and equipment; and, of course, a budget itemizing and justifying every expenditure of funds. Much of the application seemed backward: the National Science Foundation (NSF) inquired into results, contribution, and significance of the study *before* it was undertaken. I intended to conduct the research in order to provide just such knowledge—but first I needed the financial support.

Despite my initial misgivings, preparing the grant proposal turned out to be one of the most helpful steps in the entire research process. Prior to completing the NSF application, I had developed a viable theoretical framework for the study of organizational power. However, I had not considered how this framework might be implemented in the real world of organizations—a lacuna that had disturbed the members of my doctoral committee. The need for financial assistance forced me to come to grips with not only the design, methodology, and cost of the research but also its likely place in the organizational literature. It surely was not an easy endeavor, but it clarified and operationalized the inquiry to be undertaken.

The first decision concerned the selection of the sample of organizations for analysis. A continuing dilemma in the study of organizations is the trade-off between random and systematic samples. On the one hand, research based on a random sample of organizations facilitates generalization of findings. However, this design may include such different organizations with respect to size, hierarchy, goals, outputs, and so on that meaningful comparison across them may be jeopardized. On the other hand, a sample consisting of organizations of the same type (for example, steel mills) standardizes outputs across organizations, and to some extent other vital characteristics, so that comparability is ensured. Unfortunately, this limitation of the sample means that results pertain to a certain category of organization, leaving open the nagging question of whether they would hold for other sorts of organizations.

Because one of the objectives of the research was to link the distribution of power inside the organization to its outputs, the best strategy dictated a sample of the same types of organizations, so long as they produced a clear, identical output. While I considered the type of organization immaterial, the members of the dissertation committee had different ideas. Since I was a graduate student in the department of political science, they insisted on a sample consisting of public organizations. Otherwise, they argued, the research would not be distinctively "political"—and warned that political science departments interested in hiring a new faculty member might look askance (a warning that ultimately turned out to be valid). It was disappointing to learn that the boundaries between academic disciplines could be so rigid (especially after being introduced as part of my graduate training to the doctrine of the "unity of the social sciences"), but I conceded—and feared—

their point. Public transit organizations and energy-producing public utility corporations, organizations with clear outputs in the public sector, were selected initially as the focus of the inquiry.

With the sample of organizations determined, the next issue was the collection of information from them. A pair of interrelated decisions was necessary: selection of units of analysis to guide the research and development of instruments to ascertain systematic information about them. In order to remove the confounding effect of hierarchy from study results (it is a given that hierarchy awards power and authority to officials fortunate enough to hold positions higher in the pyramid) and isolate the impact of dependence on power, the major divisions of the organization were chosen as the units of analysis. These are the basic subunits into which the work of the organization is first divided horizontally, such as production, sales, finance and administration, and so on. Because each division is headed by an official at the same tier of the organizational hierarchy, typically a vice-president, any differences in power observed across them must be a product of other factors.

The study demanded a wealth of complicated information from the vice-presidents (for example, data pertaining to the dependence of every division upon each of its counterparts in the organization, influence of each vice-president in decision making across a number of important organizational issue domains, and so on). As a result, relatively simple, inexpensive methods of collecting the necessary information, such as mailed questionnaires and perusal of annual reports of the organizations in the sample, were inadequate to the task. Conducting personal interviews with division vice-presidents was the only viable method to obtain these data.

An important consequence of these decisions was to render manageable the practical agenda for conducting the research, which formerly had seemed incomprehensible. A timetable and budget for the study followed more or less directly from the study design. In order to develop standardized interview questionnaires tailored to each organization, I decided to conduct preliminary fieldwork in them. The purpose of these initial visits to the organizations was to build trust and rapport with officials; learn about the key issues, problems, and decision makers in the organization; and determine the structure of the organization and appropriate officials to be interviewed later in the study. This information would facilitate the construction of questionnaires, which would both address the needs of the study for systematic data and maintain the interest and respect of those to be interviewed during a second phase of data collection. The cost and time necessary to implement the two-phase method for obtaining information were built into the grant proposal.

The dissertation committee had no firm ideas regarding the number of organizations to use as the basis for the study. Other than to caution me to examine a minimum of two organizations to avoid obvious problems of idiosyncracies and a sufficient number to yield a "viable database" (whatever that phrase meant), determination of sample size was left to me. Ultimately, the decision was reached largely on the basis of practical rather than substantive critieria: estimates of the time and expense required to collect and process data from an organization. I considered one year the maximum period that should be devoted to these aspects of the study; I had also learned from university sources that chances of funding under the NSF dissertation grant program were greatest for proposals seeking less than $3,000 in support. Allowing a hefty margin for error and unanticipated problems, these two criteria suggested a sample no larger than six organizations. So be it.

When I completed the grant proposal, I truly felt ready to undertake the research. The design and methodology of the study had been made explicit and the attendant procedural details set. During the six months the National Science Foundation stipulated it would require to review the proposal, I planned to relieve my anxiety by conducting fieldwork in public transit organizations and energy corporations close to the University of Michigan (which was all my limited finances could afford). The time would not be wasted.

PROBLEMS IN IMPLEMENTING THE RESEARCH DESIGN: THE SAMPLE OF ORGANIZATIONS

A half-year later, the National Science Foundation awarded me the full amount of funding that I had requested. My delight was dampened, however, by difficulties encountered in the preliminary fieldwork.

The problems were of two types. First, despite the fact that they had been so carefully selected for study, the public transit organizations failed to satisfy the technical demands of the research. Visits to several of them revealed that nearly all of these organizations were quite small in size and not sufficiently complex in structure to allow an interesting test of power-dependence theory. Typically, these organizations consisted of a large operations section responsible for running the public transit system (buses, vans, and so on) and a much smaller administrative component which seemed to exist only to provide operations with support services (personnel, accounting, and the like). Fieldwork interviews left no doubt of the domination of operations in all facets of organizational life—including control of critical dependencies and power relationships. For a study predicated on varieties of dependence-power relationships between departments, these organizations were not suitable. The largest public transit authority in Michigan was an exception to this and, hence, was included in the final sample of organizations.

Fieldwork in the public energy corporations fared no better, but for a different reason. Structural complexity was not an issue, for these organizations were very large, with a maze of divisions, departments, and reporting relationships. Instead, the political environment in which these organizations operate was the source of difficulties. Just as in the early 1980s, at the time this research was conducted (1975–1976), energy corporations were at the center of controversy surrounding charges to ratepayers and stance on nuclear power. As a result, organizational leaders were less than eager to allow access to a researcher, and even when access could be arranged, trust seemed notably lacking. For example, rather than respond to innocuous questions regarding departmental dependence and power, several interviewees insisted on presenting a defense of major organizational policies. Not satisfied with my assurances of neutrality, anonymity, and confidentiality, one official asked for an affidavit that I would not reveal any information ascertained from him in a court of law. Because the data were difficult to obtain and seemed less than scrupulous, I abandoned the energy corporations as well, again with one exception: an organization which welcomed the research as a way to improve its public image.

Anticipating possible obstacles in the grant proposal, I had deliberately left vague the nature of the sample of organizations. For this reason, the collapse of the sampling frame did not strike a crippling blow to the project. I reviewed the major studies in the area of the dissertation and noted that empirical research had focused primarily on universities (convenience and access no doubt had a bearing on this result), thus raising the question of the generalizability of findings. Perhaps, then, the original restricted sample had not been advantageous, for the literature seemed open to a study based on a broader sampling of organizations. Although this design might jeopardize the comparability of the organizations finally examined, I determined to implement it.

GAINING ACCESS

The organizational literature left me totally unprepared for dealing with problems that arise in attempting to gain access to organizations for purposes of analysis. In the course of my formal education, I had not read a single study that acknowledged problems of this kind. As a result of this absence, I had taken for granted the willing cooperation of the organizations selected for inquiry. Fieldwork demonstrated that this assumption is mistaken: As organizations serve as units of analysis in studies of all types—especially in university communities—securing the necessary participation has become increasingly problematic. As evidenced by the reaction of the energy corporations to my research, cooperation even in public organizations is not always assured. When the sample was expanded to include private as well as public organizations, the situation became exacerbated.

Organizational leaders tend to be wary of researchers, and for several good reasons. First, organizational theft and/or sabotage is not an idle threat to these officials, and any intruder must be regarded with at least a modicum of suspicion. Second, while the researcher may not be a "spy," he or she may inadvertently act as one by publishing information damaging to the organization or helpful to its competitors. Surely researchers are careful not to disclose sensitive data, but simple description of one organization in a small sample may reveal its identity to a knowledgeable competitor, who may then profit from subsequent data analysis—in spite of the researcher's promises of anonymity and confidentiality to the participating organization. Third, inevitably the presence of the researcher in the organization constitutes a disruptive force. For example, a few interviewees with whom I eventually became friendly confided that they initially suspected me of acting as an informer for management. Researchers may arouse other suspicions by insisting on getting the "real story," rather than settling for a more prosaic account.

In addition to these intangible costs, the researcher consumes the resources of the organization. Ultimately, the design of this study called for personal interviews, sometimes both fieldwork and standardized, with the president, vice-presidents, and department managers in each organization, truly the key individuals in its functioning. The interviews averaged approximately one hour in length with between twenty and thirty of the highest-paid officials in the organization—not a trivial expenditure of its time and resources.

As a consequence of these liabilities, the analyst must attempt to "sell" the research to the organization. In academics, proposing a novel or provocative question had been sufficient to gain the interest and approbation of my mentors. In contrast, in many of the private organizations I contacted regarding participation in the study, officials sought demonstration that the organization stood to benefit from its cooperation. Although the organizational literature did not prepare me for this endeavor either, I found it a useful one. It was easy enough to offer these officials data obtained from their organization, a summary of major findings of the research, and any further analysis they might desire. But what use would this information be to the organization? A little thought—and a polished presentation—helped to convince skeptical officials that while a study of power-dependence relationships in the organization was unlikely to improve its profit margin, potentially it could pinpoint and ameliorate bottlenecks in organizational work flows, misunderstandings between departments, obstacles to managerial control, and failings in human relations. In addition, the openness of an organization to a researcher could be used by its public affairs office to enhance its image in the community, a fact recognized by at least one energy corporation.

One difficulty in making this presentation was that it had to be descriptive of the nature and goals of the research, yet not so explicit to alert potential interviewees to the actual information sought. Otherwise, the possibility of contamination of the data could not be ignored, for respondents might attempt to confirm or confound the expectations of the analyst (this is the problem of "reactivity"). Moreover, use of academic jargon—in which the research eventually will be codified in published reports—is a self-defeating strategy. This arcane language is foreign to those outside the academic community and serves to confirm popular stereotypes of the irrelevance of "ivory-tower" theorizing; it also leads to resistance on the part of respondents.

Armed with this knowledge, I was able to persuade the leadership of six organizations to participate in the research. Several other techniques were essential in gaining cooperation. First, the analyst must carry letters of reference from members of the university community, such as a college dean. Second and perhaps more important, reference letters from top leadership in organizations that had already participated in the study proved very effective in elaborating the research and defusing potential resistance in new organizations. Third, a memorandum from the head of the organization to interviewees explaining and endorsing the research as well as soliciting their full cooperation is essential.

Finally, I found that the chances of access are greatest at the very apex of the organization. The chief executives of the organizations in this study were well-educated individuals who had been exposed to the concept of scholarly research. As a group, they were far more receptive to the idea of research in their organizations than were subordinate officials, many of whom appeared to define their role as protecting the organization against just such intrusion. I owe a great debt to the leaders of these organizations for their support and to the officials who kindly consented to interviews.

SELECTING INTERVIEWEES AND LIVING ON A BUDGET

Even with access secured, obstacles remained. The most important—and surprising—of these was determining the organizational officials who should serve as respondents for the study. A primary requisite of the research design was to select and interview officials with first-hand knowledge of dependence-power relationships between divisions in their organization. In the few empirical studies in this area, this need had been met by obtaining data from the heads of the major divisions of the organization, such as the vice-presidents of manufacturing, sales, and so on.

Fieldwork interviews showed that the conventional approach would not suffice in the present sample of organizations, however. In describing their jobs, division vice-presidents consistently indicated that they are heavily involved in high-level organizational decision and policy making, but that this preoccupation tends to draw them away from direct oversight of the actual processing of the work of the division and coordination of its work flows with those of the other divisions. As a result, this aspect of the job is routinely delegated to a series of department managers, each reporting to the vice-president and responsible for a significant part of the operations of the division. While the participation of the vice-presidents in the formulation and implementation of policy made them an ideal source of information regarding organizational power, they were not helpful with respect to functional dependence, as the following excerpts illustrate:

Vice-president 1:   You want me to tell you about the dependence of my division on the other divisions—is that right? Well, that's a damned stupid question. I need all of them like hell. I can't hire a man without personnel, and without finance, I've got no money to do anything. . . .

Interviewer: But surely you depend upon the inputs or services of some divisions more than others?

Vice-president 1:   Not really—or at least, I can't make that distinction. Can *you*? Money or people—without either of them, I can't do a thing.

. . . .

Interviewer: How important to the operation of your division are the inputs or services provided by each of the other divisions? Do you depend on some divisions more than others?

Vice-president 2:   You sure ask some tough ones. I honestly don't know if I can answer that. . . . Look, take our dependence on sales and marketing, for instance. The most important thing we get from them—and it's very important—is how many units we have to produce by when. But a lot of the other stuff they send us—market trend reports, descriptions of our competitors' products—we usually don't even look at.

Interviewer: Okay. But do you think you could give me an overall rating?

Vice-president 2:   No. I just don't think so. Look, it's more complicated than I made it seem. Remember, this division [manufacturing] is made up of several departments which do different things. Take our quality control department: they live or die from customer feedback, which also comes from sales and marketing—but this is less important to the manufacturing department. But manufacturing really depends on the production orders from sales and marketing—which are basically irrelevant to quality control. As long as the units test out okay as they go to shipping, quality doesn't care. And let's talk about shipping—that's another of our departments.

They are dependent to a great extent on *both* customer feedback and the orders. If we bang up a unit on the dock and send it out anyway, believe me, we hear about it from the sales representative. On the other hand, the orders sometimes put unreal pressure on shipping to get the units out the door. . . .

I just don't see how I can give you *one* rating of the importance of these inputs to this division. Each of our departments depends on them to a different degree. *Why don't you ask the department managers? They could tell you far better than I.*

Because the vice-presidents were not able to summarize readily the dependence of their division on the other divisions, the advice of the second vice-president was followed: Information pertaining to intraorganizational dependence was obtained from the department managers responsible for the major work flows of the divisions. The responses of the department managers in each division were then aggregated, or averaged, to yield an overall measure of the dependence of their division on the other divisions. Since managers were extremely knowledgeable in this area (coordination with other departments is a major part of their job), this procedure facilitated a more accurate and variegated assessment of dependence. It also reduced interview time with the vice-presidents significantly.

But this solution to the problem of data collection did not come without very real costs. The inclusion of organizational vice-presidents *and* department managers as respondents swelled the anticipated sample size more than fourfold. Ultimately, I administered 163 standardized interviews and conducted another 60 fieldwork interviews to develop questionnaires tailored to the organizations. Because each organization required a different questionnaire for vice-presidents and department managers, twelve instruments were employed in all. As a result, the monetary cost of the development and reproduction of questionnaires far surpassed the amount budgeted in the National Science Foundation Grant—meaning that sacrifices would have to be made later in the project (see below).

Other costs were imposed as well. The mental and physical strain of scheduling and conducting over 200 interviews before any real progress on the dissertation could be made was enormously frustrating. Adding to the frustration was the fact that obtaining data quickly became a mundane, unrewarding, but nonetheless essential, activity. Moreover, the extensive time and travel necessary to complete this phase of the research precluded more stimulating work, such as reading and writing. As a consequence, this period was one of the least enjoyable of the research.

Once the interviews were completed, data processing began. Unfortunately, most of the funds budgeted for this endeavor had been depleted in data collection, so that I could no longer afford experienced help to assist with editing, coding, and checking the completed questionnaires. At the time, I did not consider this shortfall a serious problem, for I viewed these activities (mistakenly) as entirely straightforward. When I reviewed the work of my inexperienced assistants, I was rudely awakened to the error of my (and their) ways. The rate of gaps and errors in the data intended for sophisticated computer analysis was unacceptable. Funds were now even tighter, so that the only option was to redo the entire data processing phase of the study without hired help. With the assistance of friends trained by me, who earned my undying love and gratitude, every piece of information was checked and rechecked. Like the data-collection stage of the research which preceded it, this period was unrewarding.

Finally confident of the accuracy of the information, I arranged for keypunching, entered the data on the computer, and undertook empirical analysis. From this point on, progress on the dissertation—and with it my spirits—quickened until a successful culmination of the research just over a year later. This phase of the study had its share of frustrations and obstacles, too, but these were offset by the challenge and stimulation of confronting substantive hypotheses against actual data.

CONCLUSION

Perhaps the single most important bit of knowledge that I gained from this experience is that research rarely proceeds as it is "sanctified" in books and journal articles. Rather than the neat, logical, deductive method depicted in publications—from stimulus, to hypothesis, to research design, to data collection, to empirical analysis, to results—the research process is often nonlinear and chaotic, fraught with intellectual as well as practical hurdles. Nor is the process particularly stimulating—at least not all the time. Based on the present examination, researchers who intend first-hand collection of data in organizations will spend much of the project making contact with targeted organizations, persuading officials of the merits of their investigation, interviewing respondents, and processing the information obtained for analysis. The quality of the resulting study is just as much a product of these relatively pedestrian activities as of the insight, creativity, and scholarship that spark and guide most research. As I learned from painful experience, the investigator can afford to overlook none of these components of empirical inquiry.

A second lesson of this study is the necessity to devote significant time and resources to planning. Surely any research in ongoing organizations will encounter unexpected problems and situations, for organizations are inordinately complex and confusing, often even to their members. However, despite the substantial investment in planning and grant preparation in this research, too many surprises occurred to stymie its progress. For example, preliminary fieldwork in the energy corporations and the public transportation organizations originally selected for analysis would have revealed to me their nonsuitability for the needs of the research. Similarly, fieldwork interviews in virtually any large organization would have demonstrated the necessity to obtain data from not only division vice-presidents but also department managers (contrary to the research design commonly reported in literature in this area). Both of these facts could and should have been ascertained prior to the submission of the NSF grant proposal. They would have then been incorporated into the grant, avoiding difficulties and frustrations later in the project.

Thirdly, this study became overly preoccupied with obtaining data from a large number of cases for purposes of analysis. Certainly, the social sciences place a great premium upon quantitative analysis, and the doctoral committee overseeing this research was correct to insist on data from at least two organizations in order to combat obvious dangers of idiosyncratic findings. Yet, because of problems with the sample (for example, randomness, representativeness), I am not satisfied that an analysis strategy based on six organizations had any real advantages over one based on a smaller number. Had the number of organizations been reduced, more fieldwork could have been undertaken in each one. This design would have lent background to the study and would have helped to elucidate the *context* in which dependence and power operate in organizations.

Any study that undertakes data collection faces a difficult trade-off between breadth of sample and depth of information obtained. This one paid dearly for the breadth offered by six organizations. So much time and so many resources were consumed simply in collecting interview data that in-depth assessment of context, which could have added richness and detail to the dissertation, was not possible. In addition to this intellectual lacuna, obtaining this information was a tedious, painstaking process that deprived much of the ongoing investigation of the stimulation and enjoyment that should accompany the research experience in political science.

Finally, I gained an unanticipated benefit from this study: knowledge of the way research is actually conducted in organizations, which I have put to good use since. At the end of the project, the dissertation demonstrated some insight into power-dependence relationships in complex organizations. In addition to this substantive knowledge, it documented the process by which the inquiry had evolved from a nebulous prospectus through challenges, obstacles, false starts, and plain hard work to a credible research product. Both types of learning are valuable. As the members of my doctoral committee exited the hearing room, I did not know which of these facets had played the larger role in their favorable evaluation of the dissertation, nor did I think it terribly important.

Congratulations, *doctor*.

CHAPTER SIX

Desperate Deeds, Desperate Motives: Legal Politics in Kentucky, 1818–1832

6. "Desperate Deeds, Desperate Motives": Legal Politics in Kentucky, 1818–1832

It may seem strange that I have included an historian among the authors in this book, but I did so for two reasons.

First, many undergraduates, especially when they do political science research, do essentially historical research, albeit research on a more recent period than the early nineteenth century. Biographical research on a major leader, a case study of a local governmental decision or of a bill in Congress—these require historical research, though they address very recent history.

Second, just as I believe there is a basic unity to all political science research, I believe that unity extends to the study of history. Historians, just as much as political scientists, build their work on the basic structure of inquiry that I outlined on pages 1–5; and they, just as much as political scientists, share the task of the "true detective" as Ball portrays it.

While we are doing basically similar things, however, there is a difference in emphasis, which means that there is something important we can learn from historians and something important that they can learn from us. Political scientists usually pay a good deal more attention to theories and to the development of general propositions than historians do, while historians have usually taken much more care than political scientists to exhaust all possible empirical evidence and to be careful in using it. If historians sometimes run the danger of writing a pretty story which is not involved enough in theory or generalizations to mean anything beyond the single instance that is described, political scientists sometimes run the danger of shooting off half-cocked with a pretty theory which is supported by chance evidence of a dubious nature.

One thing to look for in Van Burkleo's essay, then, is the common basic logical structure to this and to political science. Another thing to look for is the typically careful search for evidence—an area in which political scientists have much to learn.

6A. "Desperate Deeds, Desperate Motives": Legal Politics in Kentucky, 1818–1832

SANDRA FRANCES VAN BURKLEO

Historians have long portrayed the Panic of 1819 as a traumatic moment in American economic, legal, and political development. Financial collapse, depression, and political disarray were familiar in the United States; but this panic certainly represented the most devastating crisis in thirty years of growth under a strengthened constitution. Credit and the money supply evaporated, while banks and trading houses disappeared, virtually overnight. And the effects were most pronounced in the agrarian West and South, where currency and credit shortages had been chronic: the downswing began as early as 1818, plunged deeply, and lingered well into the 1820s.[1] For those with ready cash, bargains in real estate, steamboats, and slaves were commonplace. Citizens were alarmed. Did the crisis signal permanent decline? William Waller, the Bank of Kentucky's cashier in 1818 and a river-trading panic victim, worried aloud about "combinations on foot" to undermine western finance; and the *Kentucky Gazette*'s editor, John Bradford, reported in May 1819, that his countrymen were "writhing under agonies of the severest pressure."[2]

These were tangled, darkly humorous times. Throughout the West and South, elected officials sought explanations and solutions; and in Kentucky, panic-led political reactions both resembled and departed from developments in other western states. As in Missouri and Tennessee, for instance, an amorphous "relief movement" emerged. Farmers and merchants clamored at courthouses for easy credit, cheap paper currency, and protection from bankers, the sheriff, and various "revenuers."[3] Relief agitation coincided as well with legislative reorganization. The Kentucky Assembly abruptly polarized into hostile Relief and Anti-Relief coalitions, which cut across traditional Federalist-Republican party lines. The burgeoning Relief Party gained a legislative majority and, by 1820, had captured the statehouse.[4]

Legislative debate thereafter was acrimonious and frenzied. Over the loud objections of an Anti-Relief minority, Relief members passed a sweeping statutory program aimed at the temporary suspension of contract obligations. Revised execution statutes prevented complete financial ruin at the auction block; and bankruptcy and stay laws were designed to preserve individual fortunes during years of monetary contraction in which banks were calling in, or refusing to renew, outstanding notes.[5] Legislators also created a short-lived but useful public bank (probably the Relief party's most radical innovation) to provide credit and a local currency, and to offset the practices of the Bank of Kentucky and the Bank of the United States—both bastions of "sound money" conservatism. Backed only with newly ceded Indian lands, this new Bank of the Commonwealth soon exacerbated the monetary crisis. There were public banknote burnings to restore confidence, and out-of-state merchants understandably viewed unstable, expedient paper with skepticism.[6] But the bank's real strength rested with its statutory association with the new stay law. Whenever banks refused to renew loans, Kentuckians were authorized to initiate a "replevy bond," which effectively postponed debt settlement for several years.[7]

Kentucky's list of villains was long and bewildering, and the complexity and vehemence of Relief politics quickly outstripped activity in neighboring states. Americans after 1818 were eager to find "alien" intervention in local economies; but Kentuckians outdid themselves. Politicians and financiers fastened blame upon the Bank of the United States' monetary policies, shadowy speculators cornering land and currency markets, or "Money Men" at the once-respected Bank of Kentucky. They pointed as well to designing Virginians, undercapitalized wildcat banks known collectively as the "Forty Thieves" before their demise in 1820, "tyrants" among State Court of Appeals justices, and by 1821, John Marshall's United States Supreme Court— allegedly bent upon reducing Kentucky, in Justice William Johnson's cantankerous opinion, to a state of "hopeless imbecility."[8]

But what did Virginians, John Marshall, land, and banks have to do with the Panic of 1819 and "relief"? This pantheon of enemies, while dizzying, accurately reflected Kentucky's highly atypical situation among emerging western states. Before the leadership could exert control in a financial crisis, it had to reverse decades of constitutional dependence in relations with Virginia. Its relief agenda therefore was broad, complicated, and focused frequently upon external relationships—leading, not surprisingly, to a dramatic, extremely visible course of events. Interestingly enough, the limited, remedial economic measures so characteristic of relief legislation elsewhere were the least durable consequences of Kentucky's relief activity. Bankruptcy, execution, and stay laws, for instance, were impermanent creations, temporarily softening but not reversing a legal tradition which revered scrupulous contract performance.[9] Far more important in the long run were Kentucky lawmakers' changes in land law, in redefining their constitutional relations with Virginia, and in domestic improvement—a curious legacy in the wake of an economic crisis.

Kentucky had been bound since 1792 by an extraconstitutional separation agreement through which Virginia, without formal congressional approval, had granted its westernmost province its statehood. Dutifully incorporated into the new state's constitution, the compact stipulated, among other things, that Kentuckians would do nothing to prevent the perpetual exercise of old treasury and military land warrants by Virginians in Kentucky "reserves," even when settlers already tilled the land and had been granted a well-documented but more recent Kentucky title.[10] The Assembly was free only to regulate: to oversee eviction proceedings; to assign commissioners, to suggest a length of time after which "squatters" might gain the right to argue color of title in courts of chancery, to demand compensation for good-faith improvements from successful nonresident claimants, or to confiscate and sell tracts for tax default.[11] And, for reasons that historians have not understood entirely, many Kentuckians after 1818 were no longer content to relinquish ultimate control over land distribution. A long-standing, nettlesome compact became an acute political grievance, and legislators set about defeating it with vigor—all in the name of "relief."

The four components of Kentucky's relief agenda—debtor relief, banking stabilization, land title security, and internal improvements—have been treated often as discrete issues in economic, political, and legal history.

Economic scholars have been interested primarily in the state's contributions—or resistance—to long-term modernization in the nineteenth century. And this focus, combined with compartmentalization by issue, has led to competing explanations for legislative and judicial decision making. Debtor relief laws, for example, are associated with anti-contract and anti-banking sentiment elsewhere; and banking developments, such as the creation of a public bank or Kentucky's early attempts to tax the Bank of the United States, have been viewed as contrary forces in the century-long drive toward marketing and financial centralization. Economic historians, moreover, typically interpret Relief and Anti-Relief allegiance as a struggle between relatively static camps of debtors and creditors, interrupting but not preventing modernization.[12]

In politics and law, Kentuckians win more praise. Scholars have identified incipient Jacksonian democracy in a grass-roots "relief movement," which was translated directly into Assembly politics and which culminated in party nationalization by 1828. In this view, Relief assemblymen defended angry tenant farmers against well-entrenched "monied interests," intending to democratize commerce and politics.[13] Public lands historian Paul Gates similarly views the relief years as a "delightful interlude" in American legal practice because they dramatized the process by which land law in western states became increasingly responsive to frontier circumstance. And legal scholar Morton Horwitz, who usually finds irony in legislative victories, concludes that land law evolved differently than contract law, embracing egalitarianism by century's end.[14]

Constitutional historians, intrigued primarily by the Supreme Court's behavior in the so-called Kentucky Cases and by the state's very colorful noncompliance, interpret relief sentiment as an early expression of states' rights ideology leading sadly but inexorably toward sectionalism and the Civil War. In recent accounts—histories written in the wake of legal realism, which generally associate noncompliance with "bad law"[15]—Relief supporters are seen as having courageously pursued an equitable system of private law, as well as meaningful statehood, against the Marshall Court's rigid, antiquated Federalism and its Anti-Relief empathizers. The High Court is often charged with technical error, insensitivity, and perhaps with responsibility for ominous tensions between state and federal authority, while Anti-Relief partisans were motivated mainly by nationalism or unwarranted elitism.[16]

Charles Grove Haines once called this tension between local and national interest, with its strong imputation of mutual exclusion and irreconcilability, the "central issue" in pre–Civil War constitutional politics; and the "nation versus state" synthesis is powerful—partly because historians know that the Civil War eventually came, but also because Kentuckians repeatedly made their case for local necessity in legislative and judicial chambers through the familiar language of state sovereignty. Few formal arguments appear with greater regularity in the public record throughout the century; and images of an incremental march toward war therefore compel, if only by sheer weight of evidence. Joel Silbey perceives that the war exerts a "pernicious influence" in historical studies; yet scholars still must contend with a thick wall of language allied firmly with the "nation versus state" umbrella.[17]

Taken together, then, these accounts portray Relief partisans as virtuous egalitarians, tainted mainly by the charge of debt evasion and economic obstruction, while their Anti-Relief opponents are paternalistic, sometimes treacherous entrepreneurs, exonerated only by economic foresight. The "radicals" surrounding Relief leader Amos Kendall were moved by a mixture of benevolence in debtor-creditor relations, animosity toward a monied class, sympathy for tenant farmers and democratization, and preference for a fortress commonwealth protected against outsider encroachment or external entanglement. Anti-Relief activists, on the other hand, were interested in self-preservation, elite hegemony in political and economic life (whether for benign or malevolent reasons), reactionary legalism, and increased identification with the nation, even at the expense of local autonomy. The two camps, in short, occupy very different ground.

In 1819, however, Kentuckians intended to reach outward toward national involvement rather than to retreat inward. The legislative leadership, both Relief and Anti-Relief, included merchants, bankers, planters, attorneys, and mill owners—men with a clear stake in the commonwealth's effectiveness as a unit of political and economic organization. All were entrepreneurs, or dependent upon Bluegrass entrepreneurship; and, with passage of the stay law in 1821, even old fortunes were rendered insecure. When the Clays, Crittendens, Marshalls, and others confronted economic depression, they accurately perceived that the crisis was basically financial; that only the best-capitalized individuals and institutions would survive; that access to credit was essential; and that Kentucky, mainly because of the crippling separation agreement with Virginia and its disadvantageous western location, did not enjoy full reciprocity in commercial exchange or the legal wherewithal to mobilize internal resources.

Legislators agreed that constitutional limitation was finally intolerable; and they agreed further that Kentucky's best interests as a staple-producing hinterland state rested with eventual national integration. The leadership, in other words, pursued domestic consolidation and the agreement's defeat in *order* that citizens might participate in national life more completely and less precariously. These were nineteenth-century economic thinkers: to secure private interest was to guarantee public growth and security. If leaders agreed about objectives, however, they disagreed violently about the legal and political means best calculated to secure stability and prosperity. Anti-Relief partisans adhered to restrictive fiscal policies—"sound money," tight credit, and state-licensed but privately managed banking—and to strict contract performance. And they preferred to compensate Virginians for the value of landholdings whenever their claims were found superior at law. Relief legislators urged inexpensive currency, liberal credit, and public finance. They also recommended short-run abrogations of tradition in contract law, not to undermine private fortunes, but to protect them, fearing that sacrifices of property encouraged immoral speculation and concentration.[18]

The four issues addressed during these years, moreover, were actually bound together. And the tie that bound was private banking. The land title question gained political force basically because landholdings supported individual wealth in bank stock, and because the survival of private banks depended almost entirely upon the validity of land titles backing bank mortgages.[19] Stay laws and other anti-contract legislation seriously damaged banking liquidity: an uncollectable note was at best a worthless asset and often a liability. And political identification—which was remarkably fluid rather than static—generally mirrored individual stake in, or indebtedness to, Kentucky's primary financial institution before 1818, the Bank of Kentucky. Anti-Relief support can be associated with individuals whose assets in the bank exceeded their indebtedness, while Relief partisanship correlates strongly (although not perfectly) with outstanding notes in excess of stock—a situation which drove many bank customers toward affiliation with the new Bank of the Commonwealth. Partisanship and banking affiliation, moreover, shifted with financial condition. Merchants and speculators moved as necessity dictated from one institution or coalition to another; and relief measures were supported selectively, often as circumstance dictated.[20] And a successful internal improvements program—begun years earlier but soon abandoned—required a predictable source of financing and secure land titles, neither of which were available before 1826.

Before all else, then, assemblymen had to defeat that burdensome Virginia-Kentucky compact. While the Relief Assembly enacted its various economic measures, created a new bank, and focused political wrath upon the Bank of Kentucky's "Money Men,"[21] Henry Clay and other Anti-Relief sympathizers challenged the Marshall Court's conservatism between 1821 and 1823 in the case of *Green* v. *Biddle*. Richard Biddle, a middling Kentucky planter, had been evicted by the heirs of Virginia's John Green; and Biddle's appeal tested the ongoing force of the separation agreement and, indirectly, the validity of Kentucky's statute of limitations as a route to conclusive title.[22] When the Court denounced the state's pretensions as flagrant violations of the contracts clause—a decision anticipated in Kentucky—the Assembly refused to comply. Legislators memorialized Congress for harsh restrictions of federal judicial authority in state affairs, ignored federal marshals, and hastened the High Court's incremental retreat on the land question between 1825 and 1831.[23]

Relief partisans also confronted an Anti-Relief State Court of Appeals in land and stay law litigation, lost, and refused to accept defeat. Justices had declared stay laws unconstitutional and had declined to rule on the incendiary land issue; and Relief insurgents therefore created an alternative "New Court," which sat across town from the "Old Court." The New Court was pledged to the entire Relief program, and it brought the state very near civil war before it was quietly dismantled.[24] In debtor-creditor relations, Kentuckians urged that circumstance superseded strict law, and in land litigation they similarly argued from the rules of equity, not from the letter of old state statutes, disregarding their original, purely compensatory spirit. Necessity, not antiquity or formal right, the Assembly insisted, should determine resource distribution. And this posture was strengthened by passage of a particularly belligerent land statute a year after financial collapse.[25]

Supreme Court Justice Joseph Story certainly perceived that Kentuckians intended a major legal revision, announcing in 1821 that the state's seven-year statute of limitations was "part of a *system*," the object of which was to defeat the 1792 agreement, and with it traditional deference to the common law.[26] One Relief pamphleteer even publicized this heretical idea: "It is not principles and men—it is first MEN!" he wrote, "then laws calculated for their happiness. . . . Our principal objects [are] to reestablish public spirit and to consolidate the stability of the state by the security and attachment of its husbandmen . . . to the soil."[27]

"Laws calculated for happiness," however, spelled doom—not only for many Virginians, but also for the Bank of Kentucky's stockholders. The bank's difficulties dated from 1818 when its president, Robert Alexander, contacted other western bankers in an unsuccessful attempt to create a regional protective association against the national bank's formidable resources. Profit, wrote Alexander, was "no object compared with safety."[28] And his premonitions were well founded. With legislative licensing of numerous wildcat banks in 1818, and the Bank of the United States' severe contractions shortly afterward, pressures were finally insurmountable. The bank suspended specie payments, began calling in notes, lost credibility with important trading houses in Baltimore and New Orleans, and then lost its charter to the Relief Assembly. And stock certificates, once $200, plummeted by 1821 to one-half of their face value.[29]

After 1821, Clay, Rowan, Wickliffe, and others amassed hundreds of shares of devalued Bank of Kentucky stock, either through speculative purchase or as payment for debt. Clay's certificates, for instance, equaled at least $12,000, and Rowan's about $9,000.[30] Robert Alexander privately acknowledged a stockholders' scramble at the Frankfort office; and, were stock values to be restored,[31] these shares represented a promising investment. Clay's denunciations of the Bank of the Commonwealth in a stockholders' meeting therefore reflected both ideological and material concern. Alexander expressed similar anxieties, labeling the stay law a "disaster" for bank collections; and Bank of Kentucky directors devoted much time after 1819 to research into the security of titles underpinning requests for note renewal.[32] Branch bank boards filed hundreds of suits, and clerks compiled long lists of defaulted notes in which Relief partisans figure prominently.[33] When Clay and his colleagues argued state sovereignty before the Virginia Assembly and the Supreme Court, in short, they were defending the Bank of Kentucky as surely as Richard Biddle.

The Relief legislature, suspecting collusion, stipulated in 1820 that bank directors could not serve simultaneously as lawmakers—whereupon John Crittenden, massively indebted to the Bank of Kentucky, resigned his directorship to become president of the Bank of the Commonwealth. And land speculator Humphrey Marshall, reputed to be hopelessly in arrears at the Bank of the United States, moved in and out of the new bank's directorate with dazzling speed.[34] The scene was complicated by land agents whose fortunes depended upon the validity of Virginia titles. With the opening of Indian lands west of the Tennessee River in 1818, Cuthbert Anderson, James

Marshall, and other members of a prestigious Frankfort firm solicited new business among Virginians. The firm located, surveyed, and secured large tracts for holders of old warrants, then received one-third of the acreage as payment.[35] These were the same lands, moreover, that backed the assets of the Bank of the Commonwealth and were being farmed by numerous irate farmers. Anderson and Marshall approached the Bank of Kentucky in 1819 for note renewal, were refused, and transferred stock to the cashier, presumably to cover defaulted notes. In 1822 James Marshall was elected a Bank of the Commonwealth director. One hard-pressed farmer in Princeton, Kentucky, complained to the governor that the new bank was little better than its predecessor, denying help to those with "little means," and the charge elicits sympathy.[36]

The Assembly's seemingly paranoid vision of alien encroachment—by Virginians, the Bank of the United States, or federal courts—also enjoyed a firm foundation in fact. And the central avenue by which out-of-state interests found expression in Kentucky was the lower federal judiciary. Circuit and district courts *were* a threat to local bankers and merchants; for, as early as 1818, Justices Todd and Trimble could satisfy only those whose interests originated beyond state borders. Those interests, moreover, were not limited to landholdings. By 1819 the Supreme Court was pitted firmly against contract renunciation and mobilized behind the claims of internal revenue agents and the national bank, and inferior courts adhered scrupulously to High Court guidelines.[37]

The District Court after 1817 ruled without exception in favor of internal revenue agents whose suits represented a majority of the court's caseload. After 1818 most Kentuckians failed to appear, granting the plaintiff judgment by default. Pipes of brandy, stills, and tobacco were seized regularly and sold for taxes, while steamboat owners suffered enormous losses. Kentucky traders and bankers often owned their own boats, which by 1820 were often impounded to compensate captains and crews for unpaid wages.[38] Benjamin Crandall, for instance, captain of the steamboat *Elizabeth*, won his wages by default in December 1822, as did Daniel Green and Francis Ames in a suit against the owners of the steamboat *Mars*.[39]

The Seventh Circuit Court was busier and more powerful than the district tribunal, routinely granting the claims of treasury or post office agents for amounts typically in excess of $20,000.[40] In May 1819 the Bank of the United States sought its first major judgment in a suit against land surveyor Richard Taylor—a member of Cuthbert Anderson's hard-pressed land agency—and hundreds of actions followed. On November 27, 1820, for instance, sixty-eight judgments were awarded the bank in amounts ranging from $400 to $7,000, and the deluge continued through 1823, involving such luminaries as Amos Kendall, the hapless William Waller, Humphrey Marshall, and John

Crittenden. In May 1822 the bank began seeking injunctions in chancery. On May 14 twenty-one requests were granted; fifteen more appeared the next day; and there were hundreds thereafter.[41] John J. Marshall lost a house and lot, as did Richard Taylor and several Johnsons—many as partial reimbursement for defaulted notes exceeding $10,000.[42]

In land litigation—the circuit court's weightiest chore—Virginians filed suit upon suit, relying upon the court's jurisdiction in conflicts between citizens of different states. Kentuckians again commonly stayed home, and the court just as typically ordered surveys under the marshal's watchful eye, "lest force be offered." When citizens did appear, they simply agreed to "insist upon the title only"—an agreement bound to defeat "junior" Kentucky titles—and possession was swiftly transferred to Virginians, or to Kentuckians claiming title based upon old Virginia grants. Once evicted, unhappy "tenants" were left the option of a compensatory hearing in chancery to secure reimbursement for improvements and hopefully to be relieved of rental charges.[43] Legislative memorials, newspaper articles railing against usurpation or the flight of settlers, and fears about confusion in agriculture, then, were linked as directly to lower federal court activity as to the Supreme Court's more conclusive but less constant hostilities. But Kentuckians were ingenious evaders. Compensatory proceedings were pursued sometimes only to deplete a nonresident's resources; for, if Virginians could not compensate tenants, or if improvements exceeded the fair value of land, title reverted to the occupant. Many dispossessed settlers refused to vacate, risking contempt charges, or procrastinated for years through repeated requests for leave to gather evidence.[44]

Why might Todd and Trimble have persisted so tenaciously? Surely their unyielding conservatism was compatible with the judiciary's traditional support of creditors against defaulting debtors, of the national bank, and of vested interests more generally. But the defeat of Kentucky's land law system did threaten the Bank of Kentucky as well as the Bank of the United States whenever its claims rested upon Kentucky land titles. For these justices, the Assembly's resort to the rules of equity, and in particular their unusual employment of those rules, introduced important doctrinal issues quite apart from material concern. Todd feared for the common law itself—for its conclusiveness, and for its traditional, controlling relationship with the rules of equity. Kentuckians, he concluded, had created an alternative rather than inferior, complementary, and analogous body of rules which, if left unchecked, suggested an imponderable revision: equitable injustice.[45]

Thomas Todd expressed his concerns in 1819 in a labored circuit court decision on behalf of the ubiquitous John Green. Kentucky's Bernard Gittner and others had hoped to bar Green's claim through Kentucky's statute of limitations, which allowed residents to argue color of title after seven years' occupancy and improvement. Gittner was even prepared to demonstrate twenty years' settlement, the standard at Virginia law—not simply to secure reimbursements, but as a "Compleat bar" to Green's claim. Justice Todd was unmoved. Courts of chancery, he wrote, "do not proceed upon general principles of equity; but exercise Jurisdiction on the law side of the Chancery and are governed by principles of law." It was plain to Todd, in this instance and in others to follow, that "there could be no such equitable principle as a positive bar in equity . . . independent of . . . the spirit and intentions of the Statutes," for equity regarded length of time only "as a Circumstance in guiding and assisting the conscience . . . of the Chancelors but not as a positive Bar, per se."[46]

Justice Robert Trimble refused to reopen the issue several years later, shortly after the High Court's reinforcement in *Green* v. *Biddle*.[47] And Henry Clay, interestingly, was aware of this doctrinal distinction, telling his friend Thomas Bodley in November 1821 that he had little hope for the survival of the notion that "twenty years adverse possession constitutes a Bar to a bill in equity." Clay wanted to argue the point in state courts because "many parties were interested" and because its adoption would have afforded him "particular satisfaction."[48] But arguments failed in the State Court of Appeals until 1825, when the United States Supreme Court, and then the state bench, tacitly accepted the twenty-year standard.[49] Adoption of the rule effectively resolved Kentucky's land title dilemma and soundly defeated the 1792 separation compact: Unlike common law actions of ejectment, which could be argued many times, these decrees in chancery were analogous to rulings on a writ of right—which, as Thomas Todd had noted with some anxiety, were "final and conclusive, between parties forever."[50]

With the lifting of economic hardship after 1825, the closing of the Bank of the Commonwealth, and the return of Bank of Kentucky stock to par, the Assembly was free to launch a program of road and bridge construction, river improvement, canal building, and agricultural experimentation. Working closely with the governor's office, Kentuckians even dabbled in railroads. State Senator Robert McAfee, an "American System" Whig, explained in 1827 that the legislature was "busily engaged in providing the ways and means [for] Internal improvements. . . .[O]ur table in the Senate is literally covered with projects."[51] In 1817 improvements had languished, but by 1828 private companies in which the state commonly subscribed for one-half of the stock, proliferated. Twelve acts supporting land surveys, bridges, tollgates, and other improvements appeared in 1826. A year later, there were twenty-three; in 1828, thirty-two; and by 1830, forty-seven. Old Bank of Kentucky officials and customers dominated company directorates. John Sneed, once a bank clerk, was president of the Shelbyville and Louisville Turnpike Company, while Valentine Peers, a major bank stockholder and elder statesman, directed the Maysville Turnpike Company.[52]

Circulars emphasized linkages between private and public enterprise, and between state and national interest. And many were addressed to citizens "grown weary of Monopolies."[53] The leadership of the Louisville Turnpike Company, including former Bank of Kentucky directors John Speed and William Pope, urged the company's "great and good benefits for citizens at large," and the Maysville directors, remembering that similar efforts in 1817 had "failed in effect," hailed the removal of "difficulties and obstacles hitherto held to be almost insurmountable."[54] One of those hurdles had been financial, but in 1828 the governor's office approached the national bank for assistance and found it "congenial." In the same year, Kentucky hired its first trained engineer, and asked the secretary of war for a "distinguished Officer of the Engineer Corps" to orchestrate the "madness" of railroading.[55]

Merchants foresaw a "new era" in Kentucky through domestic improvement which, "though *local,* in a great degree . . . blends with its locality, an obviously *general* interest." Roads and canals improved interconnection with Tennessee and New Orleans in the "easy and safe transmission of . . . surplus products to the several points or places of exportation."[56] The Assembly memorialized Congress to secure federal support, and merchant Lewis Vimont, an improvements booster in the legislature, imagined a blend of state and national effort on behalf of a better-integrated Kentucky. "Every day," he wrote to Valentine Peers, "we become more wedded to the opinion that roads should be a *state* concern. . . .

[W]e know of no object to which our funds can be better appropriated than that of internal improvement . . . so long neglected that the character of our state *abroad* has been rendered very disreputable. Before it will ever retain an exalted reputation it must . . . encourage industry of a *public* nature. . . . And for what purpose? We would answer to transport the mail . . . For the Members of Congress . . . to travel upon to the Metropolis . . . to convey troops in the event of war. For bringing the citizens of the East and West, the North and South, nearer together, thereby identifying more and more their interests. . . . We have never entertained any fear of the General Government.[57]

Vimont was exaggerating, for Kentuckians had long expressed extreme displeasure toward federally imposed impediments to internal development and economic recovery. But Bluegrass elites also understood the benefits that flowed from broad participation in the marketplace and general governance. When the leadership insisted upon Kentucky's right to consolidate its interior on its own terms, they sought conditions essential to a much-desired integration. And increased confident involvement was apparent in Kentucky by 1832—in party politics, local acceptance of national banking, and swift completion of improvements projects tending toward efficiency and reduced agricultural costs. Certainly the outcome of Kentucky's very complicated struggle was politically conservative and wholeheartedly capitalist: Private banking had been preserved, especially after the establishment of a Second Bank of Kentucky by 1832. Individual fortunes and private banking had been secured; and stable landholding, while an encouragement to immigrants and to vulnerable settlers in backwoods counties, benefited the "monied interests" at least as much.

But these several ends had been achieved in the midst of explosive debate, confusion, competition, and elite fragmentation, through the liberalization of property law and through the defeat of a "sacred compact" with another sovereign state. In a sense, the Kentucky Assembly exceeded its wildest expectations, managing a structural transformation rather than simple reconstruction or preservation. Historian Dale Royalty has concluded that the closing of the Bank of the Commonwealth signaled the demise of the commonwealth ideal,[58] but in reality the failure of the Relief Party's single most anti-capitalist innovation marked the achievement of that ideal. The complaint against wildcat banking in 1818 had been its terrible freedom—its complete immunity from public scrutiny and accountability, and one of the misgivings about public finance had always been its extreme publicity and its frank introversion. Kentucky's search for domestic stability—however groping and chaotic—had been predicated at every turn upon linkages between self-interest openly pursued and public enrichment. Partisans had urged repeatedly that local government lacked essential capacities in pursuit of individual and public security, even as they disagreed profoundly about what those capacities properly might be and how they might be regained or refurbished.

More abstractly, Kentucky's transformation through law strongly suggests that legal historians might fruitfully excavate beneath what John T. Noonan has called the "mask of the law" in search of the layers of interest, both intellectual and material, which found expression through law. And this search might begin in other western and southern states during those critical, half-understood years preceding the nullification crisis: If sectional breakdown in the 1830s represented a change of direction in Kentucky, then scholarly explanations of that disintegration become more difficult.[59] *Were* Bluegrass experiences atypical in every respect, unlike local sentiment elsewhere? Or were these quarrelsome capitalists merely louder, more labored, and less restricted to narrow economic remedy in the aftermath of depression?

And the rules of equity, finally, which legal historians too often ignore after the eighteenth century but which plainly lay at the heart of Kentucky's relief agenda and of federal judicial decision making, merit renewed attention. In land law particularly, the course of development probably was richer, more expansive, and more inclusive than scholars have been able to acknowledge. In Kentucky, as in the "federal city," the rules of equity and concerns about equity's significance in a common law tradition, were alive and burgeoning in 1819—thriving so thoroughly, in fact, that Thomas Todd felt compelled to denounce "desperate deeds . . . produced by desperate situations and desperate motives" in 1824.[60] He might have feared less, for Kentuckians were, before all else, old-fashioned commonwealthmen.

NOTES

1. The best source of general information about the Panic of 1819 is Murray Rothbard, *The Panic of 1819: Reactions and Policies* (New York, 1962). For its consequences in banking, see J. VanFenstermaker, *The Development of American Commercial Banking, 1782–1837* (Kent, Ohio, 1965).

2. For chronic credit and currency shortages, see Richard Sylla, "American Banking and Growth in the Nineteenth Century: A Partial View of the Terrain," *Explorations in Economic History* (1971–1972), 9: 197–227. Ralph Catterall's *Second Bank of the United States* (Chicago, 1963) describes the newly chartered bank's behavior after 1818. But collapses in areas of Kentucky's economy beyond the financial sector have not been studied carefully. For interesting commentary on commercial disruption, archival materials can be helpful. For typical examples, see John Wilie of New Orleans to John Hanna, August 11, 1818, and October 7, 1818; and Hanna to John W. Hunt, August 20, 1821; in John Hanna File, MC393, Kentucky Historical Society, Frankfort, Kentucky, cited hereafter as KHS. William Waller's remark can be found in Waller to Farmer Dewey, Cashier of the Lexington Branch Bank, Records of the Bank of Kentucky, Letter Book E, February 3, 1819, 55, Kentucky State Archive, Frankfort, Kentucky, cited hereafter as KSA. For John Bradford's editorial, see the *Kentucky Gazette,* May 7, 1819.

3. The literature surrounding relief movements is sparse. But see, for instance, Rothbard's *Panic of 1819*; Samuel Rezneck, "The Depression of 1819–1822: A Social History," *American Historical Review* 39 (October 1933): 1–29; or W. J. Hamilton, "The Relief Movement in Missouri, 1820–1822," *Missouri Historical Review* 22 (October 1927): 51–92. Kentucky's movement is best described in Paul Gates, "Tenants of the Log Cabin," *Mississippi Valley Historical Review* 44, no. 1 (June 1962): 3–31. But other valuable accounts include Arndt Stickles, *The Critical Court Struggle in Kentucky, 1819–1829* (Indianapolis, Ind., 1929), esp. pp. 29–64; Richard P. McCormick's Kentucky section in *The Second American Party System: Party Formation in the Jacksonian Era* (New York, 1973); Frank Mathias, "The Relief and Court Struggle: Half-Way House to Populism," *Register of the Kentucky Historical Society* 71, no. 2 (April 1973): 154–76; Mathias' Ph.D. thesis, "The Turbulent Years of Kentucky Politics, 1820–1850," University of Kentucky, 1971; Dale Royalty's dissertation, "Banking, Politics, and the Commonwealth, 1800–1825," University of Kentucky, 1971; Thomas Clark's *History of Kentucky* (New York, 1937); and Anti-Relief partisan George Robertson's *Scrapbook on Law and Politics, Men and Times* (Lexington, Ky., 1855), pp. 32 ff.

4. Legislative polarization is described in Gates, "Tenants of the Log Cabin," and in Stickles, *Court Struggle*. Gates explains Anti-Relief motivation as an expression of *noblesse oblige*, while Stickles posits a debtor-creditor antagonism.

5. For stay and execution laws, see *Acts of Kentucky*, 30th General Assembly, December 11 and 21, 1821, pp. 91, 136, cited hereafter as *Acts*. The substance of these measures is described with fair accuracy in Gates, "Tenants," although legal and lay meanings of the term "equity" are confused frequently. And, for typical displays of Anti-Relief indignation, see the numerous pamphlets in the Samuel Wilson Pamphlet Collection, University of Kentucky Special Collections, Lexington, Ky. Among them, see "The Rejected . . . Petition of George M. Bibb," 1824, by a "Looker On"; Green Clay's "To the People of Kentucky and of the United States," 1824; "A Few Reflections of a cool-minded Man on the present Judiciary question," 1825, anonymous; and Robert Wickliffe's "An Expose of the Relief System, by a protest and resolutions . . . refused to be printed by . . . the House of Representatives," 1824.

6. "Act to establish the Bank of the Commonwealth of Kentucky," *Acts*, 29th General Assembly, 1820, p. 55; and, for an example of banknote burnings, "Resolution," *Acts,* 38th General Assembly, 1829, p. 283.

7. For one example of the consequences of replevin laws for out-of-state merchants, see the letter of Vermont trader Elisha L. Plumb to William Plumb, April 28, 1821, Elisha Plumb File, MC764, KHS, in which Plumb complains about "twisting and turning" to affect debt collection in Kentucky courts. Records of replevy bonds issued by the state have not survived.

8. References to "Money Men" and other varieties of tyrants recur in the Relief newspaper, *The Patriot*, published between 1825 and 1827. For examples, see pages 9, 13, and 16. *The Patriot* and its Anti-Relief counterpart, *The Spirit of '76*, are held by University of Kentucky Special Collections, Lexington. For Justice William Johnson's stinging dissent in the United States Supreme Court's hearings of *Green* v. *Biddle* after 1821, see *United States Reports,* 8 Wheaton 1 (1823).

9. For a recent, disturbing study of the development of contract law in nineteenth-century America, see Morton Horwitz, *The Transformation of American Law, 1780–1860* (Cambridge, Mass., 1977).

10. For useful studies of the origins of Kentucky's irregular grant of statehood and of subsequent problems in land management, see Patricia Watlington, *The Partisan Spirit: Kentucky Politics, 1779–1792* (New York, 1972); Joan Wells Coward, *Kentucky in the New Republic: The Process of Constitution Making* (Lexington, Ky., 1979); Mary K. Bonsteel Tachau, *Federal Courts in the Early Republic: Kentucky, 1789–1816* (Princeton, N.J., 1978), esp. pp. 167–90; Richard Ellis, *The Jeffersonian Crisis: Courts and Politics in the Young Republic* (New York, 1971), pp. 123–56; Peter Onuf, "Toward Federalism: Virginia, Congress, and the Western Lands," *William and Mary Quarterly* 24 (July 1977): 353–74; and lawyer William Littell's pamphlet, *Political Transactions in and Concerning Kentucky from the First Settlement Thereof Until it Became an Independent State in June, 1792* (Frankfort, Ky., 1806). This booklet contains the separation agreement, pp. 12–17. The third article insured that "all private rights and interests in land within the said district, derived

from the laws of Virginia . . . shall remain valid and secure under the laws of the proposed state," and that disagreements would be arbitrated by commissioners sitting as a court of chancery.

11. For the several occupying claimants' statutes, see *Acts,* 5th General Assembly, 1797, p. 143; 17th General Assembly, 1809, p. 85; 20th General Assembly, 1812, p. 117; 27th General Assembly, 1818–19, p. 761; and 29th General Assembly, 1820–21, pp. 148–51.

12. See, as examples, Rothbard, *Panic of 1819,* or Catterall, *Second Bank.*

13. Political studies of this sort include McCormick, *Second American Party System,* or Lynn Marshall, "The Genesis of Grass-Roots Democracy in Kentucky," *Mid-America* 47 (October 1965): 269–87.

14. See Gates, "Tenants of the Log Cabin," p. 3; and Horwitz, *Transformation,* p. 61.

15. For extensive, probing commentary on the process by which noncompliance has come to be associated with "bad law" in the wake of Legal Realism, see Robert Gordon, "Introduction: J. Willard Hurst and the Common Law Tradition in American Legal Historiography," *Law and Society Review* 10 (Fall 1975): 9–55.

16. For typical constitutional treatments, see Charles Grove Haines, *The Role of the Supreme Court in American Government and Politics, 1789–1835* (Berkeley, Calif., 1944), pp. 463–70; Charles Warren, *The Supreme Court in United States History* (Boston, 1926), 1: 623–51; Alfred Kelly and Winfred Harbison, *The American Constitution: Its Origins and Development,* 5th ed. (Chicago, 1976), pp. 263–68; Robert J. McCloskey, *The American Supreme Court* (Chicago, 1960), pp. 54–71; Benjamin Wright, Jr., *The Contract Clause of the Constitution* (Cambridge, Mass., 1938); or C. Peter Magrath, *Yazoo: Law and Politics in the New Nation* (New York, 1966), pp. 104–5.

17. See Haines, *Role of the Supreme Court,* p. 463; and Joel Silbey, "The Civil War Synthesis in American Political History," *Civil War History* 10 (June 1964): 130–40, esp. p. 140.

18. For Anti-Relief concern and suggestions that Kentucky consider monetary settlement with Virginians, see *Spirit of '76,* pp. 14, 26, 78 ff. at University of Kentucky Special Collections, Lexington; or George Bibb's dissent in *Fisher* v. *Higgins,* 21 Kentucky Reports, 147 (1827), which denounces the legislature's 1820 land statute as "harsh" in its treatment of nonresidents—all the while agreeing that Kentuckians ought to possess ultimate control over landownership.

19. See Records of the Bank of Kentucky and Records of the Bank of the Commonwealth, particularly the daybooks, ledgers, and stockholder journals of the Principal Banks at Frankfort and of the Lexington, Paris, and Louisville branches, KSA. Collateral, usually land and slaves, is noted carefully beside many transactions. Record keeping became less meticulous after 1830, presumably because both banks were closed by that year.

20. Ibid.

21. For stay and execution laws, see *Acts,* December 11 and 21, 30th General Assembly, 1821, pp. 91, 136. After 1826 the legislature moved to secure land titles,

to eliminate the "excesses" of Relief replevin and execution statutes, and to reverse New Court rulings. These measures have received scant attention. See, for instance, "Act to Secure Actual Settlers," 35th General Assembly, 1826, p. 188; "An Act More Effectually to Guard the Occupant of Land," 36th General Assembly, 1827, p. 244, which gave title to settlers whenever lands were forfeited for taxes if settlers could pay the amount due; and an act to "prevent further confliction" in land claims, 39th General Assembly, 1828, p. 147, which granted common law title for settlers after three months' advertisement of a claim. For execution and replevin law contraction or simplification, see *Acts,* 1826, p. 123, and 1828, p. 146; and for repeal of the legislation creating a New Court, see 35th General Assembly, 1826, p. 13, and 1828, p. 51. For establishment of the Bank of the Commonwealth, see "Act to establish the Bank of the Commonwealth of Kentucky," 29th General Assembly, 1820, p. 55. The colorful rhetorical war between Relief and Anti-Relief partisans can be tracked in political pamphlets. See, as examples, Patrick Henry [pseud.], "The Bank Dinner, an expose of the Court Party of Kentucky, and the Curtain Drawn from the Holy Alliance of America," 1824; Jesse Bledsoe, "Speech on the resolutions . . . concerning Banks," 1819; or "The Devil amongst the speculators," 1823, by "A Farmer's Son"; all in the Samuel Wilson Pamphlet Collection, University of Kentucky Special Collections, Lexington; or the lengthy anonymous Relief pamphlet, "Considerations on Some of the Matters to be Acted on, or worth acting on, at the next Session of the General Assembly of Kentucky, First, the sphere of Powers of the Judiciary, second, the Ways and Means by which the People might extricate themselves from Difficulties and Raise to Happiness," 1824; in the Pamphlet Collection, Filson Club Library, Louisville.

22. For Kentucky's several occupying-claimant land statutes, see *Acts,* 5th General Assembly, 1797, p. 143, which secured financial reimbursement for improvements made by actual settlers; 17th General Assembly, 1809, p. 85, a seven-year statute of limitations on nonresident claims, after which time occupants could argue color of title; and 20th General Assembly, 1812, p. 117, which allowed settlers to retain possession during litigation and also allowed them to choose between title and payment for improvements whenever tenant investments exceeded three-quarters of the land's value. On February 9, 1819, the legislature provided further that occupants could harvest crops despite formal eviction; 27th General Assembly, 1818–19, p. 761. The 1797 statute had given the state a perpetual lien against lands on which taxes were not paid, but extensions were common. By June 1819, however, forfeitures were being enforced. See, for instance, the alarmed correspondence between members of the Brown family in Virginia and Kentucky, in Orlando Brown Papers, Folios 4 and 5, Filson Club, Louisville, in which Brown was asked to pay taxes for delinquent relatives before a deadline. See also Joseph Desha's message to the House, Executive Journal, January 12, 1820, Governor's Papers, KHS, in which Desha promises attention to tax-delinquent Virginians. Finally, see letters between Kentucky agents and Virginians in arrears conveying power of attorney, as in J. D. Sims to Edmund Taylor, October 8, 1819, Brown-Brent-Taylor Papers, MC125; John Winn to Archibald Bilbo, November 17, 1823, Bilbo File, MC70; and Felix Grundy to George M. Bibb, July 16, 1818, Felix Grundy File, MC387, KHS.

23. See *Green* v. *Biddle*, 8 Wheaton 1 (1823). The best brief account of this process can be found in Gates, "Tenants of the Log Cabin."

24. The "New Court"–"Old Court" battle has been described in Stickles, *Court Struggle*.

25. In *Acts*, 29th General Assembly, 1820–21, pp. 148–51, assemblymen suspended rental payments to absentee owners until judgments for the value of improvements had been completed, and those judgments frequently took years. Surely the most militant land statute ever passed, the measure was repealed on January 7, 1824.

26. *Green* v. *Biddle*, 8 Wheaton 1, 17 (1823).

27. "Considerations on Some of the Matters to be Acted on. . .", 1824, pp. 4, 28.

28. See Robert Alexander to Henry Lee, November 15, 1817; to A. Morehead, November 30, 1817; and to George M. Deadrick, President of the Nashville Bank, October 28, 1817; Bank of Kentucky Records, Letter Book C, pp. 58, 65–67, 75, KSA.

29. See, for instance, William Waller to Thomas L. Harman, Cashier, Louisiana Bank, December 29, 1819, Bank of Kentucky, Letter Book D, p. 187; Robert Alexander to W. R. Hynes, President of the Bardstown Branch Bank, July 25, 1818, Letter Book D, p. 129, KSA. Stock certificate values—$200 at par, and by 1821 worth about $100—are recorded in the Bank's Stockholder Journals and Stock Certificate Register.

30. Bank of Kentucky, Stockholders Minute Book A, pp. 31–32; Stock Certificates General Register, pp. 146–49, 206–9, 312–43, and elsewhere, KSA. At least half of the bank's stockholder registers and transfer books have not survived, which means that individual holdings will be underestimated. Bank of Kentucky survivals include certificates in the series 1–1746, 5801–10646, and 19398–21999.

31. Robert Alexander to James Marshall, October 26, 1822, Marshall Family Papers, Folio 13, The Filson Club, Louisville. Values, in fact, were restored by 1828; see Bank of Kentucky, Stock Transfer Book 3, 1822–33; and Stockholders Minute Book A, 123–97, KSA.

32. See Bank of Kentucky, Minute Book C, Principal Bank at Frankfort, May 22, 1820, p. 72; and Robert Alexander to Robert Wickliffe, Letter Book D, January 9, 1821, p. 54, KSA.

33. See Bank of the Commonwealth Minute Books A and B; Record Book A, KSA. And see as well Memorandum from James Weir, Cashier, to President and Directors of the Lexington Branch Bank, December 20, 1820; John Tilford to President and Directors of the Lexington Bank; Jacob Miller to President and Directors of the Richmond Branch Bank; and other documents in Bank of Kentucky and Bank of the Commonwealth Collection, 60M21, University of Kentucky Archives, Lexington. For legal maneuvering, see Bank of Kentucky, Louisville Branch, Letter Book B, pp. 12, 17, 32; Paris Branch, Firm Book, pp. 312, 416, 418, 532; Lexington Branch, Letter Book E, pp. 12, 95; Principal Bank at Frankfort, Letter Book F, pp. 15, 42–46; several volumes entitled "Notes in Suit," Frankfort, Lexington, Paris, Princeton, and other branch banks; and "Reports from Branches of Debtors of $1,000 and Upwards," 1820–22, KSA.

34. For Marshall's original indebtedness, which was not with the Bank of Kentucky according to its ledgers, see Gates, "Tenants of the Log Cabin," and for involvement with the Bank of the Commonwealth, see Minute Book A, p. 19, and Record Book A, pp. 36–37, KSA.

35. Examples of these transactions include Cuthbert Anderson to Currie, March 25, 1819; William Harper to Anderson, September 20, 1819; and J. Richard to Anderson [n.d.]; Anderson-Taylor File, MC70, KHS. This collection includes many powers of attorney, memoranda, and conveyances related to the firm's extensive dealings with nonresident land claimants.

36. For hostility toward the members of Anderson's firm at the Bank of Kentucky, and for their subsequent affiliation with the Bank of the Commonwealth, see Minutes of the President and Directors Meetings, Bank of Kentucky, Principal Bank at Frankfort, April 21, 1819, Minute Book C, p. 89; Bank of the Commonwealth Stock Certificate Register, 1821–36, p. 112; and Minute Book A, January 2, 1822, KSA. For the plaintive letter from a Princeton, Kentucky, farmer, whose signature unfortunately is illegible, see Governor's Papers, Box 36, Bundle 145, January 2, 1822, KHS.

37. The best brief summary of the Marshall Court's positions after 1801 on legal and constitutional issues involving private property is R. Kent Newmyer, *The Supreme Court Under Marshall and Taney* (New York, 1968), esp. pp. 18–88.

38. Order books and the complete record of the lower federal courts, Kentucky District, are held on microfilm at University of Kentucky Archives, Lexington. For examples of seizure of goods, see *Charles Savage and Edward Lewis* v. *Richard Ferguson,* or *Dennis Fitzhugh* v. *Same*, U.S. District Court, Order Book H, December 10, 1819, pp. 133–35, Series M-680, Box 5. Actions against steamboat owners were docketed as admiralty suits, relying upon federal court jurisdiction in wage disputes on the Ohio River—authority which the courts lost by 1825. See *Daniel Wirtz et al.* v. *Paragon and Owners* and three other cases dismissed on June 2, 1825, for want of jurisdiction, Order Book H, 340, ibid.

39. For examples of this rash of steamboat confiscations, many of which affected Kentucky's political leadership, see *Benjamin Crandall* v. *Owners of the Steam Boat Elizabeth; Richard M. Johnson* v. *Steamboat Jefferson's Owners; William S. Vernon and Martin Blake, Merchants* v. *James D. Breckenridge and Henry Shreve, former owners of the Steam Boat Post Boy,* and *Daniel M. Green and Francis Ames* v. *Daniel Mallory, et al., owners of the Steam Boat Mars;* all on December 11, 1822, District Court, Order Book H, Series M-680, Box 5, 225–68; University of Kentucky Archives.

40. For examples of these judgments, see *U.S.* v. *George Harrison,* or *U.S.* v. *Robert Respass,* May 18, 1819, U.S. Circuit Court, Order Book F, pp. 287–89, Series M-679, Box 13.

41. See *B.U.S.* v. *Richard Taylor,* May 7, 1819, 248, U.S. Circuit Court, Order Book F; and for other B.U.S. efforts, see Order Book G, pp. 101–3, 114–16, 311–34; Order Book H, pp. 171–88, 281–95; and *passim*. The possibility of state taxation of the United States Bank—declared unconstitutional by the United States Supreme Court in 1819—was broached again in *B.U.S.* v. *Richard Taylor,* May 8, 1822, ibid.,

p. 270, which perpetually enjoined the Assembly against taxation through Taylor, its sergeant-at-arms.

42. *B.U.S.* v. *John J. Marshall; Same* v. *Richard Taylor; Same* v. *Henry Johnson; Same* v. *John Johnson;* and other cases on May 14, 1822, pp. 281–89 and thereafter, U.S. Circuit Court, Order Book H.

43. Justices Todd, Trimble, and Boyle adhered scrupulously to the letter and spirit of traditional practice, and lower federal court acceptance of and deference to Kentucky's compensatory system of occupying-claimants statues varied according to the militance of the measure. Through 1823 the circuit court allowed compensatory hearings in chancery, following an action of ejectment, only under the 1797 and 1809 statutes—never under the later, more controversial 1812 or 1820 measures which allowed Kentuckians to argue color of title (or earn title through nonresident default). In *Henry Banks* v. *James C. Johnson, et al.,* December 11, 1820, U.S. Circuit Court, Order Book G, p. 412, the court rejected a commissioner's report which waived rental charges until all judgments were concluded, and the subject was not entertained again.

44. Examples of evasion abound. But see, as examples, Green Clay to John Rowan, December 15, 1822, Green Clay Papers, Folio 12, Filson Club; or Archibald Bilbo to John Winn, August 17, 1821, Bilbo File, MC70, KHS. And protests in newspapers, pamphlets, and elsewhere—particularly following the incendiary *Green* opinions in 1823—are equally abundant. See, for instance, Richard M. Johnson's protests, *Annals of Congress,* 17th Congress, 1 Session 23, December 12, 1821, pp. 67–91; January 14, 15, 1822, pp. 95–114; the *Frankfort Commentator*, April 19, 1821, and June 1, 1825; or the *Louisville Public Advertiser*, February 6, 1822. Among the numerous pamphlets, see "Speech of John Pope delivered in the Legislature of Kentucky, at the November Session, 1823 . . . ," 1824; David Trimble, "Circular," 1824; Samuel Daveiss, "Speech . . . on the . . . Decisions of the Supreme Court of the United States, relative to the occupying claimants laws . . . ," 1823; Lafayette [pseud.], "To the People," c. 1824; George Robertson, "Speech . . . in Committee of the Whole . . . on the late decisions . . . ," 1823; John Rowan, "Report . . . in relation to the late decision . . . ," 1823; James Hughes, "A Report on the Causes determined by the late Supreme Court . . . ," c. 1823; and Kentucky General Assembly, "A Remonstrance to the Congress of the United States on the occupying claimants laws of Kentucky," 1824; in Samuel P. Wilson Pamphlet Collection, University of Kentucky Special Collections, Lexington.

45. For the Supreme Court's Joseph Story, Kentucky law made a "mockery" of the lawful owner's right to the use and enjoyment of landholdings. See *Green* v. *Biddle*, 8 Wheaton 1, 17ff. (1823). Gates and others have dismissed these arguments as exaggerations, but Story likely did perceive Kentucky's intentions. For Todd's laborious discussion of proper relations between law and equity, see *John Green's Heirs* v. *Bernard Gittner, Jacob Micksell, William Elliott, Hickerson Bett, John Liter, and Jacob Liter,* June 1, 1819, pp. 376–92, Circuit Court of Kentucky, Order Book F, Series M-679, Box 3. Gittner chose to argue, quite cleverly, from the common law's relatively stringent twenty-year requirement for land title through possession and improvement, rather than from Kentucky's more liberal seven-year requirement.

46. Ibid., pp. 384–87, 389.

47. See *Jessee Noland* v. *Samuel McKean,* October 21, 1824, Order Book K, Series M-679, Box 6, pp. 175–76.

48. Henry Clay to Thomas Bodley, November 30, 1821, Henry Clay File, MC179, KHS.

49. See Supreme Court opinions in *Thomas* v. *Harvie's Heirs,* 10 Wheaton 146 (1825); *McCormick and Wife* v. *Sullifant,* 10 Wheaton 192 (1825); *Darby's Lessee* v. *Mayer,* 10 Wheaton 465 (1825); and particularly *Elmendorf* v. *Taylor,* 10 Wheaton 152 (1825), in which John Marshall quietly legitimized Elmendorf's possession-based claim at common law, thus incorporating the twenty-year principle against which Todd and Story had struggled. In many ways, these 1825 rulings—much neglected by historians—are more interesting and significant than the High Court's formal overrule of *Green* v. *Biddle* in the 1831 *Hawkins* case, in part because the former coincided with dramatic shrinkages in the district and circuit court work loads, with aggressive legislative efforts to mobilize land and monetary resources toward internal improvements, and with Kentucky's effective noncompliance in land questions.

50. *Green* v. *Gittner, et al.,* p. 389. And, for evidence of ongoing federal court awareness of Kentucky's situation and of local hardship, see *Finley* v. *Williams*, 9 Cranch 164 (1815); *Matson* v. *Hurd,* 1 Wheaton 130 (1816); or Bushrod Washington's poignant closing remarks in *Green* v. *Biddle*, pp. 93–94.

51. Robert McAfee to Joshua Wilson, May 12, 1827, McAfee File, MC412, KHS. See also his speech "In the Legislature . . . shewing his view of the policy the state should pursue, in making internal improvements," January 14, 1831, which suggests joint state and federal funding. In the same vein, see Robert Wickliffe, "Speech . . . in the Senate . . . in relation to the Tariff and Internal Improvements," 1830; Samuel P. Wilson Pamphlet Collection, University of Kentucky Special Collection.

52. See *Acts of Kentucky,* 37th through 40th General Assemblies. For examples of turnpike and other improvement company records, see Louisville Turnpike Company Minute Book, Filson Club Manuscripts Division; Basil Hobbes to John S. Snead, November 14, 1826, estimating costs and enumerating personnel for the Shelbyville and Louisville Turnpike, Basil Hobbes File, KHS; similar correspondence in the R. Higgins File, MC442, related to the Maysville Turnpike Company, KHS; and the extensive materials collected in the Maysville File, MC653, KHS.

53. "Memorial and Petition of the Citizens of Maysville by their Committee to the Senate and House of Representatives of the State of Kentucky in legislature assembled," c. 1826, Maysville File, MC653, KHS.

54. Ibid.; and Circular, "To the Citizens of [several counties] contiguous to the great Road leading from Maysville to Lexington," August 24, 1826, Valentine Peers Papers, 73M20, University of Kentucky Archive, Lexington; and Draft of a Circular, Minute Book, Louisville Turnpike Company, September 1830, p. 61, Filson Club Manuscripts Division.

55. See draft of a letter to President and Directors, Bank of the United States, Philadelphia, October 15, 1828, and letter from Richard Taylor, November 2, 1828, to the Governor, Executive Journal, 1828, p. 334, and Box 46, Bundle 13; a discussion of engineering candidates, Executive Journal, May 14, 1828, p. 242; all in Governor's

Papers; and Richard M. Johnson to Elisha Winters, March 15, 1830, Richard M. Johnson File, MC491; KHS.

56. Circular, "To the Citizens of [several counties] contiguous to the great road. . . ."

57. "Resolution" concerning support for the tariff and for cooperation between nation and state in local improvement, coinciding with state support for Henry Clay's "American System" presidential candidacy, *Acts*, 38th General Assembly, 1829, p. 287; and Lewis Vimont to Valentine Peers, November 28, 1826, Maysville File, MC653, KHS.

58. Dale Royalty, "Banking and the Commonwealth Ideal in Kentucky," *Register of the Kentucky Historical Society* 77, no. 2 (Spring 1979): 91–107.

59. John Thomas Noonan, *Persons and Masks of the Law: Cardozo, Holmes, Jefferson, and Wythe as Makers of the Mask* (New York, 1976).

60. *President and Directors of the Bank of the United States* v. *Thomas Studman, et. al.*, November 18, 1824, Circuit Court, Order Book K, Series M-679, Box 6, pp. 252–53.

PERSONAL ACCOUNT

6B. My Own "Desperate Deeds and Desperate Motives": How The Project Evolved

SANDRA VAN BURKLEO

The essay very briefly surveys a doctoral dissertation, the subject of which is legal politics in and about Kentucky in the wake of the Panic of 1819. Because the project mutated and broadened during the research process to incorporate a range of interrelated historical and methodological issues, as well as a rather sprawling body of evidence, I have chosen to paint broadly rather than deeply. Concentration upon a single issue might suggest that individual questions were answered in a neat, well-insulated fashion—which they were not—or that all questions were formulated in advance of research— which would be soothing but entirely fictitious. This project has been plagued from its inception by uninvited complication, surprise, incremental fragmentation, and serendipity. None of this is particularly elegant, but whole truths rarely are.

"Subject" is a static idea, describing situations or historical outcomes. Kentucky itself can be viewed most fruitfully as a fixed lens across which an unruly cast of characters moved, acted, and reacted, resulting in a series of durable legal and political monuments—statutes, court rulings, courthouse gatherings—with which historians have been reasonably well acquainted. Analytical objects, on the other hand, are dynamic, even slippery concepts, involving scholarly action upon or within a subject. The voice is interrogatory rather than declarative. My objects, phrased as questions, have been three: What happened? Why did various elites come to behave as they did? And how might historians circumvent the formalism so characteristic of conventional "histories of law"? Let me therefore describe the state of the art among historians of American law and then discuss how I conducted my research in Kentucky.

The British legal scholar Frederick Maitland once remarked that legal history was history first, modified by "law." He then spent a lifetime grappling with the implications of his own remark, finally concluding that the professional objectives of lawyers and historians were incompatible. Maitland would be saddened, but not particularly surprised, to learn that legal studies in the United States—long the preserve of lawyers and, to a lesser extent, of political scientists—have been invaded by historians only in recent years. As a result, there now exist two competing "traditions," each claiming guardian-ship over an "authentic" legal history.

Historians of law, many of them trained in law schools, defend the lawyers' special prerogative as interpreters of their own tradition. Histories emphasize the continuity of doctrinal or institutional development from past to present, resulting often in characterizations of past law as a miniaturization of present practice. And, despite increased awareness of politicization within legal institutions, impressions of law's separateness from politics and the economy persist. Objectives of this group of scholars include the explication (or criticism) of the inner life of a common law tradition, and its ongoing impact upon a democratic society—the development of the contracts clause as a judicial tool, for instance, or the unhappy consequences of school prayer rulings in Tennessee, suggesting that lawmakers return to the drawingboard. Their analysis rests mainly with formal historical evidence—the body of case law, statutes, constitutions, or treatises which bound the law's authority—referring often to formal language as best evidence about the motivations of historical actors. Thus, Kentucky's bout with the Supreme Court, which was couched in contract law and states' rights language, was necessarily *about* contracts and state sovereignty, for litigants and justices alike.

Legal historians, on the other hand, urge the demystification of the law—even as they trip over the intricacies of writs and land law. Their histories emphasize frequent discontinuities rooted in interconnections between the law, politics, and the economy, and in dissimilarities between past and present practice. The knowledge of judicial politicization in particular has often led them to portray justices as politicians in black robes; and the notion that lawmakers ought to be responsive to the democracy most of the time has encouraged a shift away from courts of appeal toward state tribunals and local legislatures. In Robert Gordon's phrase, legal experience in this revised mode "merges with context," at some logical extreme losing its apolitical identity altogether.[1] But the impulse is healthy. Increasingly, historians assess the significance of law *in* time, and in a lived-in world. At its best, this scholarship relies upon the private record in conjunction with formal remains, although historians have been curiously reticent about the confident use of informal documents—even when inquiring after the intentions of individuals whose greed, valor, convictions, or simple curiosity found expression *through* law, yet remain hidden beneath the law's formal language.

Surely one pursuit need not invalidate the other. The two visions differ sharply—certainly by object, and probably by subject, as "internal" and "external" approaches to historical issues so often do. In a sense, continued animosity between the two is unwarranted, and even counterproductive. It is nowhere clear, for instance, that "enlightened" legal historians, armed with knowledge of historical environment and archival evidence, improve our understanding of decision-making by past legal professionals whose values often resembled or paralleled those articulated by modern lawyer-historians. In the rush to politicize or democratize, scholars can move perilously near an improper suggestion of pervasive self-interest or politicization, and of the irrelevance of judicial public policy—all of which are demonstrably false. Problems, then, are complicated by the fact that formalism and formal evidence are appropriate and indispensable whenever scholars inquire after the internal life of institutions, or after the consciousness of legal professionals, but are usually far less appropriate when the focus shifts to the interests of those who resorted to law. No single method will do. The trick is to distinguish between questions and historical actors, marshaling evidence appropriate to wildly different political aspirations and values.

Having said that, let me retreat almost completely and confess that the Kentucky project originated in ignorance, without benefit of Maitland or very much else. It began, in fact, as a thoroughly crass attempt to fashion a reasonably interesting graduate seminar paper in the least possible time so that I might escape into "important" research. The Supreme Court's high-handed behavior in the 1821 and 1823 *Green* v. *Biddle* rulings had nagged at me in a peripheral way since my first term as a graduate student; but it pressed far less urgently than a good many other topics. I cleverly decided to focus upon the intentions of two justices—Joseph Story and Bushrod Washington—in a single case and to produce a traditional "internal" account that might lay the nag to rest. Who could be *consumed,* after all, by a limited investigation of an obscure Kentucky land case—so obscure, in fact, that historians preferred not to write about it? Conveniently enough, neglect left me with a small, well-contained secondary literature.

The plan backfired. My "clever" seminar exercise soon snowballed into a preposterous 150-page essay which concluded, rather haplessly, that I knew far too little to conclude. Even more important, Kentuckians had insinuated themselves into my graduate career; and I'm reminded, time and again, of the infuriating process by which those early efforts eventuated in a dissertation. Henry Clay and Virginia land law kept me awake at night, infiltrated concerts, and jeopardized friendships. The slightest spadework invariably yielded fresh puzzles, monkeywrenches, cryptic half-messages, or dead ends. I sometimes have viewed the historical record as a minefield pitted against professional confidence. Some years after smugly opening Wheaton's *United States Reports* to make quick work of *Green* v. *Biddle,* I can offer this beginning advice: never presume perfect intellectual control.

That original, peripheral nag is easily explained: I simply did not believe what I was reading about the Marshall Court's intentions in the *Green* case. Resistance to nationalist decisions had increased in many states after 1819, contributing to the Court's retreat by 1825. And these were seasoned jurists, well acquainted with tensions and salient political issues in the several federal circuits. Yet I learned, volume after volume, that the two *Green* decisions were unfortunate technical errors based upon a misunderstanding of the Virginia-Kentucky compact, lapses in judgment, or insensitive impositions of an antiquated Federalism upon proto-Jacksonians. And cursory readings of the opinions themselves increased my skepticism. These were tightly argued, well-documented, even poignant rulings. The federal bench usually courts congressional or state disfavor only for good reason; and Federalist pique or ineptitude seemed inadequate reason—particularly because the High Court ruled identically on two separate occasions, two years apart, the second time more firmly than the first. In short, I could not believe that skillful judges had worked carefully on an important case, and had produced decisions that were clumsy mistakes. Were all the analysts and critics wrong?

I set about reconstructing the Court's own history in land and contract appeals between 1815 and 1835, in search of the justices' experience and memory in cases like *Green* or *Wayman* v. *Southard.* I realized, oddly enough, that the land-law rulings flowed logically from the Court's practice in cases appealed from Kentucky, Tennessee, and Ohio, and was anything but the aberration or anomaly depicted in constitutional histories. There had been a pattern of increased militance from the bench after 1818 whenever common law debt or land disputes involved state statutes rooted in the rules of equity. Those rules, which define the practice of courts of chancery, traditionally worked to offset the possible rigidities and inequities of the writ system, and to accommodate evidence which courts of law typically excluded. Yet the Supreme Court seemed to be reacting—quite mysteriously, and often only implicitly—against state legislative use of the principles of equity. But I knew very little law, and couldn't puzzle out why these statutes might be problematic.

Research in Kentucky politics was therefore unavoidable. I had access only to published primary sources—memoirs, scattered letters, barebones legislative journals—and a sparse collection of local histories. Those materials revealed that legislators were obsessed with several apparently unrelated issues—among them, debtor relief, banks, and land; and I came to suspect connections between banking and land law while reading Anti-Relief leader George Robertson's self-congratulatory "Scrapbook." But I had no idea what that connection might be. I knew as well that, by 1828, Henry Clay's "American System" Whigs had placed internal improvements at the heart of their nationalist political program, and that Clay, with other Whigs, had come to support the national bank by 1828—a complete turnabout which historians were hard pressed to explain. But I had no reason to suspect links between road building and the heated political struggle in Kentucky before 1828. I also sensed that legislators of both political persuasions had defined the relief agenda more broadly than had their counterparts in other states, to include land titling and the separation agreement. But why? I couldn't even know whether this was an important observation, or merely an interesting one. At project's end, I was left with a stunning collection of mismatched pieces and could only describe chaos.

Quite apart from the Kentucky fiasco, which I had come to view as an embarrassment, I had become persuaded that historians of nineteenth-century legal development were generalizing about legal change from skewed and inappropriate evidence. The century had been characterized, before all else, by territorial expansion and rapid institutional adaptation in response to shifting circumstances; yet scholars continued to mine archives on the eastern seaboard—an area which arguably was a legal backwater by 1803. As the nation's center of gravity shifted westward, Americans discussed fencing, water rights, cattle grazing, slave labor, paper money, and homesteading; and wealth was derived increasingly, not from New England's commerce, but from southern and western agriculture. *Was* it accurate to generalize from seaboard evidence? Would Indiana settlers recognize the suggestion that legal development occurred mainly through the efforts of legislators, judges, and commercial interests working in tandem? In the absence of case studies elsewhere, it was impossible to know.

I was convinced as well that a traditional "history of law," with its emphasis upon formal records, was flawed whenever historians hoped to penetrate decision making *about* law. I began thinking more seriously about the strengths and limits of historical evidence, pressing my concerns upon a captive audience of students in my senior paper seminar who likely benefited far less than I. What could we know, for example, from newspaper evidence, which represented public information, but not public opinion? Were letters written by self-conscious elites conclusive evidence about motivation, or did testimony require corroboration through actual behavior? And what *did* public records reveal? Court records, even election returns, are evidence about conflict *resolution*. Were they tractable sources of information about political and legal thought, or about the interests which drove people into public arenas? Might not the remarkable *smoothness* in American legal development conveyed by most historians reflect reliance upon this mountainous record of historical resolution?

That group of patient seniors contributed immeasurably to my own development as a researcher. On one occasion, I posited an analogy between the research process and a criminal trial, asking my slightly incredulous students to metamorphize into lawyers, jury, and judge, and then to imagine that I represented the historical record—a witness from whom various perspectives about "facts," or the culpability of individuals, might be learned through proper questioning. It worked, and we were all a bit dazzled. The questions broached there have guided me since. What happens, for instance, if only one witness survives? Is corroboration always required? When? How much? What if no witnesses survive? Can researchers infer intentions from concrete result, as juries are cautioned not to do, or is testimony essential to conclusions about state of mind? What if evidence destroys a pet theory? Do judges and attorneys pursue the suggestion, even at the expense of a new investigation? Or do they blink, favoring the theory?

In the midst of thought about the pitfalls of legal history writing and of historical research more generally, I overreacted. With many others, I zealously preached wholesale revisionism—the complete abandonment of legal fiction, the pursuit of subterranean political and economic currents, minimization of Supreme Court activities, and fresh research in the South and West. If the field desperately needed case studies in the dynamics of legal change (or resistance to change), I would provide one. And what better place to begin than in Kentucky? I was possessed of an unresolved puzzle in legal politics, involving local and national governance as well as a major economic crisis. Kentucky was "western" by nineteenth-century standards; and the state's experience after 1818 was couched in a typically formalist literature.

I imagined the project then as an "external" pilot study in relations between law, polity, and economy at the "grass roots," carefully controlled in time and space. I wanted to inhabit the perspectives of Kentuckians, and I also hoped to experiment, rather self-consciously, with historical (as opposed to legal) methods in the writing of legal history. I presumed erroneously that an "external" approach was synonymous with a local, largely legal-political vantage point, eschewing what I took to be "internal," generally constitutional questions linked inevitably to the Supreme Court. I was, in fact, fully prepared to jettison the Marshall Court, Joseph Story, the Kentucky Cases, and the contracts clause, blissfully unaware that they would return to haunt me.

That period of detachment, however falsely construed, was invaluable. I was able to gather together the minutiae of local politics and law, untangle a good many kinship networks and legal technicalities, and basically disregard abstract doctrinal considerations long enough to master concrete detail. When it finally occurred to me, literally in the dead of night in Louisville, Kentucky, that Kentuckians were at least as concerned about judicial policy and legal principle as were Supreme Court justices—if for different reasons—and that the real quandary in studies of decision making was substantive rather than mechanical—the *content* of political consciousness brought to bear upon law rather than one's distance from it—I simply reincorporated judicial and doctrinal concerns armed with a wealth of legal and political detail.

But, at that early, zealous stage in my own development, the primary question was, "Why did Kentucky's leadership behave as it did?" I sought the reasons underlying legislative and political activity. And to address that question, the testimony typically found in private manuscript collections was essential in order that I might *interpret* a skeletal formal record. Would archival materials support such a project? I set about looking. And the research experience from that moment forward was both frustrating and fruitful beyond my wildest expectations. Over time, the dialogue between self and sources resulted in a work quite unlike anything imagined at the outset. But the practical and professional learning which paralleled the creation of a history—the need to *find ways* on unfamiliar terrain—has been more significant by far. In general terms, that second education was shaped by confrontations with four kinds of obstacles, which loosely might be categorized as the problem of false authority, problems of archival condition (which may be particular to impoverished repositories), the problem of inscrutable information, and problems of personal and professional value.[2]

Let me summarize the course of my archival research, and then describe these four areas of difficulty. I had contemplated research in original manuscripts in eight Kentucky repositories, but I actually conducted it only in four. One location was eliminated before leaving because "holdings" were merely photocopies of materials held elsewhere. Another proved a dead end upon arrival, the documents having been moved to Georgia some years earlier without a trace in manuscript guides, and a third in southwestern Kentucky was eliminated at trip's end when I abruptly ran out of funding. I learned about a fourth—the basement of a court building—while on location, through conversations with archivists, and although I did unearth a rich lode of previously unused court records, all pertained to a later period, and I turned them over to another historian. Local repositories in which I did work included a state historical society, a state archive, a state university archive and special collections department, and a private historical society. Later, I worked in the Library of Congress, but that experience, by virtue of its ease and predictability, can be distinguished from the process elsewhere.

The problem of false authority clearly was the most nettlesome and recurrent of all difficulties. It appeared in many forms, both before and during actual research—in advice from well-intended colleagues, in the catalogs and indexes used in bibliographic searches, in finding aids held within repositories, in the labels on boxes and wrappers on bundles of documents, and in curators' assessments of the value of collections. Authority, as political theorists know, is sometimes more apparent than real, and without bulldozing or otherwise alienating other professionals whose advice is often invaluable, the labels, advice, and all of the rest have to be challenged continually. Had I not been skeptical—often from plain desperation—it is fair to say that the Kentucky project would never have eventuated.

Examples abound. While trying to decide whether the thesis topic held promise, I sent a prospectus to a scholar in Kentucky. He wrote legal history, and he offered only an "amber light." Private papers, he thought, were inadequate for my purposes, and legislative proceedings (as apart from journals) had not survived. I therefore made a study of his publications and learned that his topical and period interests differed from my own. In addition, his work was based mainly upon public documents. Either archival sources were too thin to be useful or were irrelevant to his questions, or he had not consulted them. More hopefully, another historian in Kentucky volunteered that local archives were used mostly by genealogists and history buffs, and my thesis director told optimistic tales about others who had discovered buried treasure in "empty" repositories.

I also performed standard searches in manuscript guides. Collections seemed to cluster around the state's earliest years, specifically around the statehood struggle before 1792, then leapfrogging to the Civil War, with very little between. But archivists often are asked to submit descriptions only of "major" collections, and measures of significance vary widely. Did these clusters mirror the actual number or size of holdings? The curators' sense that statehood and war were most significant in the state's development? I wrote letters to several archives, describing my interests in detail. In two instances, I learned of potentially useful collections viewed as "minor" which were nowhere represented in manuscript guides. These were slender reeds—a few suggestive letters, suspicions, and contradictory eyewitness reports. But I decided to visit—literally to learn whether I had a topic or not. Fortunately, I was eligible for travel funds for a summer scouting mission. I packed my car with books and notecards, planning a three-week adventure.

I remained over three months, depleted my funds, and had to return a second time to finish work left behind. Clearly I "found" a dissertation. I also found numerous practical impediments, which might have been obviated with some forethought. There were no cheap hotels in Frankfort, for example—no boarding houses, motels with weekly rates, or "patrons" of history willing to board a visitor. I spent days searching for room and board on arrival—all in August heat—and finally moved into a hotel in Lexington, commuting daily. Later, I learned that historical society volunteers, once persuaded of a visitor's civility, will accommodate researchers: I need only have written the right kind of letter with the proper references tucked discretely between the lines.

The problem of false authority loomed time and again during those three months. At my first stop in Frankfort, I reviewed legislative journals and statute books while trying to learn something about the contents of several steel warehouses. A glance at the finding aids, prepared years before and patched together by untrained personnel, suggested inaccuracy—especially because so much was stacked in packing crates. Through conversations, I gradually gained familiarity with the repository's criteria for collecting material, and gathered clues about the crates' contents. I stumbled upon the state auditor's records, for instance, which were unlisted in finding aids, in a conversation with a worker usually hidden in the warehouse. The auditor's office was powerful in the early nineteenth century, and I approached those materials with enthusiasm, very nearly standing on my head in a wooden crate. Here, I thought, I might discover something about the treasury's condition before and after the Panic. But ledgers and treasury warrant numbers were indecipherable. I gave up.

I also discovered several hundred bound volumes of banking records—unrecorded in any manuscript guide—and was given a preliminary inventory, which was only partly accurate: size was recorded properly, while substance was not. "Record books," for example, variously meant ledgers, minute books, and miscellaneous volumes. I abandoned the inventory, having learned the collection's size, and scrutinized volumes myself. Letters were stashed in ledgers; banknotes and conversion tables were glued into letter books. In spite of its intimidating size, a full search was necessary. George Robertson had implied that banking and land were linked. Did these officials agree? Would they tell me how these issues were related? There were thirteen branch offices for each major bank and voluminous records for the wildcat Frankfort Bank. I ruled out the Frankfort Bank as a poor investment of time: it had functioned for only a few years and had generated almost as much paper as the durable Bank of Kentucky. I reasoned that most political activists would transact business near their homes, in Frankfort, Paris, Lexington, and Louisville, and I arbitrarily chose to explore the Bank of Kentucky's Frankfort office first, generally because principal branch offices often served as clearing houses for other branch bank activities.

After this process of elimination, over a hundred volumes remained. Letter books and minute books offered startling candor. I now knew that banks and land were linked through mortgaging and stockholding, and that stay laws impeded loan collection at the Bank of Kentucky. Cashiers, directors, and presidents expounded about the pernicious national bank, the scandalous debtor bank, wildcatting "nabobs," and public immorality. I found lists of notes in suits in which Relief supporters predominated. Who stood to gain by the Bank of Kentucky's survival? I gathered stock ledgers and daybooks together, comparing stock and loan records for individuals whose names I recognized. I noticed blocks of stock changing hands at the depression's peak. Were Bank of the Commonwealth clients mainly hard-pressed middling farmers? No. Records revealed pillars of the community borrowing and depositing heavily. The debtor-creditor dichotomy collapsed: These men were often debtors and creditors simultaneously, albeit at different institutions. I traced a few familiar legislators, constructing crude timelines which tracked support of relief measures with shifts in banking affiliation. Correlations appeared. I finally was able to interpret information in the state auditors' records—my first encounter with the problem of inscrutable information. Having cracked a symbol system, records were illuminated.

But I couldn't remain there indefinitely. Nor did I recognize enough names. The staff granted me permission to photocopy. I spent two weeks reading, selecting pages, making lists and cross references, and expanding the search into hinterland branch records as clues emerged—only to learn that archival policy had changed. Photocopying of selections was disallowed. I could choose between staff microfilming of selections at a steep price, or using the cameras myself for much less cost, provided that I filmed whole volumes rather than selected pages and left the master behind. I tried to remain calm, donned a technician's coat, and found myself behind sophisticated microfilming equipment under hot floodlights in a dank warehouse. Two weeks later, I had filmed over 10,000 pages, garnered prints, finished other research, and moved on to another repository. Myths had been shattered. My fingernails were permanently grimy; white blouses tended toward gray.

My journal, in which I record ideas, unanswered questions, and a running conversation with myself as work progresses, reveals naive confidence at that point in a simple, determinist relationship between banks and future political strife. Thereafter, entries reflect incremental softening as I encountered other sources, and tried to explain important exceptions to my overly-simple generalizations. What about Relief partisans, who were not customers of the Bank of the Commonwealth, or who were not indebted to the customers of the Bank of Kentucky? Why were Bank of the United States clients divided on the relief question? And what if the apparent centrality of these banks was a function of the serendipitous discovery of records at an early stage in research? Was sheer bulk masquerading as extreme significance? Other materials were fragmentary by comparison; were they therefore less important? How could I *test* my generalizations about financial institutions? Would politicians and merchants discuss banking with partners or kin, for example, in family or business papers? And a troubling new question appeared: Why did so few leaders talk about those farmers gathered at courthouses? Why no reference to one's constituents? I began thinking seriously about legislative parties as apart from constituent parties. Was this a truncated or engaged leadership? Was "relief" a homogeneous or heterogeneous concept? Could there be a "mass movement" without institutionalized leadership? Could I infer likemindedness between voters and assemblymen without concrete evidence *beyond* electoral success? Historians yearned for "democratic" advances and a spearheading elite, but was it true?

My second stop was a state historical society, where I was greeted by friendly volunteers, a classically southern librarian, and a small horde of genealogists. Yankee consonants sometimes signal alarm: doors shut very silently. I therefore spent two days learning about lives, children, family histories, local historical study groups, the society's history, and weekly apple-and-cookie gatherings behind the photocopying machine. I studied finding aids. Mostly, I *paused,* which is difficult for scholars on tight budgets. I learned that "minor collections" had been microfilmed by trained personnel, and that the all-important governor's papers had been filmed shabbily, with frequent omissions. But the originals were sealed. More important, I quickly gathered that manuscripts had been organized by family name, in part to facilitate genealogical research. And the names were a stumbling block: who was Basil Hobbes? Valentine Peers? How could I find a way around this wall of unfamiliar names? At night, I studied names in local histories; by day, I searched collections. Soon, a network of kin and business associates appeared, and I was able to move from one grouping to others with some confidence.

Fortunately, there were no crickets skittering along baseboards, no tiny worms in book bindings to be plucked away, no crickets leaping from storage crates. But there were problems of false information. I gained permission to use the original governor's papers and saw that the inventory had been prepared in the 1940s by a volunteer. Nobody knew anything about her. But whole boxes were missing, and the numbers of bundles inside boxes did not tally with the inventory. I narrowed the search to some forty boxes, then disregarded labels altogether and simply read. Materials were not in order: election returns were bundled with militia records. An invaluable letter from a disgruntled farmer resided in a bundle labeled "Applications for Position as Keeper of Tollgates."

Finally, I discovered, through a volunteer, that the "storeroom" held material that nobody had ever used. Why not, I asked? She didn't know. I was granted permission to roam in the mysterious "storeroom"—a place reminiscent of another small room in a Carolina library called "the coffin." There were cobwebs, boxes, and old books buried beneath boxes. I lifted, gently moved, and dug. There was an unlabeled register of monies received by the treasury, linked to landholdings in ways that were not clear, and the volume had not been indexed because it lacked a title page. I found five amazing minute books, kept by the Senate clerk during five sessions after 1821—but in a curious shorthand, complete with splendid caricatures of Senate speakers in the margins. More inscrutable information. I quickly photocopied them. These volumes were a reasonable substitute for long-lost legislative proceedings, providing I could penetrate the shorthand system. They listed individual votes on bills; they summarized speeches. In my hotel room, I read about early American shorthand and eventually deciphered the clerk's alphabetic coding.

At a third repository, located at a state university, another two days were given over to conversation with the staff and to generalized poking and digging in finding aids. Again, I wanted to learn something about criteria for collecting, the degree of bibliographic control, the quality of calendars and descriptive inventories. And I hoped to locate someone familiar with the contents of three huge family paper collections which had never been inventoried formally. I found a junior staff member who had processed two of the collections, and had been curious enough to absorb and jot some of the contents. She was thoughtful and meticulous. I trusted her notes and memory, and eliminated considerable searching. An enormous pamphlet collection then appeared—like so much else, not represented in manuscript guides— and, through perhaps a hundred pertinent political pamphlets and broadsides, as well as long runs of Relief and Anti-Relief newspapers, I was able to corroborate suspected relationships between banking, land, and relief statutes. I also confronted compelling evidence of local interest in and concern about federal court activities, which made necessary that reincorporation of the federal judiciary.

I had been gone well over two months, and it was clear that I would not be able to visit both repositories remaining on my list. Already I was reduced to two meals a day. I aborted a plan to drive to a small western college in order to survey three family paper collections, fragments of which had been explored in the state historical society and had proved irrelevant, and decided to concentrate remaining resources upon a private historical society in Louisville. I had grown wiser. Having found temporary housing in the city with a colleague, I again spent several days learning about staff and repository, this time also inquiring about possible "patrons" with inexpensive rooms. The staff responded admirably: Within a few days, I was ensconced in a full suite complete with marble cherubs, French lace, and two gracious hosts in a sprawling Victorian mansion. And I could anticipate three meals each day.

My weeks at this final archive were the most instructive of all. The society was underbudgeted and understaffed—an increasingly typical archival condition, but the staff was dedicated. And they chose to befriend me. Over lunch, I heard horror stories (very like those told elsewhere) about visiting scholars—the "loot and pillage" variety who storm a repository with pockets filled with dimes for photocopying, and who leave without acknowledging a debt; dependent scholars who expect curatorial workers to conduct research *for* them; lethargic historians who, when confronted with hundreds of relevant entries in a card catalog, simply leave; or gratuitous visitors who view archivists as failed historians or bright clerks. The staff habitually responded in kind, usually by refusing to volunteer information.

Correspondence collections were unusually well organized and unusually forthcoming. I located a letter, for example, which confirmed the existence of a stock scramble after 1821 at the Bank of Kentucky. Other documents necessitated backtracking to Frankfort in order to examine the letterbooks of two small branch banks previously thought to be uninteresting. While roaming the stacks in Louisville, I found turnpike, canal, and railroad company records—a treasure trove, given the discovery several weeks earlier that long-range concern about internal improvements lay at the heart of state politics as early as 1824. I now possessed an extraordinary range of evidence about those improvements programs—financial information, correspondence, the journal of a canal engineer, gubernatorial documents, the legislative record, and company journals. And my journal reveals that I was persuaded finally, after weeks of strong suspicion, that the "nation versus state" framework was anachronistic.

An unpaid volunteer offered to microfilm these improvement company records for the society's permanent collection, since they were rapidly disintegrating, and to loan the film at a later date. I peered into unlabeled boxes, discovering more pamphlets, political convention notes, and broadsides which directly addressed relief politics and federal courts. One pamphleteer was generous enough to speak directly to *consolidation* in order that Kentucky might engage in national life more completely; I could now link my generalizations directly to contemporary language. And I learned additional lessons about possible dysjunctures between archival and historical language.

At the last minute, I stumbled upon the fact that pamphlets, although viewed as manuscript sources for historians, were not catalogued in the manuscripts division, but were superintended instead by the librarian in the separate society library, because they were printed rather than handwritten. And that discovery, combined with an unfinished family paper collection, mandated a second trip.

Upon returning home, it was possible to read the formal record of litigation and legislation *from* that underlayer of human interest and political persuasion—to make of names, chronologies, and legislative resolutions an historical rather than abstractly legal fabric. The lower federal court records, for instance—which historians had rarely used—literally sprang to life. My anxiety-ridden bankers, canal company directors, and nonresident speculators moved in and out of federal courtrooms, and those movements, enriched by knowledge of context and of the ideas *behind* institutionalized behavior, made fresh sense. I could know that William Waller, whose private financial empire had collapsed, would view a successful suit by the Bank of the United States with frustration, and that his anti–National Bank posture was rooted in more than simple states' rights sentiment or political parochialism.

Kentuckians, in other words, now inhabit for me a dynamic, three-dimensional system of public and private institutions in a state of flux, within which individuals pursued a rich mixture of self-interest and social concern. This system of local and national arenas occasionally functioned smoothly, but more often its components collided noisily, often changing in response to modified interests, intellects, and imaginations. Courts were created and abandoned; banks opened their doors, then disappeared. In retrospect, and especially as I survey my journal entries, I can trace the very interesting process by which institutions softened, and literally *receded* in significance; at the outset, I presumed a relatively fixed, highly resilient institutional framework. By project's end, that framework is more tentative—simple containers within which the vital, humorous, and sometimes clumsy business of history occurred.

Not surprisingly, I'm left still with an array of unanswered questions—some of which will remain so for want of evidence or want of analytical sophistication. I have not yet resolved the "relief movement" problem, for example: Having found little evidence to support the notion that local leaders were responding primarily, or even very directly, to backwoods agitation after 1819, I can neither assert those connections nor definitively disprove them. Does the absence of testimony always mean a lack of concern? Need it suggest insensitivity? Or can it indicate a universe of presumed or shared, unarticulated concern, predicated perhaps upon the classical belief—so very prevalent in these years—that private interests, once secured, would redound to the public good? The problem recurs in political research. Kentuckians, to offer another example, were slaveholders, and after 1820 the slave versus free labor question gained considerable visibility in American politics. Yet I found no testimony about slaves, their value, or the need to defend a slave labor system—despite evidence suggesting that forced sales included slaves. Do I then presume that Kentuckians were less than vitally concerned about slavery? Of course not. But what, if anything, can I say about those slaves changing hands or gaining freedom during an economic depression? Do I resign myself to ignorance?

And a second, more purely methodological issue, remains as well. Having accused "formalist" scholars of arbitrary, mainly convenient use of private archival remains to illustrate arguments shaped almost completely by the language of law, and having self-consciously turned the method on its head, moving from the private record *into* the public, have I now duplicated the error in reverse order? Have I engaged in identically arbitrary use of formal records in order to illustrate my own, "superior" categories and arguments? I can, and likely will, insist that my categories, shaped by private testimony in advance of historical outcomes, are more profoundly "historical" whenever historians inquire after the *reasons* behind political and legal action; but the position depends critically upon the quality of the private record, the accuracy of my observations within it, and my ability to survey the formal record broadly before making selections from it. With luck, I've done that: A transcription of the work load of lower federal courts reveals, for instance, that the issues addressed by courts paralleled salient political issues in Kentucky, with remarkably little exception. This shift in direction, then, may yield better history, but mirror-image methodological distinctions can be overly precious.

These stories, and many others that might have been told, suggest two general conclusions, the second more important than the first. Problems of false information, archival condition, or inscrutable information are mechanical nuisances. They can obstruct and prevent progress, but they are susceptible to lavish applications of skepticism, elbow grease, and persistence. Other obstacles, which have to do with *conditions of mind* brought to bear upon research, are infinitely more important and more destructive.

Successful archival research, as opposed to mechanistic information gathering, can depend in large measure upon the recognition that our disciplinary categories, definitions, and priorities—shared and understood within particular scholarly communities—are actually adoptive fictions with limited application. And they can affect not only what others will teach or make available, but also what scholarly eyes will be able to see. Had I pursued my own categories in Kentucky—"legal politics," "relief agenda," or "contract litigation"—I might never have read the Basil Hobbes file. Successful research, in other words, requires an advance confrontation with the possible effects of imperialistic categories, narrowed vision, and chauvinism on unfamiliar terrain—not merely because they are unsightly or illiberal, but because they can positively prevent access and learning.

In the end, the challenge—as in scholarship more generally—is to insist upon the broadest possible vision of one's inquiry. In political research, the *idea* of an inquiry is not limited to the particulars of politics, law, or the economy. Rather, it includes an archival setting with important, sometimes half-hidden walls of language constructed *around* a universe of evidence. And the researcher has to imagine ways around those walls, in order to *inhabit* past and present politics, to ask questions, and to facilitate maximum observation. The experiences narrated here, in short, generally exonerated the aptness of that courtroom analogy discovered with students long years ago, but they also clarified the extent to which fruitful research depends upon a good deal more than disciplinary mastery of a well-formuated research topic.

In its broadest sense, science has always been a yielding, compassionate, persistently inquisitive approach to knowing. Few of us in the twentieth century can deny association with a critical tradition which continually scrutinizes received wisdom, and which seeks the closest possible congruence between observations—whether past or present—and explanations for the existence of things observed. Science moves with one ear to the ground. And this symbiotic exchange between objects and explanations can be crippled or short-circuited in practice. One story will illustrate my meaning. At the Kentucky State Archive, I met a young historical geographer in pursuit of his doctoral dissertation. His eagerness and energy were boundless. He was feverishly transcribing information from county tax records onto forms designed in advance; and the stack grew hourly, as box upon box of records were copied and returned. Curiosity prompted an introduction. "Tell me what you're doing," I said. He explained that he was testing the argument of another historical geographer, hoped to make a thesis of the results, and expected to learn that the other scholar was wrong. "But what if he's right?" I asked. He blinked, then beamed across the table, not in the least disconcerted. "Well," he answered, "I can always find another county."

NOTES

1. See Robert Gordon's "Recent Trends in Legal Historiography," *Law Library Journal* 69 (1976), esp. p. 465; and his "Introduction." In the same vein, see Harry N. Scheiber, "At the Borderland of Law and Economic History: The Contributions of J. Willard Hurst," *American Historical Review* 75 (1970): 744–56.

2. Andrea Hinding, director of the Walter Library, University of Minnesota, provided invaluable counsel while I tried to make sense of the archival experience described here.

CHAPTER SEVEN
One-Party Dominance in Legislatures

7. One-Party Dominance in Legislatures

This study is different from the others you have read in this book. Where each of the other studies is primarily an attempt to ascertain some set of facts, this one develops a theory that would be consistent with some facts that are already known. Both types of study deal with facts and theory. But whereas the other studies you have read seek out facts to test a theory, Sprague's study starts from an observation that had struck him as odd and attempts to develop a theory that could account for that observation.

The puzzle that starts Sprague off is the deceptively simple question: How is it that since World War II, while Republicans and Democrats have shared the presidency almost equally, the Democrats have nevertheless held almost exclusive control of the House of Representatives? Since approximately the same electorate is involved in both sorts of election, why have the Democrats done so much better in controlling the House than in controlling the presidency?

Sprague attempts to account for this paradox by developing a theory that would be consistent with it. He uses a mathematical theory—a frequently used device, since the precision and formality of mathematical language are well adapted to the needs of theory. In reading his paper, it is quite possible that you will strike some mathematical technique that is new to you. Should this happen, please don't feel that you must stop at that point; you may be able to continue to follow the basic argument of the paper, even if you must for now take it on faith that Sprague has in fact done something mathematically that he says he has done. Eventually, if this kind of theory building appeals to you, you will want to acquire enough mathematical training to approach work like Sprague's confidently and critically. For our present purposes, however, it is permissible if you occasionally are forced to "suspend disbelief" and continue through the paper.

Formal theoretic work of the sort represented here has become increasingly popular in political science in the last decade or so. In a useful and readable article, Morris Fiorina lists four advantages to developing theories in this way:

1. Developing a formal model forces precision in the terms of one's argument. One cannot use words with multiple or ambiguous meanings in a mathematical equation.

2. Developing a formal model requires that all of our theoretic assumptions be stated fully and explicitly. In casual arguments, assumptions may be left unstated and unexamined. In mathematical statements, however, they must be included; any inconsistencies among them will become obvious because the mathematics will fall apart.

3. A related point is that it is easier to check the validity of the logic involved in a formal model than in a more casual argument.

4. Finally, formal models should lead on to a richer set of further conclusions and applications, because the varied results that logically follow from a given set of assumptions show up readily from the mathematical statements. Without these, we might have to depend much more on the inventiveness and thoroughness of the researcher. As Fiorina puts it: "Formal models greatly facilitate carrying an argument to its logical end—bleeding a set of assumptions dry, so to speak."[1]

As you read Sprague's article, you might bear these possible advantages in mind. Does his formal modeling in fact benefit from these advantages? Are there compensating disadvantages (other than the fact that one must, of course, read mathematical work slowly)? Another question to consider—even though Sprague works from observation to the development of theory, rather than from theory to an investigation of facts—is how different are the tasks that Sprague is doing from the tasks that faced the other investigators whose accounts you have read? In his narrative, did he face different problems from them? Does he seem to have had different feelings about what he did?

NOTE

1. Morris P. Fiorina, "Formal Models in Political Science," *American Journal of Political Science* 19, no. 1 (February 1975): 133–59.

_____ RESEARCH ARTICLE

7A. One-Party Dominance In Legislatures

JOHN SPRAGUE

Democratic party domination of the United States House of Representatives coupled with competitive presidential elections is mildly paradoxical. The same voters participate in presidential elections as in congressional elections, yet the partisan distribution of voters across constituencies is such that control of the U.S. House has been consistently Democratic in the modern era, a period in which the Presidency has shifted frequently between the parties. It is reasonable to inquire into the determinants of that persistent condition in our national representative institutions. While the U.S. presidential election is in many respects a national election, the election of the House of Representatives is of course the aggregate result of elections in 435 district constituencies. In the article which follows, the consequences of the particular distribution of votes which exists in a given set of legislative constituencies over an electoral epoch are explored. Employing a simple mathematical model, I attempt to demonstrate that a number of significant consequences for partisan control of a legislature are logically entailed by the inevitably unequal distribution of safe seats between two parties. The argument is broadly applicable to two-party legislatures but empirical reliance is placed on the experience of the U.S. House of Representatives.[1]

SOME EVIDENCE

The history of partisan control in the House of Representatives is displayed in Figure 7.1 where the measure of control is the proportion of all House seats controlled by the Democratic Party from 1900 through 1970 in the session prior to a general election. The magic number of .5 is imposed on the figure to aid the eye in seeing this history (Przeworski and Sprague, 1971). The figure

_____

Legislative Studies Quarterly, VI, 2, May, 1981. Copyright 1981 by the Comparative Legislative Research Center

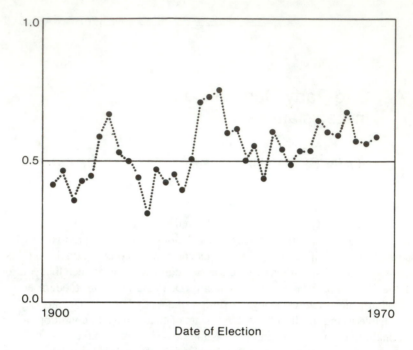

FIGURE 7.1
*Partisan Control of the U.S. House of Representatives, 1900 – 1970
(in proportions of all seats by date of election)*

reveals the truly extraordinary control majorities received by the Democrats in 1932, 1934, and 1936—they exceed all other Democratic control proportions in the 20th century, including the results of the 1964 elections—and visual inspection strongly suggests that the *system* of partisan control is different before and after these great electoral events. Prior to 1932 the pattern of control follows the presidential election results and perhaps exhibits more variation. After those remarkable three elections not only are the Democrats typically above the magic number, i.e., in control of the House, but there appears to be less variation in this control. After 1936 the points appear to move within a narrower range. These features of the data urge the wisdom of distinguishing the earlier from the later period.

To evaluate further the reasonableness of making a division of the data into periods, it is useful to remove some of the short-term variation by some smoothing of the observations in Figure 7.1. This is done in Figure 7.2, which

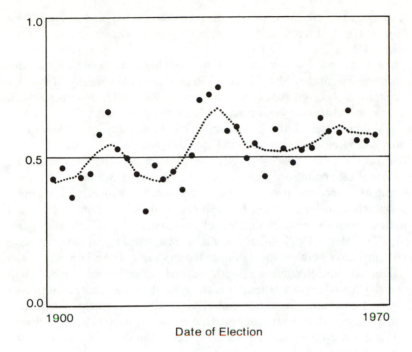

FIGURE 7.2
Partisan Control of the U.S. House of Representatives, 1900-1970
(In proportions of all seats by date of election. Dotted line is moving average[a])

[a]The moving average is unweighed, centered, and includes five values.

repeats the data of Figure 7.1 but imposes a line computed as a centered five-election equally-weighted moving average. With some short-run noise, i.e., short-run political conditions, thus suppressed, Figure 7.2 supports the notion that the epoch before 1930 should be distinguished from the years following. At no time since 1930 has the moving average taken on a value less than .5, which is in sharp contrast with the pattern before that date. The earlier moving average crosses the magic number line twice before the final crossing that ushers in the modern era.

The patterns in Figures 7.1 and 7.2 justify breaking out the period from 1930 onwards as distinct. It is characterized by an average control that is decidedly biased in favor of the Democratic party, a moving average of control which never dips below .5, an average value a considerable (statistical) distance away from the .5 value of pure competition, and less over-time variation. We shall return to these properties after a brief examination of the presidency in a comparable period.

The (same) voters who returned all but two Houses to Democratic control managed to award the White House to Republicans occasionally. Table 7.1 sets forth the observed pattern for the period 1936–1972, a convenient ten elections, and also displays the results of ten simulations of ten elections each, using a simple Bernoulli trials model.[2] The probability of a Democratic victory at any election was set equal to .65, which was determined by the belief that there are about twice as many Democrats as Republicans in the presidential electorate so that some probability around two-thirds is a good estimate of Democratic presidential election probability of success or voting support. Nevertheless, under that hypothesis there was one run of ten simulated elections in which the Republicans managed seven victories (simulation 7). Table 7.1 establishes two facts. First, presidential elections have been competitive between the parties in the modern era (the Democrats won six times and the Republicans four). Second, a totally naive model will adequately reproduce that pattern. It is clear that the same totally naive model interpreted on House partisan control history will substantially underpredict the frequency of Democratic control. That is, the Democrats have controlled the House more often than we should expect, simply on the basis of the number of Democrats in the electorate.

Now reconsider the partisan control patterns in the House in the later time period. What keeps the moving average of Figure 7.2 bounded above .5? The advantages of incumbents might explain the persistence of a pattern once established, but they do not immediately provide an explanation for the pattern of Democratic dominance—the bias in the system in favor of Democratic control. Nor do they account for the return to Democratic dominance after the two instances of Republican partisan control.

A REFORMULATION OF THE PROBLEM

If the probability of successfully reelecting members to the House by a party is proportional to the vote division, then a frequency distribution of seats by partisan vote shares gives at least a partial picture of partisan competitiveness or noncompetitiveness. When the deciles are treated as categories of competitiveness for each party, the within-party distributions may be computed and compared. This is done in Table 7.2, which immediately reveals the advantage for the Democrats in safe seats in the 1970 election.

It is apparent that the congressional districting map falls distinctively across the distribution of partisanship in the electorate. In the remainder of this

TABLE 7.1
Partisan Control of the Presidency:
Observed 1936–1972, and Simulations

Election	Observed	Simulation Trials (P = .65 = Probability of Democratic Victory)									
		1	2	3	4	5	6	7	8	9	10
1	D	D	D	D	R	D	R	D	R	R	D
2	D	R	R	D	D	D	D	R	D	R	R
3	D	D	D	D	R	R	D	R	D	R	R
4	D	D	D	D	D	D	D	R	D	R	D
5	R	D	D	D	D	D	D	D	D	D	R
6	R	D	D	R	D	D	D	R	D	D	D
7	D	D	D	D	R	R	D	D	D	D	R
8	D	D	D	R	D	R	R	R	D	R	R
9	R	R	R	D	R	D	D	R	R	D	R
10	R	D	D	D	R	R	D	R	D	D	D
Total D =	6	8	7	9	4	7	8	3	8	5	4
Total R =	4	2	3	1	6	3	2	7	2	5	6

Means across all ten simulations: $\overline{D}$ = 6.3, $\overline{R}$ = 3.7.

TABLE 7.2
Seat Safety Distributions in the U.S. House of Representatives
by Party for the 1970 Election
(based on Democratic proportions of the major party vote
by vote proportion deciles)

Vote Proportion Deciles		Proportion of Party Seats	
		Democrats	Republicans
Safe	I	0.21	0.03
	II	0.08	0.01
	III	0.21	0.13
	IV	0.30	0.48
Competitive	V	0.20	0.35
Total		1.00	1.00

article, I will demonstrate that this particular overlay of districting on partisan preferences produces a pattern of Democratic control of Congress that is different from the pattern of party competition for the presidency. A different overlay, in a different electoral epoch, or in a different country, would produce different consequences.

The Importance of Seat Safety

In the argument which follows, seat safety plays a central role. This notion will be given a precise definition. It is used to explore some logical properties of the joint system of one-party dominance, seat safety differentials, and institutionalized political behavior.

The elaboration of these interrelationships sheds light on the way in which relatively fixed structural characteristics—in this case the distribution of seat safety—bias political outcomes. The problem may be reformulated now in metatheoretic fashion. What are the consequences of committing oneself to the sentence "The Democrats have more safe seats than the Republicans" as an explanation for the observed differences in partisan control in the presidency and Congress?

The moving average plot shows that the dynamic system, whatever it is, underlying the Democratic dominance of the House since 1930, tracks to some value above .5 Democratic. Ultimately, it will be possible to calculate a precise value toward which the system moves, a system telos that behaves much like the desired setting on a thermostat, but that calculation requires an explicit model. For the time being, note that after big wins and narrow wins, and even after Republican wins, the system returns to the neighborhood of the small partisan bias in favor of the Democrats.

It is equally worth noting that this bias does not operate to push the 1936 Democratic margin any higher. This suggests in turn that the telos of the system lies somewhere between .5 and the .77 proportion of seats the Democrats controlled after the 1936 election. It is argued below in addition, following Stokes and Iversen (1967), that certain other system forces also work to reduce the Democratic advantage.

The evidence from the seat and vote share distribution in 1970 leads to the hypothesis that the telos toward which the system tracks is a function of differential seat safety between the two parties. In the modern electoral epoch it must be the case that seat safety is higher on average for the Democrats. Intuitively, this differential in seat safety is a parameter of the underlying process continually driving the partisan control of the House into Democratic hands. Thus, we seek the form of the dynamic process overlaid on the short-run factors influencing electoral outcomes which determines the system control bias in favor of the Democrats as a function of Democratic seat safety advantage. Before attempting to specify the form of this underlying process, the notion of seat safety is rendered with somewhat greater precision.

Estimating Seat Safety

I believe there is a number, a pure theoretical quantity, which gives the probability that my Congressional district will continue in Democratic hands after the next election if it is in Democratic hands before the election. Similarly, there is a number which gives the probability that my district will continue in Republican control after the next election if it is in the control of Republicans before the election. These conditional probabilities are seat safeties.

No good method of estimating seat safeties for individual districts is at hand, so we will seek some average for all districts. The focus is on Democratic advantage in control in the modern era, and for this reasonable time period it may be that seat safety is roughly constant. The stability of the moving average of control in Figure 7.2 after 1936 is consistent with this assumption. What matters, really, is not that average seat safety is constant over time but that it stays biased and bounded in a fairly narrow range so that the assumption that it is constant over time does no great harm. In fact, this assumption does very well as it turns out. The resulting measures of seat safety, d and r, once they are obtained, can be thought of as estimates of average values for each party for reasonable electoral epochs.

How can the seat safety probabilities be interpreted at the twice aggregated level of parties and electoral epochs? We defined d as the average conditional probability that an average House seat (selected at random from all House seats) remains in Democratic control after an election, given that it was in Democratic control before the election, for all elections throughout an electoral epoch. A similar definition holds for r (substitute "Republican" for "Democratic" here). These average values, d and r, are independent.

How can numerical estimates of the theoretical seat safety quantities d and r be obtained? Before any given election, the Democrats and Republicans hold known seats which do or do not continue in the control of each party after the election. The average seat safety conditional probabilities for each party at a given election can be estimated by forming the ratio of the seats controlled after an election that were also controlled before the election to the total controlled before the election. Once such a series of d and r values for particular elections are computed they may be averaged over time and the doubly aggregated seat safety values then estimated for an electoral epoch.

A numerical example will help to fix ideas. Prior to the election of 1970 the Democrats controlled 243 House seats. In the 1970 election, although they won 18 seats formerly controlled by Republicans, the Democrats lost 8 seats to the Republicans. The 18 new seats are ignored in the calculation of d, but the 8 seats lost from those formerly controlled are sufficient information along with the original seats controlled to compute a seat safety estimate. A total of 235 seats were retained in Democratic control out of the 243 originally in Democratic control. The ratio of these two numbers produces an estimate of seat safety of approximately .97. Under the interpretations which have been developed and subject to the idiosyncratic error associated with the 1970 election, this number may be interpreted to assert that in 1970 the average conditional probability that a Democratic House seat chosen at random would remain in control of the Democratic Party after the election was .97. For the same election using the same procedure, r—estimate of seat safety for the Republican party—is approximately .91. Consistent with our expectations, the Democratic seat safety is larger than the Republican seat safety. Note also the very high value of these numbers and their obvious independence. It turns out in the model developed below that these particular seat safety values for 1970 imply a long-run expected Democratic control proportion (if these values were fixed for all time) of .74, i.e., about three out of four House seats in Democratic hands. The value of .74 is between .5 and the 1936 observed Democratic control proportion of .77.

The procedure of the numerical example can be repeated for each election in the 20th century. When this is done the estimates give a portrait of the dynamics of seat safety subject to error due to short-run idiosyncratic effects associated with each particular election. A time plot of seat safety values estimated in this way is displayed in Figure 7.3. Figure 7.3 is consistent with the earlier conclusions based on partisan control with respect to the division of House partisan control history into two epochs. Seat safety in the modern era exhibits two features. First, in the modern era the mean value of seat safety for each party is higher than in the earlier era. Second, in the modern era the over-time variation in the seat safety estimates is smaller.

Aggregated over individual seats and over time, seat safety may thus be empirically estimated. Such summary numbers for electoral or party system epochs provide an empirical handle for the abstract pure theoretical construct seat safety. The price that is paid is that argument must proceed at the level of the system—a collection of districts—rather than at the level of each individual district; and at the level of time intervals—collections of elections—rather than at each individual election. In the argument that follows, average seat safeties for each party, d and r, are taken as parameters in a dynamic representation of the influence of seat safety on partisan control.

The Connection Between Seat Safety and Partisan Control

The substantive problem may now be cast as a modeling problem. How does seat safety determine partisan control? Determine is meant in a mediated sense, for clearly seat safety is itself determined by a complex of other considerations. Nevertheless, it is instructive to proceed from this fairly high level of abstraction seeking insight into the problem of one-party domination in the modern history of the House.

A slight addition to our notational baggage is useful. Let D_t denote the proportion of all House seats which are controlled by the Democratic Party immediately prior to election t. Similarly, let R_t denote the proportion of all

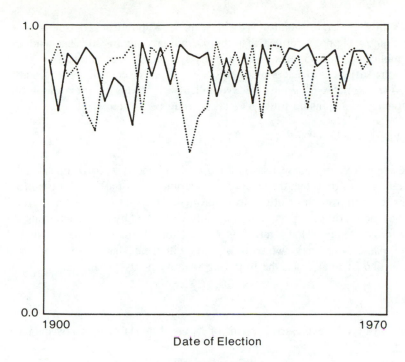

1.0

0.0

1900   1970

Date of Election

FIGURE 7.3
*Seat Safety Estimates for Democrats (solid line) and Republicans (dotted line)
in the U.S. House of Representatives, 1900-1970
(in proportions of original seats retained after each election by date of election)*

House seats which are Republican at election *t*. The phenomenon to be explained, or accounted for, or at least with which we wish to come to grips, is the time path of D_t. The graph of D_t in the 20th century was set forth above in Figure 7.1.

The simplest model that specifies partisan control as a function of party seat safeties in an era is a slight generalization of the accounting relationship which must obtain between any two sequential Congresses. The seats the Democrats control after an election are composed of those seats the party successfully defended plus seats gained from other parties. It is assumed here that the only other party is the Republican party; i.e., a two-party system is assumed for purposes of argument. Hence, the Republican seats after the election are similarly composed of the seats they defended successfully plus those won from the Democrats. Suppose a legislature of 150 seats with 100 seats in Democratic control and 50 seats in Republican control prior to election t. Suppose further that the Democrats retain 80 seats and the Republicans retain 35 seats. In a two-party system of constant total seats these facts are sufficient to determine completely legislative control at $t + 1$ and to provide estimates of d_t and r_t. Symbolically in terms of proportions this accounting relationship for two elections may be written:

(1) $$D_{t+1} = d_t D_t + (1 - r_t)R_t.$$

The implied values for seat safety are $d_t = 0.80$ and $r_t = 0.70$. Eq. (1) may be read as asserting that the level of Democratic control at $t + 1$ arises from seats retained from those originally controlled at t, i.e., total retention of seats in the amount of $d_t D_t$; plus those originally controlled by the Republicans at t lost to the Democrats at a rate $1 - r_t$, i.e., total Democratic party gains of $(1 - r_t)R_t$. Now in a two-party system with seat shares measured as a proportion of total seats, the following identity holds for any t:

(2) $$D_t + R_t = 1.0.$$

Thus, R_t may be expressed in terms of D_t and Eq. (1) may be rewritten as:

(3) $$D_{t+1} = d_t D_t + (1 - r_t)(1 - D_t).$$

Two more steps and the elementary model of party control will be in hand. First, following the discussion of seat safety and especially relying on the fact that the moving average of Democratic control never fell below .5 in the modern era (see Figure 7.2 above), assume that seat safety is fixed for both parties in electoral epochs; hence, suppress the index t on r_t and d_t. Substituting these average values, r and d, into Eq. (3) produces:

(4) $$D_{t+1} = d D_t + (1 - r)(1 - D_t).$$

The form specified in Eq. (4) can be thought of as determining the underlying effect of seat safety in an epoch after the short-run effects of particular elections are removed from d_t and r_t. It specifies, for each election, a direction of movement or stability for partisan control independent of short-run electoral forces. Eq. (4) gives the law connecting seat safety in the system as a whole to partisan control in the system as a whole. It expresses the institutional consequence, the logic, of a relatively fixed system of stable areal partisan seat continuity.

Each election, of course, has overlaid upon it the results of the particular conditions obtaining in that election, whatever they may be—Watergate or job scarcity or gasoline prices. Thus, the second step required to complete the model is to represent these short-run forces. This second step is postponed until some properties of the model in the form given by Eq. (4) have been examined.

PROPERTIES OF THE DETERMINISTIC MODEL

The model set forth in Eq. (4) can be manipulated algebraically in various ways to see what can be learned from it—what it implies. The model is a linear difference equation with constant coefficients, and it is true, happily, that the theory of such mathematical objects is complete (Goldberg, 1958) and may be exploited.

Over-Time Behavior of Model

The first question to be asked is: What is the over-time behavior of the model? What qualitative pattern does it generate? Put another way, with short-run electoral conditions suppressed, what does the model dictate in terms of partisan control? These questions may be studied both numerically and analytically.

In order to study the model's behavior numerically some explicit quantitative parameter assignments are required. In particular, the process must be started somewhere, some initial condition D_0 (the Democratic proportion of seats held at time zero, when we start looking at the process) must be chosen, and values must be assigned to d and r. Now the entire structure of the argument up to now, and the entire structure of the argument to come, rests on one fundamental relationship between Democrats and Republicans. To wit, the Democrats have more safe seats than do the Republicans. In terms of the parameters of the model of Eq. (4), this may be expressed by the inequality:

(5) $$r < d.$$

Ineq. (5) is only a hypothesis. Numbers—estimates—were computed above which are consistent with Ineq. (5) but it is an assertion of an empirical regularity. In other epochs it may be false or it may fluctuate. We take Ineq. (5) as true of the House since 1930.

If the relationship between r and d is to reflect bias in favor of the Democratic Party, no such case can be made, based on the model, for biasing the initial condition D_0 in similar fashion. Thus, choose $D_0 = .5$, which is essentially what its value was following the election of 1930—a convenient congruence between history and our technical requirements. Some estimates for r and d were given above in the discussion of seat safety and others are discussed below. For a first look at model behavior set $d = .89$ and $r = .79$—an assignment that certainly satisfies Ineq. (5).

With these particular parameter assignments and with no additional short-run electoral effects imposed on the model, a history of Democratic party control is generated and displayed in Figure 7.4 for ten elections in sequence. The future is indeed deterministic and indeed highly favorable to the Democrats under these particular numerical hypotheses. From a completely competitive initial condition the level of Democratic control moves steadily upward, evidently at an ever decreasing rate, approaching a dotted line on the graph of the figure that is labeled D^*. One can interpret the sequence of large black dots as describing a hypothetical history absent all other events—in short, absent politics.

The quantity D^* gives an equilibrium value for the process—if D_0 is set equal to D^* the process never moves from that value—toward which the process moves but never quite reaches. In fact, D^* is the only equilibrium value of the system in the example and it is stable. If the system is displaced from D^* (by short-run electoral events perhaps?) it will move back toward D^*. This is true whether the displacement is below or above the equilibrium value; i.e., it is globally stable.

The quantity D^*, the global equilibrium of the system, can be expressed analytically in the form:

$$(6) \qquad\qquad D^* = (1 - r)/(2 - d - r).$$

Eq. (6), defining D^*, shows that the equilibrium value, the telos of the system toward which the system moves, depends only on the seat safety parameters d and r. Thus, the underlying logic of the seat safety system is to move the level of Democratic control toward a value determined by Eq. (6). For the particular numerical assignments underlying Figure 7.4, D^* takes the value of .656. In the long run, if the process is left undisturbed, the Democratic Party will come to control about two-thirds of the seats in our numerical example.

This systematic and biased process is hidden by the short-run fluctuations that result from politics as usual. Each of the points on the plot in Figure 7.4 can be thought of as some initial condition, and there could be others at intermediate values or below .5, and also still others above the equilibrium value. Any election result determines a new status quo ante for a dynamic thrust toward equilibrium according to the law given in Eq. (4). Some short-run forces may speed up the approach toward equilibrium, i.e., enhance the underlying system bias in favor of the Democratic Party. Other short-run forces may slow the approach to equilibrium or even reverse it. The point to be made is that the underlying systematically-biased dynamic is always present, no matter what other short-run conditions obtain, provided only that Ineq. (5) holds, $r < d$.

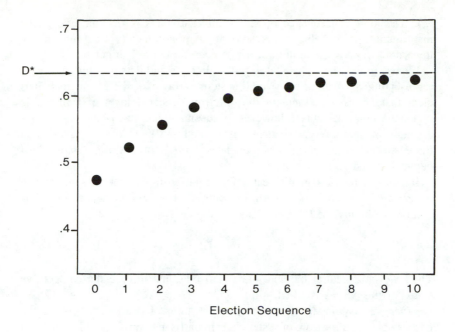

FIGURE 7.4
A Model of Democratic Control Over Time:
Proportion of House Seats Controlled by the Democratic Party
in the Absence of Short-Term Effects
$(D_0 = .50; d = .89; r = .79)$

The equilibrium value of the party dominance model of Eq. (4) defined in Eq. (6) is a candidate for characterizing the system consequences of differentials in inter-party seat safety for system partisan control. With conditions normal and politics as usual, the model moves toward an equilibrium in monotonic fashion following behavior similar to that exhibited in Figure 7.4. This normal condition may be written as:

(7) $1 < d + r.$

The principal import of Ineq. (7) is that average seat safety in the system as a whole exceeds .5. When that is true, oscillation in the time path of partisan control is precluded. For the major parties in the United States (and it turns out to be true also for major parties in at least two non-American systems) seat safety probably exceeds .5 always. Thus, the normal condition of modern House electoral politics is d and r each greater than one-half and $r < d$, Ineq.

(5). The joint consequence of these empirical facts is that the underlying institutional party habit tracks smoothly, monotonically, and inexorably toward an unknown equilibrium of Democratic control larger than .5.

I have urged the view that D^* is a likely candidate for measuring or representing the bias in the overall system in favor of the Democrats. It is clear that D^* is a measure of the long-run expected level of Democratic legislative control, but is it, however, a reasonable measure of the system bias arising from seat safety? The answer is yes and may be justified by examining three special cases of the consequences on D^* of specific relationships between d and r.

If there is no bias in the seat safety relationship in the system, then a measure of system bias in partisan control terms should be neutral. This condition obtains for D^* and it can be shown:

(8)   If d = r, then D* = .5.

Thus, D^* is a neutral measure of system bias just in case the competitive status of the parties is equal.

Whenever asymmetry in the competitive status of seat safety between the parties obtains, a measure of system bias in partisan control should reflect that fact. Is this true of D^*? It is and the following propositions hold:

(9)   If d > r, then D* > .5;
(10)   If d < r, then D* < .5.

I conclude on the basis of propositions (8), (9), and (10) that D^* is a reasonable measure of system bias in partisan control arising from party differentials in seat safety. More can be shown analytically. D^* does move in the correct direction for marginal changes in the values of seat safety for the two parties. Second, the effect of each seat safety on D^* becomes more pronounced as the seat safety parameters move away from zero.

Because asymmetry between r and d exists empirically, $r < d$, a plot of D^* as a function of the seat safety parameters will trace out a set of curves in some appropriately chosen space. To obtain a representation in two dimensions, which is technically convenient, we turn to an elaboration of the notion of institutionalized political behavior, which is substantively important (Huntington, 1965; Przeworski and Sprague, 1971).

INSTITUTIONALIZATION

Overall institutionalization of partisan seat safety may be described by the average of d and r. This number may be interpreted as giving the probability that political control conditions in the legislature will be the same after an election as they were before. It is intuitively a description of the probability that all political actors behaving in a current election reproduce the same behavior as the occupants of those same statuses did at the previous election. Institutionalization of politics means, in this formulation, the probability that all actors continue to act the same way at time t as they did at time $t - 1$ with respect to some relevant behavior.

Now if everyone acts the same way in election t that they did in election $t - 1$, with high probability, the system can be considered highly institutionalized. Defining institutionalization by the average of d and r is on all fours with this idea. If everyone acts the same way the same distribution of party control will result. What is of interest is how does D^*, our measure of system bias, vary as institutionalization varies? Define institutionalization by:

$$(11) \qquad\qquad\qquad I = (d + r)/2.$$

In order to obtain a representation in the (I, D^*) plane we generate curves for fixed differences between r and d. The results of this manipulation are set forth in Figure 7.5 for the area of the plane of empirical interest for the House in the modern era.

The curves displayed in Figure 7.5 deserve close study. First note that if a level of institutionalization is fixed, then increasing the magnitude of the difference between d and r in a direction favorable to the Democrats (moving upward through the family of curves in a vertical direction) increases the system bias. This is perfectly reasonable. Holding I fixed requires moving d upward and r downward in this case. For example, fix I at the .65 level with $d = .7$ and $r = .6$—a difference of .1 in seat safety. Then keep I fixed at .65 and set $d = .75$ and $r = .55$—a difference of .2. What happens to the value of D^*? It moves from a value of .57 to a value of .65. Increasing the difference in seat safety at a fixed level of overall institutionalization has a correct consequence.

Second, consider fixing D^* and moving across the curves in a horizontal direction from left to right, i.e., increase institutionalization while maintaining some fixed long-run advantage for the Democrats. The figure shows and numerical calculations confirm that this results in a decreasing difference between the seat safety values for Democrats and Republicans. But this means that as institutionalization increases, a smaller and smaller difference in seat safety is required to maintain the same long-run system advantage. In fact, an even stronger statement may be maintained, for it is possible that the difference between d and r may be decreased and yet D^* is increased; i.e., lowering the relative seat safety advantage of the Democrats can result in an increase in their long-run system advantage! This requires traversing the curves in Figure 7.5 in a direction from lower left to upper right. Some numerical examples are set forth in Table 7.3.

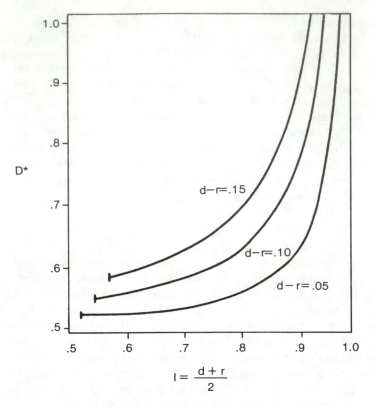

FIGURE 7.5
*System Bias in the Long-Run for Fixed Differences in Partisan Seat Safety
as a Function of Average Seat Safety for Both Parties*

The last four entries in Table 7.3 are especially instructive. A fixed advantage in seat safety of .05 yields a high system advantage just in case overall institutionalization is high, but almost no advantage when institutionalization is low. Furthermore, tracing out the curve while keeping the seat safety difference fixed results in large changes in system advantage just in case the system is already highly institutionalized, but virtually no change in system advantage at low levels of institutionalization. Those particular results characterize the curve in Figure 7.5 closest to the bottom and farthest to the right. And that curve is not very far away from the most likely empirical curve characterizing the relative position of Democrats and Republicans in the period 1930–1970. For the 1930–1970 period average seat safeties are $d = .917$ and $r = .873$. Using these values the index of institutionalization,

TABLE 7.3
Various Examples of Seat Safety, Long-Run System Bias, and Institutionalization (numerical examples in the (I, D*) plane)

Seat Safety (d)	(r)	Institutionalization (I)	Seat Safety Advantage (d − r)	Long-Run System Bias (D*)
.70	.60	.650	.10	.57
.75	.55	.650	.20	.64
.85	.70	.775	.15	.67
.95	.85	.900	.10	.75
.90	.85	.875	.05	.60
.95	.90	.925	.05	.67
.60	.55	.575	.05	.529
.65	.60	.625	.05	.533

I, takes on the value .895, the difference between *d* and *r* is .044, and the long-run system advantage, *D**, has the value .60, which compares favorably with the mean Democratic control since 1936 of .57.

The relative difference in seat safety between the parties in the House is very small but it is consequential precisely because the system is highly institutionalized. The curves in Figure 7.5 show that small differences in relative seat safety advantage are translated into large long-run system advantage in seat control only when the overall level of continuity in seat control is high for both parties. But that is the empirical condition of House electoral politics in the United States. Democratic control of Congress is to be expected because a small advantage in seat safety is embedded in a highly institutionalized system of electoral politics. These results may be summarized in the following strategic property of the system:

Principle I: Small differences in political resources lead to large differences in political advantage whenever the system is highly structured.

Consider achieving influence in the decision process in a court of law compared with influencing the decision process in a legislature. In the court of law small differences in attorneys' skills may be very important, whereas small differences in the skills of lobbyists in the legislature are not likely to be consequential. The essential difference in the two situations is the level of institutionalization, or structuring, of the influence process.

Before moving on to a model elaboration including short-run electoral conditions, one last consequence of institutionalization for the behavior of the model is considered. The question is simple: How rapidly do the Democrats approach the long-run expected advantage they have in the modern system?

Since every election can be viewed as a new initial condition or a new displacement from equilibrium, what is at issue here is the rate of first-period recovery toward equilibrium after some disturbance. The difficulty is that the rate of movement toward equilibrium is a function not only of the parameters r and d but also of the magnitude of the displacement; hence, this must be corrected for in some fashion. A trick that works is to express the first period change toward equilibrium—the first period change is the rate of movement in this discrete time formulation, relative to the displacement from equilibrium. The quantity may be written as:

$$(12) \qquad \frac{\Delta D_0}{D^* - D_0} = 2 - d - r.$$

Inspection of the result in Eq. (12) shows that when $r = d = 0$, i.e., when institutionalization is zero, the first period recovery is two times the displacement. The process wildly overshoots D^*. This represents the extreme point in the realm of oscillation where there is undamped but nonexplosive change with the parties exactly recovering their original partisan strength every other election. The interested reader should turn back to the model of Eq. (4) and reconstruct the pattern of D_0, $1 - D_0$, D_0, . . . , and so forth. As r and d move from zero through average values less than one, the first period recovery still overshoots, but this is in the realm of damped or convergent oscillation in the model. Finally, the realm of smooth system response is for average values of seat safety above one, i.e., politics with at least some non-pathological institutionalization, and within this range the first period recovery toward equilibrium is some (decreasing) proportion of the displacement. And that is the essential point as the graph in Figure 7.6 shows. As institutionalization approaches its maximum of one, the rate of proportional recovery goes toward zero and we have another strategic property of the system, which is summarized in the following:

Principle II: Under conditions of highly institutionalized politics the price of system advantage in the long run is a slow rate of approach to that advantage in the short run.

The system, then, "exhibits a contradiction Comrade," for the properties that give a long-run expected advantage to the Democrats—a slight advantage in seat safety rate coupled with a high level of system institutionalization—also imply that the approach or recovery will be slow. Now every election is subject to short-run electoral effects, and hence this short-run slow recovery rate is just like the system bias in the long run—ever present. We will return to this slow response feature of the House partisan control system under the guise of system memory after elaborating short-run effects.

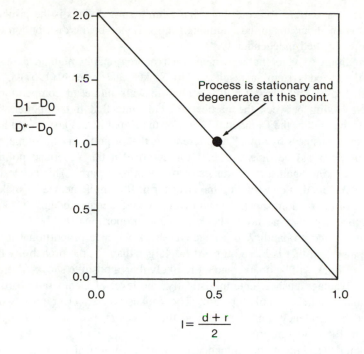

$$\frac{D_1 - D_0}{D^* - D_0}$$

Process is stationary and degenerate at this point.

$$I = \frac{d + r}{2}$$

FIGURE 7.6
First Period Recovery as a Function of Institutionalization
(measured in proportions of displacements from equilibrium)

The deterministic model, elementary in form as it is, nevertheless turns out to be quite rich analytically. At least one qualitative result is surprising, Principle I, and the general behavior of the model shows a consistent set of relationships between system partisan control and the driving parameters of seat safety. It is time to add some short-run politics.

A LONG-RUN STRUCTURE FOR SHORT-RUN ERROR

To simulate realism, a stochastic component can be added to the model as an additive random shock. If the shock is too large it will overwhelm the deterministic component, and if the shock is too small no realism will be achieved. The magnitude of shock and its variance are in part a function of voter habit, and this is represented in simulations as a fixed probability interpreted as the likelihood of not switching between parties on the average.

A value of about .75 for voter habit has been assumed. This is the principal regulator on shock magnitude, although the variance of the distribution also can be controlled independently.

In addition to voter habit, which must be reasonably high in a highly institutionalized system, a result due to Stokes and Iversen (1967) is exploited. Stokes and Iversen utilize a random walk model of competition to simulate voting between the parties and conclude that if the model were correct, then either the Democratic Party or the Republican Party would have been out of business by now. The inference is that as partisan control margins (vote proportions) become extreme, forces arise in the American political system working against the fortunes of the dominant party. This suggestion may be exploited in constructing the error term. It is implemented by making the sign of the random shock depend inversely on the magnitude of D_t. Thus, the probability of a negative shock is made proportional to $1 - D_t$ and, conversely, the probability of a negative shock is made proportional to D_t. But in a system that is biased toward $D*$ larger than .5, the probability of a negative shock will be on average more likely than a positive shock. The seat safety advantage pushes, deterministically, the level of Democratic partisan legislative control steadily upward. The Stokes-Iversen error term works against this tendency, and the more so the higher D_t becomes—a long-run structure for short-run error.

Making the sign of the influence of short-run political fortunes depend (probabilistically) on the magnitude of D_t is the essence of the Stokes-Iversen error conception. As D_t approaches high values, like the 1936 value for House Democratic partisan control, the probability of a negative counterforce becomes larger and larger. This gives the push and pull so characterisic of the 1936 to 1938 drop or the 1964 to 1966 drop. When short-run forces (by accident or design) push the partisan control level to an extreme value, the return movement is nearly certain, and the Stokes-Iversen error term tries to capture that reality. The bigger the aberrant displacement the more certain the system retaliation. This logic also may be used to ape off-year on-year Congressional voting turnout effects (the presence of the President is a random shock that is positive) but, most importantly for our purposes, it copies the off-year fall-back in House seat control when some President (Roosevelt in 1936 or Johnson in 1964) has particularly long coattails. And so the push and pull in the model copies in a simple abstract fashion the interaction of institutional seat safety biases and short-run electoral effects.

Will this elementary and now stochastic model reproduce the essential pattern of legislative control in the modern House? The answer is yes if pattern is used to mean expected frequency of partisan control in an epoch. The relevant history and two simulation runs are set out in Table 7.4. In the

TABLE 7.4
**Simulated and Observed Time Paths of Democratic Proportions
of the House of Representatives**

Congress	First Simulation		Second Simulation		Observed, 1930–1970
	D_t	Shock	D_t	Shock	
0	.50	—	.50	—	.50
1	.55	.00 +	.46[a]	− .09	.72
2	.55	− .03	.51	− .02	.74
3	.59	0	.55	0	.77
4	.53	− .08	.61	.03	.60
5	.57	.00 +	.64	.01	.61
6	.60	0	.65	.00 +	.51
7	.51	− .11	.65	0	.56
8	.53	− .03	.56	− .10	.43[a]
9	.47[a]	− .10	.49[a]	− .10	.60
10	.53	0	.49[a]	− .05	.54
11	.61	.04	.57	.02	.49[a]
12	.58	− .05	.50	− .09	.53
13	.49[a]	− .11	.59	.03	.54
14	.56	.01	.64	.03	.65
15	.58	− .01	.54	− .10	.60
16	.60	.00 +	.58	0	.59
17	.62	0	.60	0	.68
18	.56	− .07	.59	− .03	.57
19	.64	.04	.63	.01	.56
20	.52	− .12	.64	0	.59

For Simulations: $D_0 = .5$; $d = .89$; $r = .79$; probability of shock at $t = .8$; $D^* = .656$; probability shock is positive is $1 - D_t$.

[a]House controlled by Republicans.

two simulations displayed in the table, the Republicans controlled two Houses and three Houses, which is in close agreement with the observed frequency. The model, with the addition of a Stokes-Iversen error representing short-run electoral effects, will produce the basic descriptive facts which motivated its development. An inspection of the magnitudes of partisan control as they pass through time in the two simulations also have an intuitively reasonable appearance. Some results, varying r and d, with other conditions the same, are shown in Table 7.5. I conclude that the model will represent adequately the dynamics of partisan control at the level of the system for the special but important pattern of frequency of partisan control.

In terms of the model, the elections of 1932, 1934, and 1936 must have included very rare short-run events. Events of such magnitude have some very long-run consequences in highly institutionalized systems, as I will now try to show.

TABLE 7.5
Frequency of Republican Control of House of Representatives,
In Simulations with Varying Parameters

Parameters	Simulations												
	1	2	3	4	5	6	7	8	9	10	11	12	13
d	.77	.97	.97	.97	.93	.93	.93	.87	.89	.89	.89	.89	.89
r	.69	.91	.91	.91	.77	.77	.77	.79	.79	.79	.79	.79	.79
Frequency of Republican Control	1	6	3	0	0	0	0	8	2	0	3	1	2

SYSTEM MEMORY

There is a particular representation of the output of a linear system such as that specified by Eq. (4) that provides insight into the long-run consequences of particular extraordinary events like the election of 1936. The current level of Democratic partisan control can be decomposed into its components from some origin in terms of a sum of weighted system inputs, e.g., the particularly large positive shock in 1936. Define U_t as the system input at time t and W_i as its weight. The weighting sequence representation of current system output, i.e., the current level of Democratic partisan control, can be written as:

$$(13) \qquad D_t = \sum_{i=0}^{i=t} W_i U_{t-i}.$$

For $t = 3$, the definition in Eq. (13) produces, when written out:

$$(14) \qquad D_t = W_3 U_0 + W_2 U_1 + W_1 U_2 + W_0 U_3.$$

It can be shown (Cortes *et al.*, 1974) that the W_i for the system in the representation of Eq. (13) are given by:

$$(15) \qquad W_i = (d + r - 1)^i.$$

The intent of Eq. (13) and its significance can now be seen by recalling that both r and d are relatively high; hence, the W_i are proportions close to one raised to successive powers. Because they are close to one they die out slowly, and Eq. (14) shows that each input is weighted by a proportion to a power of i with the power increasing as the age of the input increases. Old inputs, that is to say old short-run effects, are discounted many times and thus contribute a smaller component to current output than more recent short-run effects or inputs. At least they would contribute less if all shocks were of the same magnitude. However, a 1936-style shock is of uncommon magnitude, and this occurs in a highly institutionalized system, i.e., one in which the average of d and r approaches one. If the institutionalization of the system is about .9, more than 10 percent of an input (a short-run electoral effect) still survives after 40 years (20 elections)! Short-run events have long-run consequences under conditions of highly institutionalized politics. This interpretation of the system consequence of highly institutionalized politics is consistent with common views of the importance of incumbency (but see Mann, 1978).

CONCLUSIONS

Static facts like Democratic legislative hegemony in the modern Congress may be explained or at least investigated by means of dynamic representations. The strategy of attack used was to construct the property of Democratic partisan control as a process in time.

The theory asserts three propositions. (1) There is a fixed structure of areal seat safety which determines partisan seat control. (2) This connection is dynamic. (3) There is asymmetry in seat safety between the parties.

The theory was modeled in the most elementary manner. A representation of partisan control was defined, D_t, two pure theoretical quantities were defined for seat safety, r and d, and these were connected by an accounting relationship which specified a dynamic rule. The model could not have been constructed of simpler elements.

The elementary model turns out to lend itself to manipulation, however, and a number of analytic quantities of interest were derived from it. Elementary as the model is, its deductive consequences are quite rich. Ease in obtaining these consequences arises from the ability to exploit the rather complete mathematical theory available for the particular model form.

The most important quantity to emerge from the deductive manipulation is D^*—a measure of the bias in the system of partisan control given by the fixed structure of the seat safety system. The behavior of this quantity as institutionalization varies was surprising, but the number itself emerges as a useful summary of an important underlying tendency of electoral systems measured in the coin that counts, partisan control of legislatures.

The substantive results depend on the model, jointly with the data, and also depend for much of their force on two empirically tested hypotheses. First, central to the argument is the hypothesis that r is less than d. Second, equally central to the more surprising results, is the empirical hypothesis that r and d tend toward high values. These empirical hypotheses find their summary in the statement that there is asymmetry in seat safety between the parties, and that the institutionalization of electoral behavior is high in the congressional electoral system.

Two propositions emerged from the analysis that seemed of sufficient generality to set out as principles. First, small differences in seat safety between the parties under conditions of high levels of institutionalization lead to large long-run partisan seat advantages. The language in which the principle is stated above is more general. The second principle asserts that high levels of institutionalization enforce a trade-off between short- and long-run system advantages.

There were a few other assertions that emerged along the way that are worthwhile recalling. The long-run system advantage of the Democratic Party in the House of Representatives in the modern era is $D^* = .60$. That is a number to remember. It summarizes a fundamental property of the modern era. The analysis of the logical structure of the model considered as a linear system produced a result based on the memory of the partisan dominance system—the persistence of the influence of past events. Under typical modern conditions in the House, i.e., under conditions of high institutionalization of politics, some effect from short-run electoral disturbances survives for a very long time. Probably the effects of the 1936 election were still felt 40 years later in 1976.

Why do the Democrats dominate the modern House? Because the Democrats have more safe seats then the Republicans. And we now have some insight into the logical consequences of that explanatory sentence. But these results may be interpreted more generally. The basic result is that small seat safety biases produce one-party dominance under conditions of highly institutionalized behavior. If the seat safety biases are stable over time, as they must be, then one-party dominance in legislatures is not at all surprising. One-party dominance in legislatures is typical, not atypical. It is the behavioral norm. It is what should be expected. It should be expected because politics in the electoral-legislative system is highly institutionalized and because symmetry in seat safety between the parties must occur with probability zero. Under these conditions, long periods of one-party dominance in legislatures are to be expected.

NOTES

Roger Robert Huckfeldt, now of the Department of Political Science of Louisiana State University-Baton Rouge, collected a major portion of the data used for the analyses. Accordingly, I am happy to hold him responsible for errors in these data. The opportunity to present the lecture on which this paper is based was provided by the Department of Political Science and the Benjamin F. Shambaugh Fund of the University of Iowa. I wish to thank G. R. Boynton for the opportunity and Gerhard Loewenberg for his ruthless editorial advice.

1. One-party dominance of the House as a phenomenon of substantive interest is closely related to several other scientific concerns by investigators of both congressional behavior and mass electoral behavior. Indeed, my original interest in this problem was first motivated by the difficulty of reconciling, to my own satisfaction, arguments and results by Stokes (1967) on the nationalization of electoral forces with the apparent imperviousness of incumbent congressmen to electoral attack reported by Cummings (1966). This issue has been reopened and forcefully presented to the scientific community most recently by Mann (1978). A related set of issues turns on incumbency effects, i.e., the electoral advantages of incumbency in House elections and, also related but not identical, the time pattern of the frequency distribution of electorally marginal seats, vanishing or not. The *opus classicus* on marginals is Mayhew (1974) which should be read in conjunction with Ferejohn (1977) and Fiorina (1977). Incumbency effects have been studied intensively from a variety of perspectives (Erikson, 1971; Kostroski, 1973; Abramowitz, 1975; Cover, 1977; Nelson, 1978; Born, 1979). There has also been the long-standing and continuing concern of political scientists with the drawing of district lines (Erikson, 1972; Bullock, 1975; Niemi and Deegan, 1978). Finally, it should be mentioned that political scientists have been concerned with the behavioral consequences of some of these empirical conditions (Burnham, 1975; Fiorina, 1974; Sinclair, 1976; Kuklinski, 1977; Sullivan and Uslaner, 1978; Brady *et al.,* 1979). The development below is probably most closely related to the scientific literature on incumbency advantages, although no direct use is made of results in that area.

2. The results in Table 7.1 for the simulation amount to the experiment of 100 trials of flipping a biased coin where the probability of heads, say, interpreted as a Democratic victory, is set equal to .65. The model is deliberately totally naive.

REFERENCES

Abramowitz, Alan I. 1975. "Name Familiarity, Reputation, and the Incumbency Effect in a Congressional Election," *Western Political Science Quarterly* 28: 668–684.

Born, Richard. 1979. "Generational Replacement and the Growth of Incumbent Re-election Margins in the U.S. House," *American Political Science Review* 73: 811–817.

Brady, David W., Joseph Cooper, and Patricia A. Hurley. 1979. "The Decline of Party in the U.S. House of Representatives, 1887–1968," *Legislative Studies Quarterly* 4: 381–408.

Bullock, Charles S., III. 1975. "Redistricting and Congressional Stability, 1962–1972," *Journal of Politics* 37: 569–575.

Burnham, Walter D. 1975. "Insulation and Responsiveness in Congressional Elections," *Political Science Quarterly* 90: 411–435.

Cortes, Fernando, Adam Przeworski, and John Sprague. 1974. *Systems Analysis for Social Scientists.* New York: Wiley-Interscience.

Cover, Albert D. 1977. "One Good Term Deserves Another: The Advantage of Incumbency in Congressional Elections," *American Journal of Political Science* 21: 523–541.

Cummings, Milton C. 1966. *Congressmen and the Electorate: Elections for the U.S. House and the President, 1920–1964*. New York: The Free Press.

Erikson, Robert S. 1971. "The Advantage of Incumbency in Congressional Elections," *Polity* 3: 395–405.

———. 1972. "Malapportionment, Gerrymandering, and Party Fortunes in Congressional Elections," *American Political Science Review* 66: 1234–1245.

Ferejohn, John A. 1977. "On the Decline of Competition in Congressional Elections," *American Political Science Review* 71: 166–176.

Fiorina, Morris P. 1974. *Representatives, Roll Calls, and Constituencies*. Lexington, Mass.: D.C. Heath.

———. 1977. "The Case of the Vanishing Marginals: The Bureaucracy Did It," *American Political Science Review* 71: 177–181.

Goldberg, Samuel. 1958. *Introduction to Difference Equations: With Illustrative Examples from Economics, Psychology, and Sociology*. New York: John Wiley and Sons.

Huntington, Samuel P. 1965. "Political Development and Political Decay," *World Politics* 17: 386–430.

Kostroski, Warren L. 1973. "Party and Incumbency in Postwar Senate Elections: Trends, Patterns, and Models," *American Political Science Review* 67: 1222–1233.

Kuklinski, James H. 1977. "District Competitiveness and Legislative Roll-Call Behavior: A Reassessment of the Marginality Hypothesis," *American Journal of Political Science* 21: 627–638.

Mann, Thomas E. 1978. *Unsafe at Any Margin: Interpreting Congressional Elections*. Washington, D.C.: American Enterprise Institute.

Mayhew, David R. 1974. "Congressional Elections: The Case of the Vanishing Marginals," *Polity* 6: 298–302.

Nelson, Candice J. 1978. "The Effect of Incumbency on Voting in Congressional Elections, 1964–1974," *Political Science Quarterly* 93: 665–678.

Niemi, Richard G. and John Deegan, Jr. 1978. "A Theory of Political Districting," *American Political Science Review* 72: 1304–1323.

Przeworski, Adam and John Sprague. 1971. "Concepts in Search of Explicit Formulation: A Study in Measurement," *Midwest Journal of Political Science* 15: 183–218.

Sinclair, Barbara Deckard. 1976. "Electoral Marginality and Party Loyalty in House Roll Call Voting," *American Journal of Political Science* 20: 469–482.

Stokes, Donald E. 1967. "Parties and the Nationalization of Electoral Forces," in William Nisbet Chambers and Walter Dean Burnham, eds., *The American Party Systems: Stages of Political Development*. New York: Oxford University Press, pp.182–202.

Stokes, Donald E. and Gudmund R. Iversen. 1967. "On the Existence of Forces Restoring Party Competition," in Angus Campbell *et al.*, eds., *Elections and the Political Order*. New York: John Wiley and Sons, Inc., pp. 180–193.

Sullivan, John L. and Eric M. Uslaner. 1978. "Congressional Behavior and Electoral Marginality," *American Journal of Political Science* 22: 536–553.

7B. The Origin and Tortuous Progress of One-Party Dominance in Legislatures

JOHN SPRAGUE

The natural history of "One-Party Dominance in Legislatures" extends embarrassingly long in time. From a first recognition and statement of the problem through a tentative solution to a final finished written product covered more than a decade of my professional life—perhaps twelve or thirteen years—which surely provides a bad model of scientific productivity. On the other hand, the finished article is mature and self-contained just as is the motivating problem, and the argument had the benefit of occasional public airings in academic settings before finally being cast in written form. The final written result, in a first finished draft, which even so omitted reporting a considerable development of the analytic structure of the error term of the model, ran just shy of ninety pages. The time rate of production then amounted to eight pages a year when amortized across the period of creation. Such a production rate certainly would never lead to favorable tenure decisions if that was all one did.

There is probably nothing special about the history of this research except the length of its period of gestation and two eureka experiences along the way—one early, one late. Indeed, the origin of the problem emerged from a discrepancy or puzzle in existing literature and the effort from the outset was to somehow satisfactorily resolve the puzzle. This pattern follows textbook descriptions. Thought, theory, and modeling came first. Then came model manipulation. Finally, data collection and analysis followed in three stages, each occasioned by the necessity of making public presentations of the problem, argument, model, and deductive model results—always made more believable if empirically embedded.

We work in a profession of empiricists who dearly love to see the descriptive facts. I rely on this tendency when asked to give a colloquium or a lecture and always try to have some data-based tables and graphs to accompany my presentations. Thus, data collection is a necessity of the public nature of our discipline, though of course it may also be intrinsically rewarding. It remains true, nevertheless, that my collection of data relevant to the model was motivated by the public nature of science rather than a desire to "test" (dreary word) the model. As it turned out, the data were somewhat more satisfying than I had any reason to hope or expect.

What follows is an attempt to reconstruct retrospectively the conditions obtaining at the time of discovery, the possible informational inputs, and a sketch of the chronology leading to final publication of a portion of the results. The most elegant result, unappreciated by reviewers and editors, remains unpublished, but perhaps some of it can be smuggled in here past hawkeyed (no pun intended) Shively.

PROBLEM ORIGIN

In the late 1960s I was a beginning assistant professor engaged in two programs of professional upgrading. First, I was in the middle of a long-run program to improve my technical, particularly mathematical, understanding. This program continues, if with less investment of time, today. Second, I was casting about intellectually in an attempt to escape the field of public law, judicial behavior, and things mostly legal, to some alternative focus on American politics, especially in its institutional manifestations. This latter activity coincided with the desirability of a departmental offering of a graduate seminar in legislative politics and thus the public interest turned out, as usual, to be consistent with my private interest—on this occasion an institutionally focused program of personal study. Ken Shepsle had not yet joined our department, and for a year or so it looked as if legislative politics would be an interesting line of investigation to pursue. Although my personal history ultimately did not go in that direction the reading for, and teaching of, that one seminar *did* furnish the basis for the puzzle of persistent one-party dominance of Congress.

At about this time a number of graduate students at Washington University developed interests that touched on some of my own—Karl Kurtz, Virginia Gray, Louis P. Westefield, Chuck Bullock, Rich DeLeon, and Dan Mazmanian. Some of these students were in that seminar (I refuse to dig up the old grade book to determine which ones), and discussions with them no doubt were important. Two other influences are easier to isolate—one a book and the other a person. The book was William McPhee's collection of essays *Formal Theories of Mass Behavior* (1963), which remains the single most intellectually exciting book I have ever read. The person was Adam Przeworski, who taught at Washington University before leaving for that pernicious institution, the University of Chicago, and with whom I still maintain some collaborative research interests.

It was in this context that the problem or puzzle was developed. My reading program was geared in a loose fashion toward the phenomenon of underlying, persistent, broad-gauge patterns of behavior—institutionalized behavior or practices. In reading for the seminar I juxtaposed Cummings (1966) with Stokes (1967), and it was clear that something was amiss. If Stokes's thesis was correct, the congressional constituency was increasingly being nationalized. How then could this thesis be reconciled with Cummings's data which showed lack of sensitivity to national politics when measured by the yardstick of incumbent reelection success, which apparently was on the increase? This led, in turn, to some desultory data collection so that election survival rates for the House could be plotted, varying conditions at entry for different cohorts (the most interesting condition was the artificial cohort of those elected at special elections). What strikes one from such plots is the overwhelming stability of House membership, and hence it seemed to me that if voting in congressional elections was becoming more nationalized (Stokes's result), the power of incumbency was still more powerful. This was not yet the problem or puzzle of one-party dominance, but it was bordering on it in terms of empirical materials.

Reflecting on these first empirical forays and on the conflicting—or so it seemed to me—analytical results of Stokes in contrast with Cummings's data, it was a very short step to the actual problem of legislative partisan dominance. The key fact to be recognized was that when Republicans gained control of the House in the modern era (twice), incumbency was not sufficient to insure their prolonged control. Why not? The problematic nature of this observation was particularly compelling when coupled with the close electoral margins in presidential elections and the notable success of the Republican party in securing control of the presidency. Thus the same electors produced a noncompetitive House and a competitive presidency. How could that be? The problem was in hand. Evidently the two electoral systems were distinct in some interesting ways. At the same time that I saw the problem *as a puzzle* the idea occurred that the long-run pattern of partisan dominance resulted from fixed underlying habit, that is, as institutionalization commonly labeled seat safety.

With the problem thus formulated there were two components for analysis. First, why did the presidency exhibit competitiveness? Second, why did the House show partisan persistence or continuity? Although ultimately profoundly substantively interesting, the first question at the abstract level of the system can be simply modeled, and in any event Dean Burnham was a colleague at the time. The second question was the one that attracted my attention and commanded my time. It is worth pointing out that some of this discovery of the problem and its formulation was worked out in the context of that seminar with active participation by captive graduate students.

THE MODELING ATTEMPT

Although the dominance of the House by the Democratic party is a big, fat static fact of modern political experience, it was clear from the outset that the central feature of the phenomenon was that it was a process in time, that is, it was a dynamic phenomenon. Hence, the modeling strategy consisted of attempts to connect observed cross-sectional one-party dominance with its presumed source in the distribution of seat safety and *its* dynamics. How soon or quickly results came I can no longer remember; however, some features of the process bear emphasis.

In this situation my style of work is to run through yellow writing tablets in a great chaos of sentences, brief notes, algebraic expressions, references that come to mind, tactical hypotheses, and so on. Pages judged worthless or wrong-headed are immediately discarded while those that are judged to have promise are numbered. All work is also dated, which turns out to be very useful when going back to notes that have been set aside because of the press of other obligations or other opportunities. At the end of a morning or a day or an evening one has a record of activity and also some sense of whether one has gotten any further with the problem at hand. After one session or thirty as the case may be, one either has results, however partial, or one has been stumped. If I have results, my habit is then to consolidate them carefully into a systematic (dated) set of notes suitable as a basis for presenting to colleagues or students the essentials of the argument and model results.

For a few brief beautiful years when Adam Przeworski was a colleague (and when he happened to be in residence), intermediate results would have been shared with him and useful progress would usually result. We had a remarkable ability to interact profitably over modeling problems, which I now understand was a truly rare condition. The key, I think, was a mutual willingness to suspend disbelief in discussion in order to see what the kernel of insight was that so interested the other. In any event, Przeworski's role for this particular modeling attempt was straightforward in another regard. He provided me with my first opportunity to trot out the results in a seminar he was conducting. This privilege was extended in spite of his frequently chiding me for studying anything so narrow as Congress.

My program of personal study and particularly the influence of McPhee's book (1963) entered the modeling strategies I pursued. In the course of my self-improvement I had worked through the marvelous difference equations text by Goldberg (1958), motivated by a reference to it in one of McPhee's essays. The lasting lesson of the McPhee essays for me was that mathematics could be used informally and without pomposity to attack successfully fundamental and broad-gauge questions of social science, that is, with genuine insight while remaining readable and empirical. I know of no better counterargument to the charge that to quantify or model in social science is to trivialize human behavior than to read these splendid essays of McPhee. Frequently his models include some dynamic components. I had recently studied a dynamics text. These were both tools I had at hand and inspiration for the possibilities of such analysis. It was natural, then, to attack the problem as one in dynamic modeling both for general substantive reasons and for reasons of personal intellectual experience.

After I made an initial presentation to Przeworski's seminar, the model and a few crude plots were consigned to the files (after all, the problem was now solved) and stayed there for perhaps three years. Occasionally some version might be shared with my own graduate students to make an instructional point but no serious *research* effort was undertaken for some time. Here matters stood until it was time to travel.

EMPIRICAL DEVELOPMENT AND SIMULATION

The initial opportunity to go professionally public with this model, albeit in an early version, was provided by an invitation to visit the University of Kentucky and present a colloquium. This was arranged by Virginia Gray, long since gone to Minnesota, and provided immediate stimulus to tidy up my thesis concerning one-party dominance. All in all, the presentation itself went very poorly; it was badly attended and not well understood. That is of minor consequence in light of the industry to which I was inspired, for the invitation led to a hurried though systematic data collection, an explicit programming of the naive presidential model for purposes of simulation, and serious work on the model itself as I prepared a program for simulation.

Of these three tasks the first and second were routine and necessary to provide motivation for the problem as I had formulated it. The third task, developing the simulator for the model, that is, adding to the beautiful and clear deterministic logic some stochastic realism, was both a major task and the occasion for much discovery. Those readers who have never written computer code for a set of logical ideas they thought they understood well have still ahead of them one of their potentially more instructive personal experiences. The code was written for an early precursor of today's desk-top mircocomputers, which I had managed to wheedle from the dean (a political scientist) ostensibly for the use of the Department of Political Science. To get some notion of how much better life has become, that machine cost about $12,000 in 1970 currency and could be matched in performance today for perhaps a tenth of that amount and by tomorrow for an insignificant fraction.

The challenge of the coding was developing a sensible yet well-behaved error term. This is briefly discussed in the article as Stokes-Iversen error, which references a paper (1967) by them. The brief discussion in the article gives no hint of the amount of time and effort that went into developing what amounts to a simple heuristic rule. The importance of the stochastic component is that it must bear the theoretical burden of representing *all* of short-run politics. An explanation of the long-run institutional bias in favor of the Democratic party is what I sought, but the instrumentality for showing that bias and its presumed source in the seat safety distribution is to show that it emerges in a model world that also includes other factors, that is, politics as usual. Hence, the development of a publicly justifiable error term was crucial to a defense of the entire mechanism of the model and the thesis that seat safety was the key determinant of dominance.

I am no statistician, but it was clear at the time even to me that the error could not be simply additive and independent—the error could not be Gauss-Markov. Although the occurrence of a random shock could be made independent of the state of the system (level of Democratic dominance), its magnitude needed to be controlled, obviously, and hence at a minimum the distribution would be truncated. But if the insight of Stokes and Iversen (1967) was to be used as a basis for modeling short-run electoral forces, it was equally clear that the sign of the stochastic disturbance had to depend on the state. To wit, when the Democrats did really well, the probability of a contrary short-run force should go up, and conversely.

This nonadditivity of the error has a twofold implication. First, constructing the error term for the simulation was an important and time-consuming task. It required thought and a little subtlety. Second, the possibility of an empirical test of the reasonableness of the error structure assumptions being made for the simulation was presented. If the error structure assumptions were closer to reality than a standard Gauss-Markov hypothesis then it could in principle be shown by an appropriate experiment. What was required was a demonstration that an estimation procedure that used the information in the Stokes-Iversen formulation would defend itself more adequately than a procedure making the Gauss-Markov assumptions. I developed such a procedure and ran some experiments, which are partially reported in the original long manuscript written some years later (Sprague, 1980a: 34–35). One result of these manipulations was to strengthen my belief in the reasonableness of the short-run stochastic structure used in the simulations. Of course the material was not the sort of thing for a substantive colloquium but it did shore up my confidence.

The technically inclined reader might like to attempt a development of the expected value of the error and its variance. I would be interested in seeing such results. In particular, the behavior of the error as a function of both seat safety party difference and average seat safety magnitude (institutionalization) would be interesting to plot.

Working through the empirical material for this first professional presentation provided the first eureka experience of dealing with this problem: the nonlinear behavior of the limiting system bias as a function of average seat safeties set out in the article in Figure 7.5 and Table 7.3 and summarized as Principle I. Lovely! Here was a payoff in substantive insight growing directly out of the model *and* the empirical situation being studied. Those plots reveal the system level mechanism by which the Democrats translate a modest advantage in seat safety into a persistent bias in legislative control and on reflection show how incumbency effects enhance the dominance of the Democrats in the House by increasing overall safety for both parties.

After this flurry of activity was completed the model went back to the files for further maturing. Once more it may have come out from time to time and was occasionally inflicted on students for instructional purposes but mainly it lay fallow. Another generation of graduate students came along including Tom Likens, Carol Kohfeld, Michael Wolfe, and Bob Huckfeldt. The first two had occasion to use the model in teaching a special small freshman course for students interested in quantitative social science and it taught successfully in that context. Huckfeldt and Wolfe were in the unfortunate position of being my research assistants for several years and hence were mercilessly exploited in several respects both by being subjected to this and other models on my mind and also by gathering various appropriate data when occasion demanded.

Sometime in the late 1970s, perhaps academic 1977–1978, an opportunity to give some colloquia at the University of Minnesota was presented. Bill Morris arranged the invitation (he has since left academic life for practical politics), and one of the seminars I offered was organized around the model of one-party dominance. This provided an opportunity to commission Huckfeldt to gather data anew. At this point I was also seriously considering going to the trouble of translating the notes into writing. If that were to be done, the data collection would have to be done from scratch and very systematically. These new data were not actually used in the Minnesota presentation, but that visit furnished the occasion for the construction of a small but carefully developed data set. The occasion also provided the stimulus to work through the model once more, to elaborate further some of the algebra, and to reconsider the overall motivation for the problem. Others may testify to the contrary but my recollection of the seminars as a whole is that they went very well, were well attended by both faculty and graduate students, and provided me with both sharp criticism and new suggestions. I believe both Stan Feldman and John Freeman were graduate students there at the time and had (no doubt skeptical) worthwhile comments to make. (The editor of this collection was also in attendance.)

The aftermath of this second elaborated development of the research on one-party dominance was not, unfortunately, to forge ahead and write the thing up. Other research took priority, and once more the materials were filed although now the file section was getting quite fat. One further stimulus was needed to get the matter into written form. It came in the form of a phone call from G. R. Boynton at the University of Iowa, who invited me to spend a week with his department and give a series of lectures sponsored by the Shambaugh Fund. I agreed, and we scheduled for the spring of 1980.

WRITING

One of the advantages of a systematic set of notes, which have served as the basis for lectures and seminars and have had the benefit of the resulting comments, is that they are more than adequate as an outline for writing. It was natural to include the substance as one of the Shambaugh lectures, since the site was the University of Iowa with its specialists in legislative politics. It was natural to seize on the occasion as an opportunity finally to put it all together in one written piece for two reasons. First, Boynton wanted the lectures written down and furnished to his faculty ahead of time (I furnished him a book's worth ultimately). Second, there would be no page constraints, and I was of the belief then (and still am now) that it was important to have a very carefully developed motivation, and page space is necessary for that purpose. In the finished article it takes two figures, two tables, and six pages to motivate the problem.

So finally I wrote it all down. Well, not *quite* all and not *just* from my notes. One of the great difficulties with writing is that it is invariably stimulating to the intellect and typically produces more questions to pursue than satisfactions with what is going down on paper. It also has another important property. It forces putting in all the logical connections in a line of argument and hence allows one to exhibit one's real argument. This is not just useful for potential readers, for its greatest virtue is in how transparent one's thoughts are made to oneself. This process produced a draft document that excluded one important section of the notes—a section that develops the Stokes-Iversen error term as a problem in estimation by analyzing geometrically the error bias induced by differential seat safety—and that added a section based on the analysis of some comparative materials that constituted a generalization of the model which was suggested in the process of writing. I will comment on each, but this latter generalization was the second eureka experience encountered in the long history of this small project. The finished draft included, after preliminaries, forty-three pages of text, thirteen pages of tables, eleven pages of figures, and twenty-one pages of technical appendices. All in all, I was very pleased with the finished paper and after one redrafting, I sent it off to Boynton.

A good example of the serendipitous stimulation that came from the act of writing itself and the knowledge that space was unconstrained was included in the original paper but not in the published (much shorter) version. In the course of writing the problem motivation and developing the definition of seat safety, some scatterplotting of Republican seat safeties on Democratic seat safeties was done. This suggested, in the middle of writing, a formulation of the frontier of interparty competition as analogous in form to a Cobb-Douglas production function. At that point writing stopped temporarily and the necessary analyses were done. This involved transforming seat safety measures for each party into interparty competition measures by subtracting them from unity. Geometrically this moved the scatterplot close to the origin and changed the probable convexity of the functional form to be fitted. Substantively it changes the focus to *losses* to the other party rather than seat retention, that is, it focuses attention on the margin or area of competitive interchange. The form

$$C = (1 - r_t)^a (1 - d_t)^{(1 - a)}$$

was then estimated for the constants C and a and the resulting curve imposed on the scatterplot—no eureka experience but very satisfying. These manipulations are detailed in the original Shambaugh lecture draft (Sprague, 1980a: 13–15, 57–58).

What the ability to fit to those data demonstrated was the empirical dependence of the logically independent seat safety measures. The plots and fitted curve also suggested quite forcefully the increasing impenetrability of each party's electoral base as election swings become extreme. Each party does have a large relatively safe base. On the other hand, immediately vivid substantive interpretations of the parameters did not jump forward, and the analysis was fundamentally static. What the episode illustrates is how far from finished work may be, even when it is familiar territory, as certainly the model, its motivation, and the notion of seat safety were to me at the time of writing. It was a worthwhile and intellectually satisfying digression in the course of writing up the overall results but one which could be sacrificed when it came to publication without loss of continuity in the flow of the narrative.

The original notes had included an extensive geometric analysis of the behavior of the estimation bias that would be introduced in a standard regression procedure from a small margin in seat safety in favor of the Democrats jointly with a Stokes-Iversen error term. The Stokes-Iversen error is as likely to be positive as negative when the control level is at .5. This is the expected value in the model only if seat safety probabilities are identical for the parties. But, with Democrats mildly favored in seat safety, the expected value of partisan control moves (in the deterministic version) to something larger than .5. This means that the Stokes-Iversen error will, probabilistically, be more frequently negative than positive because the level of Democratic control will be more frequently above .5. Furthermore, this tendency is enhanced as control magnitudes become extreme. The relationships are highly interdependent.

The problem analyzed geometrically in the notes is this: How do these two conditions influence the estimated slope and intercept if the model is fitted to a time series of, say, Democratic partisan control measures? How will the recovery of the essential parameters, r and d, from the regression constraints be influenced by this bias? If one draws some careful pictures of a regression scatter under the joint hypotheses that Stokes-Iversen error operates and that d is slightly greater than r, the geometry gives insight into these issues. I urge the reader to draw some pictures scattering D_{t+1} on D_t, keeping in mind that almost all the data points in the empirical situation of interest—House elections since 1930—lie above .5. You should be able to persuade yourself on the basis of the resulting geometry and some very trivial algebra that: (1) the slope is biased downward, (2) the intercept is biased upward, (3) r is underestimated, and (4) d is correctly estimated only if the downward bias in the slope exactly equals the upward bias in the intercept and otherwise, that is, always, is biased up or down. My own empirical results indidate that the slope bias is roughly twice as large as the intercept bias (Sprague, 1980a: Table 11). These results are all obtained by reasoning from pictures and hence lack rigor even though they are quite persuasive. They were excluded from the original Shambough lecture writeup largely to avoid a long and fruitless debate about statistical issues at the time of presentation, which would divert from a substantive focus. As the article makes clear, there is an alternative and cleaner estimation strategy available.

Serendipity produced the interparty competition curve at the time of writing and tactics of presentation suppressed the error geometries. A planned bit of generalization—only sketched as a possibility in my original notes—furnished new analyses and a second eureka experience. I had the foresight to have coerced Huckfeldt into gathering data from three countries other than the United States in order to see how difficult extension to proportional representation systems would be. The results of these efforts were summarized as

Principle III. The comparative advantage of one party over another arising from stability or continuity in seat control is extremely sensitive to the multiplicity of parties. As the number of parties grows, the system advantage arising from seat continuity differentials decreases sharply. (Sprague, 1980a: 39–40)

TABLE 7.6
Partisan Seat Shares in the Second House of the Swedish Riksdag,
1952–1964, in Proportions of Major Party Seats

	Parties				Total Number of Major Party Seats
Election	Social Democrats	Center	Liberal	Conservative	
1952	.489	.116	.258	.138	225
1956	.471	.084	.258	.187	225
1958	.491	.142	.168	.199	226
1960	.502	.150	.176	.172	227
1964	.509	.158	.189	.144	222

Note what this implies for the United States. Even with high institutionalization, if the number of parties were increased, the Democratic seat safety advantage would be less consequential. But, of course, seat safety is possible because of our single-member district system, that is, no multimember seats and no proportional representation, and single-member districts are well known to be highly correlated with two-partyism (Duverger, 1963; Rae, 1967; Riker, 1982; Sprague, 1980b). The eureka experience came at the end of the analyses leading to this proposition and involved about thirty minutes total time to the office and returning home with fifteen minutes of computing work at my university. I shall try to reconstruct this event. First I take a description of the analysis justifying Principle III from my original writeup and then point out exactly where and when the delicious eureka event occurred.

A reasonable approximation to the seat safety measure used in the United States can be constructed for Sweden. Within each province a multicandidate proportional representation party list system operates. This allows aggregating the party seat-holding survival rates within each Swedish province. The procedure is analogous to the areal survival measure utilized in the U.S. The Swedish Riksdag was transformed into a unicameral legislature in 1970, and the data studied here are for the second house of the Riksdag prior to that date.

Ignoring minor parties, the virtual stasis of partisan seat shares in the second house immediately prior to the advent of unicameralism is set forth in Table 7.6. The table exhibits very little variation in relative partisan seat shares in the two decades leading up to 1970. In particular, the Social Democrats maintain virtually the same share of all major seats, and the number of major party seats is virtually unchanged. The constancy of the seat share of the Social Democrats is remarkable.

Seat safety numbers for each of the four major parties may be computed as

TABLE 7.7
Sweden. Seat Safety Matrix, S, and Limiting Distribution, P, for the
Four Largest Parties. Second House System Based on Averages for
Elections of 1928–1964.*

	Social Democrats	Center	Liberals	Conservatives
Social Democrats	.967	.011	.011	.011
$S =$ Center	.030	.911	.030	.030
Liberals	.037	.037	.888	.037
Conservatives	.047	.047	.047	.859
$P^* =$	.526	.195	.155	.123

indicated, and the questions presented are two. First, what is the algebraic generalization of the original model? Second, toward what limiting distribution, if any, does the system move? First the model is set out, and then the second question is addressed.

If the same simplifying assumptions that were used for the U.S. are maintained for Sweden, that is, that aggregation over time and constituencies is reasonable, then single parameters characterizing partisan seat safety may be assembled in a square matrix. The main diagonal can be interpreted as specifying the probability that a seat held in an average province is kept, on the average, after an election. The off-diagonal elements specify the flow from a row state to all the other states; that is, they specify the loss rate of seats to other parties. This requires a simplifying assumption in empirical work for the off-diagonal elements, but that turns out not to be critical. The important facts are the very large entries—entries approaching one—on the main diagonal of this matrix representation of seat safety numbers and loss rate relationships. In analogy with the original model the main diagonal numbers are equivalent to the parameter d and the off-diagonal elements play a role similar to that of $1 - d$, a quantity that does not show up in the original model.

Let the matrix of safe seat probabilities be denoted by S and the vector describing partisan seat shares at an election by P_t. In the case of Sweden the matrix S is four by four and the vector P_t is one by four. The model may be written as the matrix equation

$$P_{t+1} = P_t S$$

This equation is formally identical to a Markov chain, provided the matrix S meets certain conditions of regularity, which will typically be met under the interpretation employed here. The theory of finite Markov chains similar to that defined here is complete (Kemeny and Snell, 1960) and a few theorems can be exploited for one empirical result. Before completing that exercise an alternative formulation is instructive for the motivation it provides.

It is possible to treat the Swedish situation as made up of only two parties—the Social Democrats and all other competitors. If that is done, the seat safety rate for Social Democrats may be mapped to the parameter d, say d^*, in the original model and the average seat safety for all other parties to the parameter r, say r^*. This produces, for Sweden, an $r^* = .89$ and a $d^* = .97$, which in turn imply a long-run expected advantage for the Social Democrats of .79 *under the counterfactual hypothesis that Sweden is a two-party system*. This argument asserts that, if Sweden were a two-party political system, then the Social Democrats would control four out of five seats in the long-run equilibrium. A cursory inspection of Table 7.6 shows that this is far from the empirical truth, and furthermore, the system looks very much as if it were very close to equilibrium. The two-party model is not consistent with the Swedish observations.

It turns out that the four-party model of the Markov chain formulation produces a very different result—one wholly consistent with the observed lack of movement in partisan seat shares displayed in Table 7.6. The only problem standing between an application of the Markov chain model to these data and a computed result is an assignment of numerical values to the off-diagonal entries for the matrix S. The off-diagonal entries represent losses to other parties, and the simplest assumption is that these losses are distributed to other parties equally probably. With this assumption of the equal probable distribution of the off-diagonal, the matrix S has a certain regularity property, and the general theory of finite Markov chains guarantees that there is a fixed limiting distribution toward which the system moves. Instead of a single equilibrium value the theory guarantees the existence of an equilibrium vector—the long-run values for the entries in P_t, call it P^*. If placed at P^* at time t, the matrix S will simply generate P^* again as the next distribution at time $t + 1$. A routine technology is available for computing this vector or fixed point.

The results of carrying out the appropriate calculation for Sweden are set forth in Table 7.7. The first thing to note is that the limiting distribution P^* is very similar to the observed distributions of Table 7.6. In particular, the value for the Social Democrats is within 2 percent of the 1964 observed value. What is the difference, then, between the two-party and the four-party models? This is the second thing to note: The four-party model recovers a much more believable limiting behavior. These results led to the formulation of Principle III.

Where was eureka? It was in the sudden decision to calculate the generalized model fixed point. I was home on a Sunday starting to write the section on the comparative generalization. I calculated the limiting value analogous to $D*$ for Sweden under the two-party simplifying assumption for the Social Democrats and noted the extraordinary discrepancy between the observed stable magnitude of Social Democratic party seat shares and the long-run equilibrium or expected value from the model. The model value was grossly high. Immediately it occurred to me that the complexity of the party structure might be implicated. At school I had an old Markov chain program still implemented on the now obsolete machine on which I had done the original simulations a decade before. It was a matter of minutes to sit down and construct the matrix for the four parties with care and compute the equally probable off-diagonal entries. With very high excitement I went out the front door and walked to my office (about seven minutes away), went to our data lab, searched out an old minitape with the Markov chain program on it, hit start, entered the matrix, and shouted hooray at the almost immediate output, $P*$, reproduced in Table 7.7. The discrepancy had disappeared. Institutional party structure apparently was crucial in ameliorating the effects of seat safety or continuity bias. No wonder Republicans have such a hard time gaining control of the House!

Within a half-hour's time I was back at my typewriter at home. I finished the section including the results just shown and finished the paper. It was exciting. It was fun. It had also been about twelve years.

PUBLICATION

I spent an enjoyable week at Iowa City in early April 1980. The lectures went as well as could be expected, and I learned a great deal. The paper on one-party dominance went over particularly well with Gerry Loewenberg, who manages the production end of the *Legislative Studies Quarterly*. At dinner one evening and again the next day he urged me to submit it to that journal for consideration. I did so by giving him two copies to send along to Malcolm Jewell, the editor, at the University of Kentucky. The journal, it might be noted, was not in existence when the model was first publicly presented. Loewenberg and I discussed the excessive length, and he agreed to try his hand at editing—a ruthless hand. In particular all the comparative materials were struck out. In due course I benefited from the comments of an anonymous reviewer, and Jewell agreed to publish it. Without any further hitches the edited version was finally objectified in May 1981.

This process reduced the original ninety pages of manuscript to twenty-seven journal pages. On rereading the article after a year has elapsed, I find no particular changes I would like to make. It is the best I was able to do with the problem and as is sometimes said in political science perhaps it was "close enough for government work."

CONCLUSION

The only moral that seems worth drawing is that self-contained as problem, argument, and model solutions are, the contingent nature of science is nevertheless everpresent. If the interested reader refers to Figure 7.2 in the original article, he or she will observe the next puzzle jumping from the page. How is the lack of stability in partisan dominance in the House prior to 1930 to be explained?

REFERENCES

Cummings, Milton C. 1966. *Congressmen and the Electorate: Elections for the U.S. House and President, 1920–1964*. New York. The Free Press.

Duverger, Maurice. 1963. *Political Parties: Their Organization and Activity in the Modern State*. Trans. Barbara and Robert North. New York: Science Editions, John Wiley & Sons. First English translation published in 1964.

Goldberg, Samuel. 1958. *Introduction to Difference Equations: With Illustrative Examples from Economics, Psychology, and Sociology*. New York: John Wiley & Sons.

Kemeny, John G., and Snell, J. Laurie. 1960. *Finite Markov Chains*. Princeton, N.J.: University Series in Undergraduate Mathematics, D. Van Nostrand.

McPhee, William N. 1963. *Formal Theories of Mass Behavior*. London: Collier-Macmillan Ltd. and The Free Press of Glencoe.

Rae, Douglas W. 1967. *The Political Consequences of Electoral Laws*. New Haven, Conn., and London: Yale University Press.

Riker, William. 1982. "On Duverger's Law: An Essay on the History of Political Science." Paper presented at the annual meeting of the American Association for the Advancement of Science, January 5, 1982.

Sprague, John. 1980a. "One-party Dominance in Legislatures." Political Science Paper No. 49. St. Louis, Mo.: Washington University.

————. 1980b. "On Duverger's Sociological Law: The Connection Between Electoral Laws and Party Systems." Political Science Paper No. 48. St. Louis, Mo.: Washington University.

Stokes, Donald E. 1967. "Parties and the Nationalization of Electoral Forces," in *The American Party Systems: Stages of Political Development*, eds. William Nisbet Chambers and Walter Dean Burnham. New York: Oxford University Press, pp. 182–202.

Stokes, Donald E., and Iversen, Gudmund R. 1967. "On the Existence of Forces Restoring Party Competition," in *Elections and the Political Order*, ed. Angus Campbell et al. New York: John Wiley & Sons, pp. 180–193.

Name Index

Subject Index

The Research Process in Political Science was typeset, printed, and bound by Braun Brumfield, Ann Arbor, Michigan. Cover design and internal design by F.E. Peacock Publishers art department. The typeface is Times Roman with Helvetica display.